TIMOTHY D. KANOLD
Series Editor

COMMON CORE
Mathematics
in a PLC at Work™

GRADES K–2

Matthew R. Larson
Francis (Skip) Fennell
Thomasenia Lott Adams
Juli K. Dixon
Beth McCord Kobett
Jonathan A. Wray

FOREWORD BY Rebecca DuFour

A Joint Publication With

NCTM

NATIONAL COUNCIL OF
TEACHERS OF MATHEMATICS

555 North Morton Street
Bloomington, IN 47404

800.733.6786 (toll free) / 812.336.7700
FAX: 812.336.7790

email: info@solution-tree.com
solution-tree.com

Visit **go.solution-tree.com/commoncore** to download the reproducibles in this book.

Printed in the United States of America

16 15 14 13 12   2 3 4 5

FSC
www.fsc.org
MIX
Paper from
responsible sources
FSC® C011935

Library of Congress Cataloging-in-Publication Data

Common core mathematics in a PLC at work. Grades K-2 / Matthew R. Larson ... [et al.] ; foreword by Rebecca DuFour ; Timothy D. Kanold, series editor.
    p. cm.
  Includes bibliographical references and index.
  ISBN 978-1-936765-97-3 (perfect bound : alk. paper) -- ISBN 978-1-936765-98-0 (library ed. : alk. paper)
  1. Mathematics--Study and teaching (Primary)--Standards--United States. 2. Professional learning communities. I. Larson, Matthew R. II. Kanold, Timothy D.
  QA13.C5656 2012
  372.702'1873--dc23
                              2012005553

Solution Tree
Jeffrey C. Jones, CEO
Edmund M. Ackerman, President

Solution Tree Press
President: Douglas M. Rife
Publisher: Robert D. Clouse
Vice President of Production: Gretchen Knapp
Managing Production Editor: Caroline Wise
Senior Production Editor: Joan Irwin
Copy Editor: Sarah Payne-Mills
Text Designer: Amy Shock
Cover Designer: Jenn Taylor

Acknowledgments

To Tammy, who supports my being gone from home way more than I have a right to expect.

—Matthew R. Larson

To the memory and impact of Tom Rowan and John Van de Walle.

—Francis (Skip) Fennell

Any testament of my success would be incomplete without a statement of thanks to Larry, Blake, Phillip, and Kurt. They help me believe that the impossible is possible.

—Thomasenia Lott Adams

To my children, Alex and Jessica, who have helped me to see mathematics through their eyes and to my husband, Marc, who supports my efforts to do so.

—Juli K. Dixon

To Tim, Hannah, and Jenna—thank you for all of your love and support.

—Beth McCord Kobett

To Alanna, Jordan, and Annika, who are among America's first elementary school–aged Common Core pioneers.

—Jonathan A. Wray

My heartfelt thanks to Thomasenia, Juli, Skip, Matt, Beth, and Jon for their dedicated, creative, and tireless effort to turn the idea of this book into a collaborative reality.

Personal thanks to Solution Tree—Jeff, Douglas, Gretchen, Joan, and Sarah—for their time, tireless effort, commitment, and belief in the importance of this work for the mathematics community.

Sincere thanks to the National Council of Teachers of Mathematics and the Educational Materials Committee for their support of this series and their leadership in the mathematics education of teachers and students.

Finally, thanks to all of the authors and reviewers for this series. Many of their great ideas surface across the books and serve to bring coherence to the Common Core mathematics message.

—Timothy D. Kanold

Solution Tree Press would like to thank the following reviewers:

Edna Bazik
Associate Professor, Department of
  Curriculum and Instruction
National-Louis University
Lisle, Illinois

Juanita Copley
Professor Emerita
University of Houston
Houston, Texas

Rebecca DuFour
Author and Consultant
Moneta, Virginia

Marcy M. Myers
Mathematics Resource Teacher
Robert Moton Elementary School
Westminster, Maryland

Jennifer M. Bay-Williams
Chair and Professor
Department of Middle and Secondary
  Education
University of Louisville
Louisville, Kentucky

Denise Walston
Director of Mathematics
Council of the Great City Schools
Norfolk, Virginia

Visit **go.solution-tree.com/commoncore** to download the
reproducibles in this book.

Table of Contents

CHAPTER 3

Implementing the Common Core Mathematics
Content in Your Curriculum **63**

CHAPTER 4

Implementing the Teaching-Assessing-Learning Cycle **107**

CHAPTER 5

Implementing Required Response to Intervention **129**

About the Series Editor

Timothy D. Kanold, PhD, is an award-winning educator, author, speaker, and consultant. He is former director of mathematics and science and superintendent of Adlai E. Stevenson High School District 125, a model professional learning community district in Lincolnshire, Illinois.

Dr. Kanold is committed to equity and excellence for students, faculty, and school administrators. He conducts highly motivational, high energy professional development leadership seminars worldwide with a focus on turning vision into realized action that creates greater equity for students through the effective delivery of professional learning communities in the service of mathematics education and improvement.

He is a past president of the National Council of Supervisors of Mathematics and coauthor of several best-selling mathematics textbooks over several decades. He has served on writing commissions for the National Council of Teachers of Mathematics and has authored numerous articles and chapters on school mathematics, leadership, and development for education publications.

In 2010, Dr. Kanold received the prestigious international Damen Award for outstanding contributions to the leadership field of education from Loyola University Chicago. He also received the Outstanding Administrator Award from the Illinois State Board of Education in 1994 and the Presidential Award for Excellence in Mathematics and Science Teaching in 1986. He serves as an adjunct faculty member for the graduate school at Loyola University Chicago.

Dr. Kanold earned a bachelor's degree in education and a master's degree in mathematics from Illinois State University. He completed a master's in educational administration at the University of Illinois and received a doctorate in educational leadership and counseling psychology from Loyola University Chicago.

To learn more about Dr. Kanold's work, visit his blog Turning Vision Into Action at http://tkanold.blogspot.com, or follow @tkanold on Twitter.

To book Dr. Kanold for professional development, contact pd@solution-tree.com.

About the Authors

Matthew R. Larson, PhD, is a school district administrator, author, and nationally known speaker. He is the K–12 curriculum specialist for mathematics for Lincoln Public Schools, in Lincoln, Nebraska, where part of his work focuses on implementing effective professional learning communities to improve mathematics instruction and student achievement.

Dr. Larson has taught mathematics at elementary through college levels and has held an honorary appointment as a visiting associate professor of mathematics education at Teachers College, Columbia University. He is the coauthor of several elementary mathematics textbooks, professional books, and articles in mathematics education publications.

He is a member of the Board of Directors for the National Council of Teachers of Mathematics and has served on a variety of NCTM committees and task forces. Dr. Larson is a frequent and popular presenter at national and regional mathematics conferences, and his presentations are well known for their application of research findings to practice.

He earned his bachelor's degree and doctorate from the University of Nebraska–Lincoln.

Francis (Skip) Fennell, PhD, is the L. Stanley Bowlsbey professor of education and graduate and professional studies at McDaniel College in Westminster, Maryland, where he directs the Elementary Mathematics Specialists and Teacher Leaders Project (ems&tl). A mathematics educator who has experience as a classroom teacher, principal, and supervisor of instruction, he is a past president of the Association of Mathematics Teacher Educators and the National Council of Teachers of Mathematics.

Widely published in professional journals and textbooks related to elementary and middle-grade mathematics education, Dr. Fennell has also authored chapters in yearbooks and resource books. In addition, he has played key leadership roles for the Research Council on Mathematics Learning, Mathematical Sciences Education Board, National Science Foundation, Maryland Mathematics Commission, and U.S. National Commission on Mathematics Instruction. Dr. Fennell served as a writer for the *Principles and Standards for School Mathematics*, the *Curriculum Focal Points*, and the Common Core State Standards. He also served on the National Mathematics Advisory Panel, chairing the Conceptual Knowledge and Skills Task Group.

He has received numerous honors and awards, including Maryland's Outstanding Mathematics Educator, McDaniel College's Professor of the Year, the Glenn Gilbert National Leadership Award from the National Council of Supervisors of Mathematics, the Council for Advancement and Support of Education's Carnegie Foundation Professor of the Year, and the Association of Mathematics Teacher Educators' Distinguished Outstanding Teacher Educator.

He earned a bachelor's degree from Lock Haven University of Pennsylvania, a master's degree from Bloomsburg University of Pennsylvania, and a doctorate from Pennsylvania State University.

Thomasenia Lott Adams, PhD, is a professor of mathematics education and the interim associate dean of research in the College of Education at the University of Florida, Gainesville. Dr. Adams's research focuses on mathematics professional development and multicultural issues regarding teaching and learning mathematics.

Dr. Adams's scholarship includes funded grants; a commendable list of publications; and a vast array of international, national, regional, and state conference presentations. She has authored three publications with the National Council of Teachers of Mathematics and contributed to many other mathematics publications.

Her service to the discipline of mathematics education includes editorial and leadership roles in several NCTM journals. She has served as a board member of the Association of Mathematics Teacher Educators and the School Science and Mathematics Association and as president of the Florida Association of Mathematics Teacher Educators. Dr. Adams has reviewed proposals from the National Science Foundation and is a standing reviewer for the Fulbright Specialist Program. She is a recipient of the Mary L. Collins Teacher Educator of the Year Award for the Florida Association of Teacher Educators.

She received a bachelor of science in mathematics from South Carolina State College and a master of education and doctorate of philosophy in instruction and curriculum (with a focus in mathematics education) from the University of Florida.

Juli K. Dixon, PhD, is a professor of mathematics education at the University of Central Florida (UCF) in Orlando. She coordinates the award-winning Lockheed Martin/UCF Academy for Mathematics and Science. Dr. Dixon has also taught secondary mathematics at the University of Nevada–Las Vegas and mathematics in urban school settings at the elementary, middle, secondary, and postsecondary levels.

Dr. Dixon is an active researcher focused on professional development in mathematics and science. She has contributed to a multitude of publication, including books, textbooks, book chapters, articles, and international-, national-, and state-invited presentations. She has served her discipline at the national level as the chair of the National Council of Teachers of Mathematics Student Explorations in Mathematics Editorial Panel and as a member of the Board of Directors for the Association of Mathematics Teacher Educators. At the state level, she has served on the boards of directors for the Nevada Mathematics Council and the Florida Association of Mathematics Teacher Educators.

She received bachelor's degrees in mathematics and education from SUNY–Potsdam, a master's degree in mathematics education from Syracuse University, and a doctorate in curriculum and instruction with an emphasis in mathematics education from the University of Florida.

Beth McCord Kobett is a mathematics educator and consultant. She is a former classroom teacher and mathematics specialist for Howard County, Maryland, public schools. Kobett is an assistant professor of education at Stevenson University, where she teaches courses in mathematics education for preservice teachers. She is also serving as the lead consultant for the Elementary Mathematics Specialists and Teacher Leaders Project. She serves as an adjunct faculty member at McDaniel College, where she teaches graduate-level courses in mathematics education.

Kobett conducts extensive professional development with elementary and middle school teachers focusing on diagnosing student needs and developing conceptual understanding through problem-based teaching. She also serves on the board of the Maryland Council of Teachers of Mathematics. Kobett has received the Maryland Council of Teachers of Mathematics' Outstanding Educator Award, the Johns Hopkins University Excellence in Teaching Award, and the Stevenson University Rose Dawson Excellence in Teaching Award.

She earned her bachelor's degree from the University of Missouri-Columbia and her master's degree from the Johns Hopkins University.

Jonathan A. Wray is a mathematics instructional facilitator in the Howard County, Maryland, public school system. He is president-elect of the Association of Maryland Mathematics Teacher Educators and past president of the Maryland Council of Teachers of Mathematics. Wray also serves as the manager of the Elementary Mathematics Specialists and Teacher Leaders Project and chair of the Core Learning Community's Core Challenge. He has experience as a primary and intermediate elementary classroom teacher, gifted/talented resource teacher, mathematics supervisor, grant project manager, and educational consultant.

Wray is professionally engaged in NCTM, serving on the board of directors. He also served on the editorial panels of *Teaching Children Mathematics* and *ON-Math* for NCTM. Named NCTM's Outstanding Teacher Mentor, he has also been recognized for his expertise in infusing technology in mathematics teaching, receiving the Outstanding Technology Leader in Education award for his school district from the Maryland Society for Education Technology (MSET).

He earned his bachelor's degree at Towson University and holds a master's degree from the Johns Hopkins University.

To book Matthew R. Larson, Francis (Skip) Fennell, Thomasenia Lott Adams, Juli K. Dixon, Beth McCord Kobett, or Jonathan A. Wray for professional development, contact pd@solution-tree.com.

Foreword

The publication of *Common Core Mathematics in a PLC at Work*™ could not be more timely as educators across the United States are gearing up to make the new standards the foundation of their mathematics curriculum, instruction, assessment, intervention, and professional development processes. The series editor and his team of authors are not only some of the United States' most highly regarded experts in the field of mathematics, but they also have a deep understanding of the steps educators must take to bring these standards to life in our classrooms. They recognize that if students are going to learn these rigorous skills, concepts, and ways of thinking that are essential to their success, then the educators serving those students must no longer work in traditional isolated classrooms but rather work as members of collaborative teams in schools and districts that function as professional learning communities (PLCs). As the authors state on page 12:

> It is one thing to be handed a set of written standards—even if the standards are clear, concise, coherent, focused, and individually understood. It is quite another to ensure that everyone on your team has a shared understanding of what those standards mean and what student demonstrations of that understanding, fluency, or proficiency look like.

Picture an elementary teacher working in a traditional school. He or she will likely be provided a copy of the Common Core document, may receive a few hours of training from someone in the district, and then essentially will be left to work in isolation for the rest of the year to interpret, teach, and assess each standard to the best of his or her ability. The degree to which the students assigned to that traditional classroom learn each standard will almost exclusively depend on that teacher's understanding of each standard and how much time and energy he or she is able and willing to devote to teaching the new standards.

Now imagine a team of teachers working in a school that embraces the PLC process. Each teacher will be provided a copy of the Common Core document and will become a student of the standards with his or her collaborative teammates. Teams will be provided time and support to study and discuss each standard in order to clarify, sequence, pace, and assess the standards in a common way across each grade level. Each team will be provided time to collaborate vertically with teams in the grade levels above and below its own to build a strong scope and sequence and a common language for mathematics as students progress from one grade to the next. Leadership at the school and district levels will not only provide each team with the necessary time, support, and ongoing training to engage in this critical collaborative work, but it will also put structures in place and empower staffs to build schoolwide systems of intervention, extension, and enrichment for students—providing time and support for each student to take his or her own learning to the next level.

I am honored to write the foreword for this book, written and edited by dear friends and respected colleagues. I am confident it will provide you, my heroes working in schools and districts each day, with information, strategies, tools, and resources to help you bring the Common Core for mathematics to life for the students entrusted to you each day.

—Rebecca DuFour

Introduction

These Standards are not intended to be new names for old ways of doing business. They are a call to take the next step. It is time for states to work together to build on lessons learned from two decades of standards based reforms. It is time to recognize that standards are not just promises to our children, but promises we intend to keep.

—National Governors Association Center for Best Practices &
Council of Chief State School Officers

One of the greatest concerns for mathematics instruction, and instruction in general in most school districts, is that it is too inconsistent from classroom to classroom, school to school, and district to district (Morris & Hiebert, 2011). How much mathematics a kindergarten, first-, or second-grade student in the United States learns, and how deeply he or she learns it, is largely determined by the school the student attends and, even more significantly, the teacher to whom the student is randomly (usually) assigned within that school. The inconsistencies teachers develop in their professional development practice—often random and in isolation from other teachers—create great inequities in students' mathematics instructional and assessment learning experiences that ultimately and significantly contribute to the year-by-year achievement gap (Ferrini-Mundy, Graham, Johnson, & Mills, 1998). This issue is especially true in a vertically connected curriculum like mathematics.

The hope and promise of *Common Core Mathematics in a PLC at Work, Grades K–2* is to provide the guidance and teacher focus needed to work outside of existing paradigms regarding mathematics teaching and learning. The resources in this book will enable you to focus your time and energy on issues and actions that will lead to addressing well the Common Core State Standards (CCSS) for mathematics challenge: *All students successfully learning rigorous standards for college or career-preparatory mathematics.*

Most of what you will read and use in this book, as well as this series, has been part of the national discussion on mathematics reform and improvement since the National Council of Teachers of Mathematics (NCTM) release of the *Curriculum and Evaluation Standards* in 1989. In 2000, NCTM refocused the U.S. vision for K–12 mathematics teaching, learning, and assessing in *Principles and Standards for School Mathematics* (PSSM), and the National Research Council (NRC) followed by providing supportive research in the groundbreaking book *Adding It Up* (NRC, 2001). The significance of these developments for your professional development is discussed in chapters 2 and 3.

So, what would cause you, as a classroom teacher, to believe the national, state, and local responses to the CCSS for mathematics will be any different this time than previous reform efforts and recommendations? What would cause you to think that your professional learning opportunities and activities will be any different this time than those that accompanied previous changes in standards and curriculum programs?

The full implementation of the previous mathematics teaching and learning frameworks and standards was limited by the lack of a coherent vision *implementation* process at the local level. School districts and school leaders were *invited* to implement research-affirmed changes in mathematics grade-level content, instruction, and assessment, but it was not a mandate to change. In many cases, the very system of the states' previous mathematics *assessments* caused local district resistance to teaching the deeper, richer mathematics curriculum described in the CCSS. This resistance was primarily due to the number of state standards and preparation for state testing in the intermediate grades that reflected only the lower cognitive procedural knowledge aspects of the states' standards. In many school districts, it often felt like a race to get through the grade-level or course curriculum expectations.

Since 1989, mathematics teaching and learning in the United States has been mostly characterized by *pockets of excellence* that reflect the national recommendations for improved student learning in mathematics. The lack of coherent and sustained change toward effective practice has been partially caused by a general attempt to make only modest changes to existing practices. In this context, professional development opportunities were often limited or, in some cases, nonexistent. This situation is defined as *first-order change*—change that produces marginal disturbance to existing knowledge, skills, and practices favored by faculty and school leaders who are closest to the action.

The CCSS expectations for teaching and learning usher in a new opportunity for unprecedented *second-order change*. In contrast to first-order change, second-order change requires working outside the existing system by embracing new paradigms for how you think and practice (Waters, Marzano, & McNulty, 2003).

Although prekindergarten standards are not addressed in the CCSS for mathematics, that does not imply mathematics is not important for preK students. In general, prekindergarten childcare and early education services are funded and regulated by agencies outside state and district institutions, and are not subject to standards mandates. Thus, preK standards are not part of the CCSS. However, the significance of mathematics instruction for young children is highlighted in other standards documents that preceded CCSS. *Curriculum Focal Points for Prekindergarten Through Grade 8 Mathematics* (NCTM, 2006) served an important function in enabling schools and districts to improve mathematics curriculum and instruction beginning with prekindergarten. Similarly, the National Association for the Education of Young Children (NAEYC) affirms the importance of high-quality mathematics education for three- to six-year-old children in *Early Childhood Mathematics: Promoting Good Beginnings* (NAEYC, 2010). NAEYC acknowledges that young children in childcare or other early childhood education settings can have significant experiences with mathematics. Research on children's learning in first six years of life indicates that these experiences can have long-lasting outcomes (Bowman, Donovan, & Burns, 2001; Shonkoff, & Phillips, 2000). The emphasis on early learning has prompted several states to create their own preK standards as part of the 15 percent of additional mathematics that states may add to the CCSS. Examples of preK standards from two states—New York and Maryland—are provided in appendix A (page 153), and this book does address some insight into preK standards issues and questions in chapter 3.

However, this book, *Common Core Mathematics in a PLC at Work, Grades K–2* is designed to help K–2 teachers and teacher leaders collaboratively build a sound mathematical foundation for their students. The five chapters focus on fundamental areas required to prepare every student and teacher for the successful implementation of CCSS for mathematics leading to the general improvement of teaching and learning for all students. These areas provide the framework within which second-order change can be successfully achieved. The five critical areas are the following.

1. **Collaboration:** The CCSS require a shift in the *grain size of change* beyond the individual isolated teacher or leader. It is the grade-level or course-based collaborative learning team (collaborative team), within a Professional Learning Community (PLC) at Work culture that will develop the expanded teacher knowledge capacity necessary to bring coherence to the implementation of the CCSS. The grain size of change now lies within the power and voice of the collaborative team in a PLC.

2. **Instruction:** The CCSS require a shift to daily lesson designs that include plans for student Mathematical Practices that focus on the process of learning and developing deep student understanding of the standards. This change requires teaching for procedural fluency *and* student understanding of the grade-level CCSS content. One should not exist at the expense of the other. This will require your collaborative team commitment to the use of student-engaged learning around common high-cognitive-demand mathematical tasks used in every classroom.

3. **Content:** The CCSS require a shift to *less* (fewer standards) is *more* (deeper rigor with understanding) at each grade level. This will require new levels of knowledge and skill development for every teacher of mathematics to understand *what* the CCSS expect students to learn at each grade level or in each course blended with *how* they expect students to learn it. What are the mathematical knowledge, skills, understandings, and dispositions that should be the result of each unit of mathematics instruction? A school and mathematics program committed to helping all students learn ensures great clarity and low teacher-to-teacher variance on the questions, What should students learn? How should they learn it?

4. **Assessment:** The CCSS require a shift to assessments that are a *means* within the teaching-assessing-learning cycle and not used as an *end* to that cycle. These

assessments reflect the rigor of the standards and model the expectations for and benefits of formative assessment practices around all forms of assessment, including traditional instruments such as tests and quizzes. *How will you know* if your students are prepared for the more rigorous state assessment consortia expectations from the Partnership for Assessment of Readiness for College and Careers (PARCC) and the SMARTER Balanced Assessment Consortium (SBAC)?

5. **Intervention:** The CCSS require a shift in the team and school response to intervention (RTI). Much like the CCSS vision for teaching and learning, RTI can no longer be invitational. That is, the response to intervention becomes R²TI—a required response to intervention. Stakeholder implementation of RTI programs include a process that *requires* students to participate and attend. How will you *respond* and act on evidence (or lack of evidence) of student learning?

Second-order change is never easy. It will require your willingness to break away (or to help a fellow teacher break away) from the past practice of teaching one-standard-a-day mathematics lessons with low cognitive demand. This change will require teachers to break away from a past practice that provided few student opportunities for exploring, understanding, and actively engaging, and one that used assessment instruments that may or may not have honored a fidelity to accurate and timely formative feedback. Now every teacher will be required to embrace these new paradigms to meet the expectations of the CCSS in grades K–2.

Based on a solid foundation in mathematics education research, *Common Core Mathematics in a PLC at Work, Grades K–2* is designed to support teachers and all those involved in delivering meaningful mathematics instruction and assessment within these five areas of second-order change. It is our hope that the suggestions in these chapters will focus your work on actions that really matter—for you and your students.

Above all, as you do your work *together* and strive to achieve a PLC at Work school culture through your well-designed grade-level or vertical collaborative learning teams, your collective teacher knowledge capacity will grow and flourish. Each chapter's Extending My Understanding section provides resources and tools you can use in collaborative teams to make sense of and reflect on the chapter recommendations. Then, as a collaborative learning team, make *great decisions* about teaching, learning, assessing, and how your response to learning will impact student mathematics achievement. We hope this book will help you make those great decisions—every day.

CHAPTER 1

Using High-Performing Collaborative Teams for Mathematics

Far too frequently, your mathematics professional development experience as a preK–2 teacher likely feels inadequate. Why? It could be because you receive little or no professional development time dedicated to teaching, assessing, and learning mathematics. Unless you are in the process of implementing a new mathematics curriculum, which may happen every six to eight years, the focus of most professional development time is in another major area of need—literacy.

To be certain, professional development in literacy for grades preK–2 is essential. After all, the evidence is clear that students who struggle to read in your class often struggle in mathematics as well. Skill in reading is necessary for success in mathematics (Gersten, Jordan, & Flojo, 2005; Jordan & Hanich, 2003). However, in order for you to transition to the Common Core State Standards for mathematics, you will need to shift the same amount of priority time to your professional development in mathematics (National Governors Association Center for Best Practices [NGA] & Council of Chief State School Officers [CCSSO], 2010).

Think about your most recent professional development experience in mathematics. What was it like? Was it a collection of short-duration and disjointed *make- and take-it* workshops or *try-this* games? Or was it a robust and collaborative professional development experience that focused on tasks designed to improve the quality of instruction, connect to important mathematics, and advance student learning?

The expectations of the CCSS content standards and the CCSS Mathematical Practices (NGA & CCSSO, 2010), as well as the research on highly effective mathematics instruction, will require a new professional development learning emphasis on mathematics instruction for you and your colleagues who teach in grades preK–2. This will require using professional development resources—and, most significantly, your *time*—to learn the content and pedagogical shifts needed to teach for the depth and conceptual understanding expectations outlined in the CCSS for mathematics. And you should not do so alone. This opening chapter examines the first of the second-order paradigm shifts necessary for successfully implementing the CCSS mathematics standards—the need for you to work within grade-level collaborative learning teams to expand your knowledge capacity and bring coherence to your interpretation and implementation of the CCSS. This opening chapter examines the role and activities of collaborative teams in making the necessary accommodations in professional development to ensure successful implementation of these new mathematics content standards and practices. Working together with your colleagues, you will be able to expand your knowledge and bring mutual understanding to CCSS implementation. Together, you will develop a common vocabulary that helps you to communicate more effectively about changes in your instructional practices.

Effective Mathematics Professional Development

There is new clarity as to what constitutes effective professional development. Linda Darling-Hammond (2010) provides one of the best summaries of the research on effective professional development for teachers:

> Effective professional development is sustained, ongoing, content-focused, and embedded in professional learning communities where teachers work over time on problems of practice with other teachers in their subject area or school. Furthermore, it focuses on concrete tasks of teaching, assessment, observation, and reflection, looking at how students learn specific content in particular contexts. . . . It is often useful for teachers to be put in the position of studying the very material that they intend to teach to their own students. (pp. 226–227)

In other words, effective mathematics professional development is sustained and embedded within professional learning communities and focused on the actual tasks of teaching using the same materials you use with students. What is meant by *sustained?* It means *effective professional development*—programs that have demonstrated positive and significant effects on student achievement (gains of more than 20 percentile points) and somewhere between thirty and one hundred hours of contact time with teachers over the course of six to twelve months (Darling-Hammond, Wei, Andree, Richardson, & Orphanos, 2009; Garet et al., 2010).

We know with certainty that the most effective professional development immerses you in collaboratively studying the curriculum you will teach in a structured way with other teachers, as well as in assessing how your students will acquire that curriculum. This kind of professional learning is *embedded* in your practice. At the lesson level, this approach ultimately leads to your deeper understanding and thus wider adoption of the curricular and instructional innovations sought (Penuel, Fishman, Yamaguchi, & Gallagher, 2007; Wayne, Kwang, Zhu, Cronen, & Garet, 2008). The capacity to provide this type of sustained and focused collaborative professional development for you as an early childhood teacher must be the vision for future professional development if mathematics instruction is to significantly improve and the vision of the CCSS for mathematics is to become a reality.

Professional learning communities have become ubiquitous in education, and you may equate PLCs with teacher collaboration. At the same time, various definitions and understandings regarding a PLC *culture* abound. In this book, we use the work of DuFour, DuFour, and Eaker's (2008) *Revisiting Professional Learning Communities at Work* and DuFour, DuFour, Eaker, and Many's (2010) *Learning by Doing* to define the conditions for collaborative mathematics learning teams in an authentic PLC culture. For our purposes, we will refer to grade-level groups of teachers working together in a PLC as *collaborative teams.*

Professional Development Paradigm Shift

An often-troubling problem with mathematics instruction and assessment is that they are too inconsistent from classroom to classroom, school to school, and district to district (Morris & Hiebert, 2011). Is this the case at your school? Would you be comfortable if your own child were assigned any first-grade teacher in your building?

How much mathematics a first grader in the United States learns, and how deeply he or she learns it, in many schools is largely determined by the student's school and, even more directly, the first-grade teacher to whom the student is assigned. Sometimes, the inconsistencies teachers develop in their isolated practice can create gaps in curriculum content with consequent inequities in students' instructional experiences and learning (Kanold, 2006). Noting that isolation is the enemy of improvement, Eaker (2000) observes, "The traditional school often functions as a collection of independent contractors united by a common parking lot" (as cited in Schmoker, 2006, p. 23).

Your students come to school with many challenges, and you are expected to ensure each student receives, understands, and masters the more rigorous content standards outlined in the CCSS. One of the characteristics of high-performing elementary schools that are successfully closing the achievement gap is their focus on teacher collaboration as a key to improving instruction and reaching all students (Education Trust, 2005; Kersaint, 2007). Only through a collaborative culture are you provided both the instructional knowledge and skills required to meet this challenge, as well as the energy and *support* necessary to reach all students (Leithwood & Seashore Louis, 1998). Seeley (2009) characterizes this challenge by noting that "alone we can accomplish great things . . . but together, with creativity, wisdom, energy, and, most of all commitment, there is no end to what we might do" (pp. 225–226).

Collaborative learning teams provide you the supportive environment necessary to share your creativity and wisdom and to harness the energy and persistence necessary to meet the demands of students' needs and the challenges of the CCSS.

Adequate Time for Collaborative Teams

Thus, mathematics professional development at the early childhood school level must help you to work in a grade-level collaborative team within a PLC school culture. The best hope for you and your students to be successful in the era of the Common Core State Standards for mathematics *requires* this shift. The effectiveness of your collaborative teams will depend on how well the standards are implemented. Effective implementation begins with the provision of adequate time for you to collaborate. Research indicates that significant achievement gains are only achieved when teacher teams are provided with sufficient and consistent time to collaborate (Saunders, Goldenberg, & Gallimore, 2009).

The world's highest-performing countries in mathematics or sustained educational improvers—Singapore, Hong Kong SAR, South Korea, Chinese Taipei, and Japan—allow significant time for elementary school mathematics teachers to collaborate and learn from one another (Mourshed, Chijioke, & Barber, 2010; Stigler & Hiebert, 1999). This requires that school districts shift their priorities to support weekly collaborative professional development opportunities in the form of grade-level teacher collaboration time (Hiebert & Stigler, 2004). Teaching the K–2 Common Core State Standards for mathematics is a much more complex endeavor than generally perceived if done with fidelity, and your collaborative team needs regular time to meet as you address the successful implementation of the CCSS.

How much time? You should have a dedicated block of grade-level collaborative team time once a week, and each session should be at least sixty minutes in length. This time needs to be embedded within your professional workday, that is, ideally it should not be scheduled in the stereotypical arrangement of *every Tuesday after school, once a week* (Buffum, Mattos, & Weber, 2009). When such "professional development" is scheduled beyond the normal workday, after you have spent the entire day working with students, there are two problems. First, it sends the message to you and parents that your professional learning is not that important; if it were, it wouldn't be an add-on to a full day. Second, as you know, teaching is hard work, and teachers are tired at the end of the day. The type of collaborative work that needs to take place in grade-level collaborative teams requires you to be fresh and focused on the task at hand. Collaborative professional development work simply cannot be done as effectively in an after-school session at the end of a long day of hard work.

Some school systems in the United States that are implementing the PLC process have early-release or late-start days. There are objections to late-start or early-release schedules, particularly at the early childhood level, when students cannot provide their own transportation, and there are concerns about the loss of instructional time. In addition, financial constraints may make it difficult for schools to implement late-start or early-release schedules. However, schools committed to teachers working collaboratively in learning teams have found a number of ways to find collaboration time that do not require money or result in a loss of instructional time (DuFour et al., 2010). Consider the following. (See www.allthingsplc.info for additional collaborative time scheduling ideas.)

- **Parallel scheduling:** Grade-level teachers can have a common preparation time by assigning specialists (music, art, physical education teachers, and so on) to work with students across the entire grade at the same time. The grade-level team then can designate one day each week for collaborative planning rather than individual planning.

- **Shared classes:** Students across two different grade levels can be combined into one class while the other team engages in collaborative work once a week.

- **Extended faculty meeting time:** Time can be scheduled for teams to work together during faculty meeting time, changing the focus of faculty meetings from administrative communication to professional learning for teachers.

As an early childhood teacher, you face another unique time challenge: how should you split collaborative team time equitably between literacy and mathematics? Note that the assumption is that you will work within your collaborative team to address *both* mathematics and literacy instruction for student learning. This is not an either/or choice but rather a matter of how you can most effectively do both. Literacy and mathematics both have new Common Core State Standards. Although new consortia assessments in both literacy and mathematics will not assess students until grade 3, it is crucial that the third-grade accountability assessment be viewed as a preK–3 assessment. In many ways, preK–2 grades are the most important with respect to literacy and mathematics instruction. In fact, some research indicates that the impact of having a highly effective kindergarten teacher can be detected in the salaries of students thirty years later (Chetty et al., 2010). Students' ultimate success in school in grades K–12 and beyond is a function of the effectiveness of literacy and mathematics instruction in grades preK–2, and therefore both subjects must be addressed within grade-level or cross-level learning teams. The world's most successful school systems recognize this reality (Mourshed et al., 2010).

Lezotte (1991) argues that one of the characteristics of the most effective schools is their willingness to declare that some subjects are more important than others and to assign more instructional time to those that are considered most important. It is time that administrators and faculty in K–2 schools finally heed this advice and prioritize student instructional time, intervention time, and your professional learning time accordingly in favor of literacy *and* mathematics. In many school systems, because literacy typically dominates professional development time, this will require an increase in both the instructional focus and professional development work devoted to mathematics instruction.

There are three possible models you can follow when allocating your collaborative team time to literacy and mathematics. These include:

1. Implementing an alternating schedule, designating every other week for mathematics or literacy

2. Spending two consecutive weeks a month on mathematics and two consecutive weeks on literacy

3. Spending half the time during each collaborative team session on literacy and half on mathematics

Regardless of the model you select, note that the third model—splitting each session between literacy and mathematics—is not recommended in the first year of implementation. The type of work outlined here requires significant and focused work, which cannot be effectively done in a once-weekly thirty-minute session. In the first year of implementation, you may consider devoting one semester of collaborative team time to mathematics and the other to language arts to allow sufficient time to focus on and experience the benefits of all the steps in the collaborative team process in one content area before tackling another.

The challenge of developing the content knowledge and content-specific pedagogical knowledge necessary to become a highly effective teacher of reading, language arts, and mathematics, particularly in the upper intermediate grades, is daunting. This has led some school districts to adopt a model in which individual teachers in the upper intermediate grades specialize in either literacy or mathematics instruction. Compelling arguments have been made in support of this organizational approach for mathematics instruction (Reys & Fennell, 2003). Although some research indicates that this model can have a positive effect on student achievement and that these achievement gains are cumulative across two to three years (Campbell, 2011), the research on the overall effectiveness of this approach is not substantial (National Mathematics Advisory Panel [NMAP], 2008). It may be that the most critical factor is your selection and implementation of effective instructional strategies, not the nature of your assignment. It is also worth noting that content specialization can isolate teachers and does not promote a collaborative school culture.

Therefore, particularly after year one of implementation, the most effective model to consider is the first—alternating weekly focus between literacy and mathematics instruction. As described later in this chapter and more fully in chapters 4 and 5, much of your work in collaborative teams is focused on responding to your students' performance on collaboratively developed assessments. Waiting two weeks to discuss students' performance on assessments and planning appropriate instructional responses in mathematics lets too much time pass between collaborative sessions and defeats the timely intervention response of collaborative teams.

Grade-Level Collaborative Mathematics Teams

Your collaborative work focuses on reaching agreement on the answers to the four critical questions of learning (DuFour et al., 2008):

1. What mathematics (content and practices) should students learn? (See chapters 2 and 3.)

2. How should we develop and use the common and coherent assessments to determine if students have learned the agreed-on curriculum? (See chapter 4.)

3. How should we respond when students don't learn the agreed-on curriculum? (See chapter 5.)

4. How should we respond when students do learn the agreed-on curriculum? (See chapter 5.)

It might seem that the CCSS have answered once and for all what students should learn and how they should engage in mathematics as they develop competence within the content domains and through the Mathematical Practices. To some degree, this is true, but there are still significant issues that you need to discuss in your grade-level collaborative team and reach agreement with respect to what students should learn and when they should learn it. While the CCSS at the elementary level (K–5) outline a clearly defined and coherent set of grade-level standards within the mathematics domains, all teachers at each grade level in your school should have a deep across-grades understanding, a deep grade-level understanding, and a deep understanding of the shifts in emphasis recommended in the CCSS.

Knowing how to read the CCSS grade-level standards is an important first step in developing a common vocabulary within the collaborative team. Figure 1.1 defines the key terms used in the CCSS and identifies the domains presented in K–2.

The focused nature of the CCSS, and the careful attention paid to students' developmental learning progressions, means that some of the topics you traditionally taught in certain grades have been moved to other grades, and some topics have simply been eliminated from the elementary school curriculum. For example, the CCSS emphasize fractions beginning at the third-grade level and delay probability until the middle grades. Traditionally, both of these topics were introduced in the primary grades and remained topics in each elementary school grade. The purpose of this more focused curriculum is to provide you more time to teach fewer critical topics in greater depth. Not continuing to teach content that you may have traditionally taught in the primary grades will be critical for successful implementation of the CCSS. Not teaching content extraneous to the CCSS provides the instructional time necessary to teach for depth and student understanding.

Standards define what students should understand and be able to do.

Clusters summarize groups of related standards. Note that standards from different clusters may sometimes be closely related because mathematics is a connected subject.

Domains are larger groups of related standards. Standards from different domains may sometimes be closely related. The domains for K–2 are Counting and Cardinality (kindergarten only), Operations and Algebraic Thinking, Number and Operations in Base Ten, Measurement and Data, and Geometry.

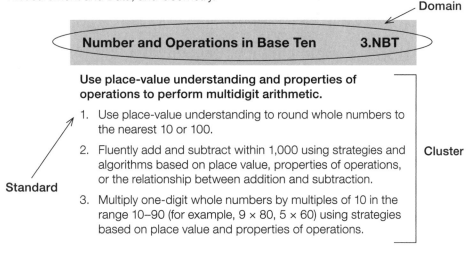

Source: Adapted from NGA & CCSSO, 2010, p. 5

Figure 1.1: How to read the grade-level standards.

Visit **go.solution-tree.com/commoncore** for a reproducible version of this figure.

You need to spend time in your collaborative team reviewing and reaching agreement on the grade-level scope and sequence you will use to ensure the alignment of the mathematics content with your district's expectations as well as the CCSS. You should also spend some collaborative team time in vertical discussions. For example, if you are a first-grade teacher, you should meet vertically with the kindergarten and second-grade teachers to ensure appropriate articulation across grade levels.

One of the primary purposes for taking time to discuss the CCSS content standards in grade-level collaborative teams is to develop *shared teacher ownership* of the CCSS content standards and Mathematical Practices. This means discussing each domain and standard cluster as a team to develop a common understanding of what each standard means and what student understanding and proficiency with each standard look like. For example, in kindergarten, one of the CCSS content standards for the domain Operations and Algebraic Thinking states that students will "decompose numbers less than or equal to 10 into pairs in more than one way, e.g., by using objects or drawings, and record each decomposition by a drawing or equation (e.g., $5 = 2 + 3$ and $5 = 4 + 1$)" (NGA & CCSSO, 2010, p. 11). Simply reading this standard might be a language issue, as you or your teammates may not have typically used this exact phrasing of the standard. It is crucial that every kindergarten teacher understands what this means, what he or she expects students to learn, and what it will look like when students have learned it. It is one thing to be handed a set of written standards—even if the standards are clear, concise, coherent, focused, and individually understood. It is quite another to ensure that everyone on your team has a shared understanding of what those standards mean and what student demonstrations of that understanding, fluency, or proficiency look like.

It is most important that your collaborative team spends significant time discussing the CCSS critical areas for instructional emphasis at your grade level. It should be noted that these critical areas are directly connected to the *Curriculum Focal Points* (NCTM, 2006), so they may present a common ground for discussing grade-level priorities and focus. Consider the following four critical areas for instructional emphasis in grade 1:

1. Developing understanding of addition and subtraction within 20.
2. Developing understanding of whole number relationships and place value, including grouping in tens and ones.
3. Developing understanding of linear measurement and measuring lengths as iterating length units.
4. Reasoning about attributes of, and composing and decomposing geometric shapes. (NGA & CCSSO, 2010, p. 13)

Your collaborative team needs to ensure that the mathematics content you teach students, as reflected in your pacing documents, lessons, assessments, judicious review activities, and intervention time, are all consistent with the CCSS emphasis on these four critical areas. Two series from the National Council of Teachers of Mathematics—*Teaching With Curriculum Focal Points* (NCTM, 2008–2011) and *Developing Essential Understanding* (NCTM, 2010–2012)—are excellent resources to support you as you work with your colleagues to develop highly effective lessons aligned with the identified critical areas of the CCSS.

Resources for Developing Highly Effective Lessons

Developing Essential Understanding **(NCTM, 2010–2012):** This sixteen-book series addresses topics in preK–12 mathematics that are often difficult to teach but critical to student development. Each book gives an overview of the topics, highlights the differences between what students and teachers need to know, examines the big idea and related essential understandings, reconsiders the ideas presented in light of connections with other ideas, and includes questions for reflection.

Teaching With Curriculum Focal Points **(NCTM, 2008–2011):** This series supplements *Curriculum Focal Points* with detailed guidance on instructional progressions, ways to introduce topics, and suggestions to build deeper understanding of essential topics. It includes grade-level volumes for preK–8 and grade-band volumes for preK–2, 3–5, and 6–8.

Considering the unprecedented clarity of the CCSS for mathematics, DuFour et al. (2010) verify why it is essential to take *action* in your collaborative team to develop a shared understanding of the content to be taught, because doing so:

- Promotes clarity among your colleagues

- Ensures consistent curricular priorities among teachers

- Is critical to the development of common pacing required for effective common assessments

- Ensures that the curriculum is viable—that it can be taught in the allotted time

- Creates ownership among all teachers required to teach the intended curriculum

Change in Instructional Emphasis

The Common Core State Standards for mathematics call for a different, and in some cases radically different, way of approaching the content as embodied in the Mathematical Practices. This significant change in instructional emphasis implies an increased need for pedagogical decision making and consistency as you work with your colleagues in your collaborative team to create equitable environments for students in which you use the Mathematical Practices as a vehicle to promote student learning with understanding.

A 2011 review of the Common Core State Standards for mathematics found that the standards represent an instructional shift toward higher levels of cognitive demand than traditionally represented in many state standards (Porter, McMaken, Hwang, & Yang, 2011). The cognitive demand of mathematical tasks matters. Higher student achievement is associated with more challenging mathematical tasks (Schmidt, Cogan, Houang, & McKnight, 2011). Traditional mathematics instruction is often characterized by low-level cognitive-demand tasks that do not support students in developing a deep understanding of mathematics (Silver, 2010). Consequently, it will be critical for you to work within your collaborative team to carefully design your mathematics instruction to engage students with the Mathematical Practices. This will be critical during initial planning, and especially after analyzing student learning, in order to increase the cognitive demand and effectiveness of the selected instructional tasks. *How* the mathematics content is approached to engage students in doing mathematics, as articulated in the Mathematical Practices, is as important—if not more important—than *what* is taught (Schmoker, 2011). Teachers working within grade-level collaborative teams are uniquely positioned to support one another in meeting the challenges associated with implementing the CCSS Mathematical Practices.

Mathematics education in the United States has a long history of confidence in standards and curriculum programs as the primary means to improve student achievement (Larson, 2009). But reliance on standards and materials alone to improve student achievement has not resulted in dramatic improvements in student learning over time. If implementation of the CCSS is to be more than merely superficial (little more than a content-standards mapping), and instead is to result in real improvements in student learning, then implementation efforts need to be more about *how* you approach the Mathematical Practices and not solely the curriculum or content standards.

Ultimately, how you teach the curriculum has a greater influence on student learning than the curriculum itself (Stein & Kaufman, 2010). As Wiliam (2011) contends, "Pedagogy trumps curriculum. Or more precisely, pedagogy *is* curriculum, because what matters is how things are taught, rather than what is taught" (p. 13). As school districts work to interpret and implement the CCSS, there will be a rush to adopt new textbooks, supplemental materials, intervention programs, and online materials as *the* solution to the transition and implementation challenges of the CCSS. Textbook publishers will be poised to offer their latest digital or text-based solutions. Innovative materials alone, no matter what publishers promise, will not—nor will they ever—improve mathematics instruction (Cohen & Ball, 2001). Student achievement is not solely a function of the agreed-on curriculum and the adopted commercial program.

Student achievement is more highly correlated with the nature of classroom instruction —how mathematics is taught rather than what program or materials are used (Slavin & Lake, 2008). An instructional approach that emphasizes high-cognitive-demand tasks that provide opportunities to reason, justify, analyze, and model mathematics—which are expectations in the CCSS Mathematical Practices and NCTM's Process Standards (NCTM, 2000)—is associated with higher student achievement (Stein & Smith, 2010). The CCSS Standards for Mathematical Practice are (NGA & CCSSO, 2010):

1. Make sense of problems and persevere in solving them.
2. Reason abstractly and quantitatively.
3. Construct viable arguments and critique the reasoning of others.
4. Model with mathematics.
5. Use appropriate tools strategically.
6. Attend to precision.
7. Look for and make use of structure.
8. Look for and express regularity in repeated reasoning. (pp. 6–8)

For the full descriptions of the Standards for Mathematical Practice, refer to appendix B (page 157).

Figure 1.2 outlines some high-leverage processes linked to the CCSS Mathematical Practice (Franke, Kazemi, & Battey, 2007; Hiebert & Grouws, 2007; Leinwand, 2009; NCTM, 2007; Stein, Remillard, & Smith, 2007; Stein & Smith, 2010; Teacher Education Initiative Curriculum Group, 2008; Weiss, Heck, & Shimkus, 2004).

- An instructional emphasis that approaches mathematics learning as problem solving (Mathematical Practice 1)

- An instructional emphasis on cognitively demanding conceptual tasks that encourages all students to remain engaged in the task without watering down the expectation level (maintaining cognitive demand) (Mathematical Practice 1)

- Instruction that places the highest value on student understanding (Mathematical Practices 1 and 2)

- Instruction that emphasizes the discussion of alternative strategies (Mathematical Practice 3)

- Instruction that includes extensive mathematics discussion (math talk) generated through effective teacher questioning (Mathematical Practices 2, 3, 6, 7, and 8)

- Teacher and student explanations to support strategies and conjectures (Mathematical Practices 2 and 3)

- The use of multiple representations (Mathematical Practices 4 and 5)

Figure 1.2: High-leverage mathematics instructional practices linked to CCSS Mathematical Practices.

Visit **go.solution-tree.com/commoncore** for a reproducible version of this figure.

The implementation of new standards—in this instance, the CCSS content standards—cannot once again be used as a distraction from a needed laser-like focus on *instruction* (that is, instruction that results in developing students who are proficient with the Standards for Mathematical Practice) if the goal is improved student learning (Noguera, 2004; Schmoker, 2006, 2011). Traditionally, mathematics educators have focused on standards and curriculum because they are easier to address than instruction. Make no mistake, standards, curriculum, textbooks, and related instructional materials are crucial tools for teaching and learning, but to truly improve student learning, the quality of mathematics instruction must improve, and that quality must become consistent across all grade levels.

To effectively implement the CCSS Mathematical Practices, you will need to acquire knowledge and ways of reasoning that enable you to analyze and make sense of your teaching, curricula, and students' mathematical thinking in new or more intense ways than you likely have previously done. In order to adopt the high-leverage instructional practices outlined in figure 1.2, you also have to align your beliefs with this vision for instruction and decide that the change in your practice is worth the effort (Gresalfi &

Cobb, 2011). Collaborative teams are perfectly structured to support you as you work to analyze and make sense of your teaching, come to identify with this new vision of teaching, determine that the change is worthwhile, and find the support necessary to change. This is only possible if the *how* of mathematics instruction—how students do mathematics, embodied in part by the Standards for Mathematical Practice—becomes a significant focus of the collaborative work accomplished in your collaborative team.

Research indicates that effective instruction rests in part on careful planning and that you should consider investing more of your work time in intentionally and systematically planning mathematics lessons with your grade-level colleagues (Morris, Hiebert, & Spitzer, 2009). One of the most effective strategies within collaborative teams to support your adoption of the high-leverage instructional practices (figure 1.2) is the use of a modified form of Japanese lesson study. Japanese lesson study is a highly structured process for designing and improving mathematics lessons (Fernandez & Yoshida, 2004) first introduced on a wide scale in the United States by Stigler and Hiebert (1999). Teachers collaboratively examine *problems of practice* and design lessons to address those problems (Little & Horn, 2007). Describing the process of formal lesson study in detail is beyond the scope of this book, but using some of the concepts of lesson study within your collaborative team is an effective way for you and your colleagues to begin to analyze how you will teach critical grade-level topics.

Consider the following scenario, which describes a second-grade collaborative team engaged in much of the work this book recommends you undertake in your collaborative team as you work to implement the CCSS.

A collaborative team of second-grade teachers is meeting during its common planning time. The teachers know from work they have previously conducted this year that one of the CCSS second-grade critical areas for instructional emphasis is for students to "use their understanding of addition and subtraction to develop fluency with addition and subtraction within 100" (NGA & CCSSO, 2010, p. 17). The team also knows, based on its review of last year's assessment results, that this is an area in which students have traditionally struggled to demonstrate fluency. Even more concerning to the team is its belief that students struggle to develop fluency because they lack a deep understanding of place value that would enable them to use generalizable strategies with efficiency and understanding. The team recognizes that in order to develop deeper student understanding and fluency with adding and subtracting, teachers need to improve the lessons they use to teach this concept, and this means they too need to develop a deeper understanding of the concepts.

So, the team members begin by discussing some reading the teachers have done outside of their collaborative team on the topic using the book *Developing Essential Understanding of Addition and Subtraction for Teaching Mathematics in Prekindergarten–Grade 2* (Caldwell, Karp, & Bay-Williams, 2011). This background reading has deepened the teachers' understanding of addition and subtraction and embedded essential concepts and sparks a productive discussion of new instructional tasks, representations, and questions they can use with students to engage them with the concepts and to check to make sure students understand the concept as the lesson unfolds. By the time the collaborative team is done, team members have written comprehensive lesson plans to introduce these concepts, which include detailed lesson notes, tasks and examples, key questions, anticipated student responses and their planned responses, guided practice tasks, summary questions, adaptations for English learners (ELs) or students with disabilities, and formative assessment strategies to determine if students have accomplished the instructional objective.

Each team member commits to using the lesson with his or her students, and the team has agreed to watch a video together of one team member teaching the lesson in order to evaluate the lesson's effectiveness. The team plans to focus its next collaborative team session on discussing the effectiveness of the designed lesson, based on student performance so teachers can both plan necessary responses to student learning and make modifications to the lesson so that teachers can further improve on the lesson prior to teaching it next year.

Intensive lesson planning as described in the preceding example is not only a high-leverage strategy to support you as you work to change your practice but is also an effective strategy to prevent the degradation of collaborative team discussions into mere story and material swapping or activity sharing (Perry & Lewis, 2010; Stein, Russell, & Smith, 2011). This type of intense collaborative lesson planning is time consuming and difficult to do for each lesson that is taught annually; unfortunately, you do not have that kind of planning time. However, the lack of time to devote to carefully planning and reflecting on all lessons cannot be used as an excuse to *never* collaboratively learn, plan, and reflect on the effectiveness of certain key lessons per standard cluster. Your goal must be to collaboratively design and refine more and more lessons over time. Effective planning is so important that Wiliam (2011) believes that "sometimes a teacher does her best teaching before the students arrive in the classroom" (p. 49). In order to begin the process of improving instruction, your collaborative team should determine the two to three most critical lessons that will be your focus in each unit and commit yourselves to collaboratively planning these key lessons, designing necessary interventions based on student learning, and revising these critical lessons for future use. Which lessons should be selected? The lessons selected for intensive planning and reflection should be focused on those standards students have struggled with most in the past, based on your analysis of prior student assessment results, and the CCSS critical areas for instructional emphasis.

Gradually, year after year, your collaborative team creates and revises more and more highly effective lessons, thereby continuously improving your instruction in small manageable chunks with shared energies rather than in isolation. Simultaneously, as your collaborative team works on lessons—hopefully side by side with other grade-level teams—and uses the refined lessons, you reduce the variation in instructional quality among teachers in your school by following a process that is similar to how other professions in the United States continually improve and develop consistency (Morris & Hiebert, 2011). This process involves collaborative sharing of the same problem for which a product offers a solution, making adjustments to improve the product, and continuously improving the product with contributions from everyone in the system.

This collegial approach is comparable to that of the PLC process, as well as lesson study, which is a strategy that can be conducted within the framework of the professional learning community.

Over the course of a decade, a team of second-grade teachers might amass nearly one hundred highly effective lessons, in addition to more effective interventions for students who struggle and challenges for gifted students. The potential cumulative impact of this work on instructional effectiveness and student learning would be truly remarkable. Now imagine this process being carried out by each collaborative team of teachers within your school district. The powerful cumulative effect of students receiving more and more effective instruction, which can only be accomplished through this system of continuous improvement, has the potential to substantially eliminate the differences in student achievement due to inconsistencies in the quality of instruction and differences in socioeconomic status (Rivkin, Hanushek, & Kain, 2005).

Assessing What Students Should Learn

Once your collaborative team has agreed on the content you intend to teach students and the Mathematical Practices you intend to develop, you must next collaboratively create assessments and scoring rubrics that will indicate whether or not your students have learned the agreed-on content standards. The National Mathematics Advisory Panel recommends using weekly formative assessments with elementary students as a key strategy to support struggling students, provided the assessment results are used to adapt instruction based on student progress (NMAP, 2008).

This recommendation is based on a wealth of research on effective instructional interventions in mathematics; research on the power of formative assessment to impact student achievement; and research on the practices that are in place at schools that are successfully raising the achievement of all students while simultaneously closing the achievement gap (Baker, Gersten, & Lee, 2002; Hanley, 2005; McCall, Hauser, Cronin, Kingsbury, & Houser, 2006; Popham, 2008; Wiliam, 2007b, 2011; Wiliam & Thompson, 2007; Williams, 2003). Researchers have found that the use of formative assessment processes (described fully in chapter 4) as a component of mathematics instruction is one of the most effective educational interventions (Black & Wiliam, 1998).

It is important to recognize that every assessment you use in grades K–2 can and should serve a formative function because the results can be used to provide students with targeted additional support. But before your collaborative team can modify instruction and provide students with targeted additional support, it is necessary to clearly identify individual students' specific mathematics weaknesses and strengths (Hanley, 2005). Chapter 5 provides in-depth guidance on structuring intervention. The focus now is to explain why it is important for you to spend time collaboratively developing assessments and scoring rubrics within your collaborative team.

When you meet in your collaborative team to discuss and plan a phase of instruction, you need to begin your planning with the end in mind (Wiggins & McTighe, 2000).

Once your collaborative team has identified what you want your students to learn, and before you begin to collaboratively plan the first lesson of a *unit* (a period of instructional time, not content), it is crucial your team works together to build the common formative and summative assessments you will use during that unit. During that time, your team will both determine if your students are making progress learning the agreed-on curriculum (by using formative assessment for regularly monitoring and improving understanding) and acquiring agreed-on curriculum at the end of the instructional unit (by using summative assessment to provide an indication of understanding, proficiency, fluency, and problem-solving skill).

It is essential that these assessments be collaboratively created *and* that each member of the collaborative team agrees to use these assessments and scoring rubrics. During the process of creating these common classroom assessments and scoring rubrics, each member of your team clearly defines and solidifies his or her own expectations for student performance, and more important, each team member develops a shared expectation for student performance, how it will be measured, and how it will be recorded—removing one of the instructional inconsistencies that plagues teaching and learning.

Consider an example. One of the critical areas for instructional emphasis in the grade 1 CCSS is that students will develop an "understanding of addition, subtraction, and strategies for addition and subtraction within 20" (NGA & CCSSO, 2010, p. 13). Unless you work together as a team to develop and use common assessments, one teacher may plan to administer a series of timed procedural addition and subtraction basic fact tests while another teacher may require students to write a series of related facts and explain how the different equations are related, emphasizing the conceptual relationship between addition and subtraction. The qualitative difference in depth of knowledge expectations between these two approaches is significant and has a tremendous impact (from an equity perspective) on what students will learn.

If your team collaboratively writes the assessments and scoring rubrics with agreed-on depth of knowledge expectations, then each member of the team shares an understanding of what is expected of students, and more important, *the same performance level is expected of all first-grade students* no matter which teacher the students are assigned. Equally important—by starting with the development of the assessments—all members of your team from the beginning know how students will be assessed. This in turn affects how you will teach. The assessment must focus on conceptual understanding, as CCSS require, and each teacher must know this before teaching the lessons. The collaborative team commitment to using the common assessments and scoring rubrics in turn demands that daily mathematics instruction must also focus on conceptual understanding.

Student performance on these common assessments will be shared with everyone in the collaborative team in order to plan appropriate and targeted intervention. The common unit assessments provide a powerful incentive to make sure that both the same content is taught and the same high level of student performance is expected of all students—procedural *and* conceptual learning goals. In this sense, assessment not only informs instruction but actually directs instruction.

The type of formal formative assessment suggested here is to be relatively short in duration—ten minutes, at most, only covering material taught in the previous two to three lessons—and its use does not result in a significant loss of instructional time. This use of formative assessment as an instructional tool should not be distinguished from the act of effective instruction; in fact, the evidence suggests that the use of formative assessment actually leads to increased precision in how instructional time is used (NMAP, 2008). It is important to keep in mind that formative assessment is a continuous process and not characterized by the use of any specific pencil-and-paper assessment instrument (see chapter 4 for details).

Response to Intervention

An assessment is only formative if you use the results to inform and improve your instruction; effective assessment requires you to take action (respond) when it is determined that students have not learned some component of the agreed-on curriculum. The response also has to be directive; all students who need additional support must be provided the additional support they need (Buffum et al., 2009). DuFour et al. (2008) outline four practices that a school must do to truly ensure learning for all:

1. Implement intervention plans that provide students with additional time and support for learning as soon as they experience difficulty

2. Implement systematic processes to ensure students' learning needs are addressed schoolwide rather than according to the discretion of individual teachers

3. Implement timely procedures to identify and respond to students who need additional time and support

4. Implement directive interventions, meaning students are not *invited* to receive additional support but rather are *required* to receive additional support

The collaborative team process outlined in this book, with its grade-level sessions focused on mathematics lesson planning and the development and analysis of common assessments, is designed to support you in implementing a systematic and timely system of intervention for all students in need of such assistance.

RTI should not be viewed as a program "but rather [as] a system for meeting all students' needs" (Buffum et al., 2009, p. 23). One of the most effective interventions in mathematics at the K–8 level is an approach to instruction that carefully monitors student acquisition of the agreed-on curriculum based on collaboratively designed formative assessments. Ideally, the "formal" formative assessments (recall that formative assessment is a continual process) should be administered at least once a week, with the results of those formative assessments used to form smaller groups of students who should receive *additional* instruction in the skills and concepts with which they are struggling (Baker et al., 2002).

Much of the required targeted additional instructional support will occur during Tier 1 core instructional time (see chapter 5). However, the evidence is clear concerning the positive impact of providing students with an additional period of well-targeted mathematics instruction at the elementary level when it is necessary at Tier 2 and Tier 3 (Slavin & Lake, 2008). But this is the important point: the well-targeted supplemental instruction must take place *in addition to* whole-class instruction instead of *in place of it*. Interventions need to be supplementary in nature and not replace the core program but instead provide additional, more targeted instruction in the core concepts (Buffum et al., 2009). In too many cases, traditional elementary school interventions have failed because they are not done *in addition to* whole-class instruction but *instead of it*. The RTI-tiered preventative approach is designed to minimize the number of students who require Tier 2 or Tier 3 intervention in your PLC.

When students struggle in mathematics, you traditionally respond in one of two ways:

1. You slow the pace of instruction for all students until each student has enough time to master content—"going as fast as the slowest student."

2. You "cover" the content—racing through it and ignoring the fact that some students get it while others do not.

Given the accountability requirements of No Child Left Behind (NCLB), racing through the curriculum without ensuring that students have demonstrated mastery of essential content is no longer an option. This is one of the positive consequences of NCLB. But slowing down the pace of instruction is not a viable alternative. All too often, schools that serve large numbers of struggling students emphasize slowing down the pace of instruction and end up teaching less mathematics content to the very students who most need more instruction in order to learn more content (Walker, 2007).

Strategic efforts must be made to ensure that all students have an opportunity to learn the agreed-on grade-level curriculum and simultaneously guarantee each student the instructional time and support he or she needs to learn it well. Intervention time must be allocated from within the regular school day. There are as many different ways to find the additional instructional time needed for Tier 2 or Tier 3 interventions during the school day as there are schools. Compacting the curriculum can provide the additional mathematics instructional time recommended in the models in figure 1.3 (page 22). The same focus and coherence applied to the CCSS for mathematics curriculum need to be applied to all subjects in the elementary curricula.

There is simply too much content in the elementary school curriculum, both within subjects and across subjects. Selecting and focusing on fewer essential standards can free up the time necessary for a daily differentiated instruction block in mathematics (Schmoker, 2011). The bottom line is that in instrumental subjects—reading, writing, and mathematics—instructional time must expand so that the learning becomes constant for all students (Buffum et al., 2009). Figure 1.3 describes four successful models for finding additional instructional time for mathematics intervention in grades K–2.

Model One: Additional Total Mathematics Time That Individual Teachers Administer

Some schools dedicate additional total time to mathematics instruction. For example, they allot the equivalent of seventy-five minutes of daily math instruction in grades K–2. However, teachers spend sixty minutes daily on new instruction and collect the leftover time to have a thirty- to forty-five-minute differentiated math block of time twice a week in which they address individual student needs based on weekly formative assessments. Individual teachers work with their own students.

Model Two: Additional Total Mathematics Time That Grade-Level Collaborative Teams Administer

Other schools allocate time as in model one, but the teachers work as a team to regroup students so each teacher is not trying to teach as many topics to as many different small groups of students. The teachers meet in their grade-level collaborative teams to determine which students need additional instruction and support in what topics and then regroup the students during the differentiated instruction block. Teachers can then focus their reteaching on fewer targeted topics, and many of the students have the opportunity to learn the concept or skill from a different teacher.

Model Three: Curriculum Compacting to Gain a Weekly Intervention Day

Some schools compact the social studies and science curriculum in grades K–2 by focusing only on the essential objectives, eliminating up to 20 percent of the curriculum. They then use this time to provide all students with a weekly period of additional mathematics instruction to meet individual needs.

Model Four: Compacting Curriculum to Gain Daily Intervention Time

Some schools have left the traditional sixty-minute daily allocation for mathematics instruction intact but compacted other parts of the day to create a daily thirty-minute differentiated instruction block of time. In the most successful implementations, teachers meet in grade-level collaborative teams to identify student needs based on weekly formative assessments and regroup students so each teacher is teaching a smaller set of skills or concepts.

Figure 1.3: Intervention time models in grades K–2.

Visit **go.solution-tree.com/commoncore** for a reproducible version of this figure.

An advantage of the last model is that it allows one teacher in your collaborative team to use the differentiated instruction block to work with those students who have demonstrated high levels of proficiency with the content, permitting these students to study topics in more depth as well as to explore additional but connected concepts. When you work as a collaborative team to regroup students for targeted additional instruction and support (or extended learning), you also ensure every team member carries out interventions and that every student receives either necessary intervention or extended learning time, thereby removing all perceptions that *intervention* is a punishment. An additional benefit of the collaborative team approach to intervention is that you have the opportunity to brainstorm, share, discuss, and develop alternate instructional strategies to meet the needs of individual students. As Buffum et al. (2009) argue, "The vast majority of educators teach the very best way they know how. . . . Most teachers re-teach using the same instructional practices that failed to work the first time" (p. 68). Collaborative teams are uniquely structured to provide you the support and opportunity you need to expand and improve your instructional practices.

The Future of Mathematics in Your School

Transitioning to and implementing the Common Core State Standards is a paradigm-shifting opportunity for you and your students. If the implementation of the CCSS is to have a longer life than previous reforms (Reys & Reys, 2011), then the implementation effort will require you to engage with your colleagues in an ongoing process of professional development and learning as a PLC. Well supported by research, this book outlines deliberate steps that you can take as you work with your colleagues to improve your own mathematics instruction, improve the quality of mathematics education in your school, and help all students develop a deep understanding and proficiency with Common Core for mathematics. Your collaborative team functioning within the designed culture of a PLC is the most effective way to successfully improve mathematics instruction in grades K–2 and meet the challenges of transitioning to and implementing the Common Core State Standards for mathematics.

As you begin to work together with your grade-level colleagues to plan more effective mathematics instruction, it will be critical that you focus on the CCSS Mathematical Practices. The Mathematical Practices (see appendix B, page 157) provide the overarching habits of doing mathematics that all learners at every grade level should experience. In the chapters that follow, we will unpack the Mathematical Practices and the CCSS content standards (see appendices C, D, and E, pages 161, 165, and 171) and explore the role collaborative teams play in implementing and supporting all students' successful acquisition of these new standards through highly effective instruction, assessment, and intervention practices. In addition, you will discover tools that you can use in your collaborative team as you work to make the vision of the Common Core State Standards a reality for your students.

Chapter 1 Extending My Understanding

1. Compare the current model of collaborative professional development used in your school or district with that of Darling-Hammond's (2010) definition of effective professional development (page 6).

   ○ How much time and what time of day (before, during, or after school; late start or early release) is devoted to effective professional development each school year? Each month? Is this time spent in grade-level or vertical collaborative teams?

   ○ What evidence exists to support or improve your existing model?

2. Discuss what an instructional shift toward higher levels of cognitive demand looks like in terms of mathematical tasks and measures of formative assessment.

What is the relationship between higher levels of cognitive demand and the Mathematical Practices?

3. Examine the high-leverage instructional practices linked to the CCSS Mathematical Practices in figure 1.2 (page 15). How do these practices compare with the individual and group philosophies of staff in your grade-level or vertical collaborative team? How might you use this information to identify a starting point for your work with the Mathematical Practices?

4. Use figure 1.3 (page 22) to discuss the advantage and disadvantages of each intervention time model. Which model for finding and using additional instructional time might work best in grades K–2 in your school? What modifications in scheduling might be needed to implement these changes?

Online Resources

Visit **go.solution-tree.com/commoncore** for links to these resources.

- **"A Professional Collaboration Model" (Jenkins, 2010; www.nctm.org /publications/article.aspx?id=27410):** This article describes a well-defined structure to guide the efforts of grade-level collaborative teams as they work to promote positive changes to instructional practices.

- **The Center for Comprehensive School Reform and Improvement (www .centerforcsri.org/plc/websites.html):** Here you can peruse a collection of resources to support an in-depth examination of professional learning communities.

- **Inside Mathematics (www.insidemathematics.org/index.php/tools-for -teachers/tools-for-coaches):** This portion of the Inside Mathematics website helps mathematics coaches and specialists support the professional learning teams they lead. Tools to support lesson study and teacher learning, including video vignettes that model coaching conversation, are available.

- **Inside Mathematics (www.insidemathematics.org/index.php/tools-for -teachers/tools-for-principals-and-administrators):** This portion of the Inside Mathematics website is designed to support school-based administrators and district mathematics supervisors who are responsible for establishing the structure and vision for the work of grade-level and cross-grade-level learning teams or PLC collaborative teams.

- **Learning Forward (www.learningforward.org/standards/standards.cfm):** Learning Forward is an international association of learning educators focused on increasing student achievement through more effective professional learning. This website provides a wealth of resources, including an online annotated bibliography of articles and websites, to support the work of professional learning teams.

CHAPTER 2

Implementing the Common Core Standards for Mathematical Practice

The Common Core State Standards for mathematics include standards for mathematics content as well as standards describing expectations for mathematical practice. As the Common Core State Standards (NGA & CCSSO, 2010) state, "The Standards for Mathematical Practice describe varieties of expertise that mathematics educators at all levels should seek to develop in their students" (p. 6). The Standards for Mathematical Practice are presented in appendix B (page 157). Implementation of the Standards for Mathematical Practice addresses the second required paradigm shift: a shift to include within your daily lesson plans intentional strategies to teach mathematics in different ways—in ways that focus on the process of learning and developing deep student understanding of the mathematical content. Your goal will be to develop in students both conceptual understanding *and* procedural fluency of the CCSS content through the collaborative selection of high-cognitive-demand mathematical tasks with a focus on engagement with the Standards for Mathematical Practice.

Your ultimate goal is to equip students with particular expertise that will help them be successful across the mathematics curriculum and at every level of their mathematics learning. In this chapter, we interpret the CCSS Mathematical Practices to provide you guidance as you work in your collaborative team. This chapter helps you develop understanding for each of the eight Mathematical Practices as you work collaboratively to design lessons that embed these practices into your daily mathematics instruction and make pedagogical decisions necessary to create environments in which the practices enhance instruction focused on student learning.

The CCSS Mathematical Practices are based on the National Council of Teachers of Mathematics (2000) Process Standards (problem solving, reasoning and proof, communication, connections, and representation), and the National Research Council's (2001) Strands of Mathematical Proficiency (adaptive reasoning, strategic competence, conceptual understanding, procedural fluency, and productive disposition). NCTM's and NRC's groundwork is reinforced and further refined in the CCSS Mathematical Practices.

The CCSS Mathematical Practices describe what *students* are *doing* as they learn the CCSS for mathematics content standards. How should students engage with the mathematics and interact with their fellow students? By creating a classroom culture that extends beyond traditional, teacher-centered instruction, you can successfully facilitate students' engagement in mathematics learning that leads to proficiency in the Standards for Mathematical Practice. The Standards for Mathematical Practice are not a checklist of teacher to-dos but rather support an environment in which the CCSS for mathematics content standards are enacted and are framed by specific expertise that you can use to help students develop their understanding and application of mathematics.

The CCSS Mathematical Practices

By first defining each CCSS Mathematical Practice through exposure to its meaning and examples and then addressing each of the questions in figure 2.1 by working in your collaborative team, you can make sense of a particular CCSS Mathematical Practice, generate ideas for how to support the CCSS Mathematical Practice, and analyze ways to assess students' success with the CCSS Mathematical Practice. The questions in figure 2.1 are designed to guide your work in your collaborative team as you explore the eight CCSS Mathematical Practices.

---

1. What is the intent of this CCSS Mathematical Practice?

2. What teacher actions facilitate this CCSS Mathematical Practice?

3. What evidence is there that students are demonstrating this CCSS Mathematical Practice?

Figure 2.1: Key questions used to understand the CCSS Mathematical Practices.

Tasks for collaborative teams are provided for each CCSS Mathematical Practice. The purpose of these tasks is to facilitate your work in collaborative teams by suggesting activities you can complete within your classroom settings or between collaborative team meetings. Your collaborative team can choose to complete the tasks in the order they are provided, address one each team meeting, group tasks together, or pick and choose tasks that best meet the goals of your team.

Mathematical Practice 1: Make Sense of Problems and Persevere in Solving Them

The first step in exploring CCSS Mathematical Practice 1, "Make sense of problems and persevere in solving them," is to provide a clear definition of what a problem is as it specifically relates to mathematics instruction (NGA & CCSSO, 2010, p. 6). A *problem* is defined as a *situation,* be it real or contrived, in which a challenge (question or unknown) that requires an appropriate response (such as an answer, solution, explanation, or counterexample) is presented and for which the person facing the challenge does not have a readily accessible appropriate response (Kantowski, 1980). That is, according to Lester (2010), problem solving is "the process of coordinating previous experiences, knowledge, and intuition in an effort to determine an outcome of a situation for which a procedure for determining the outcome is not known" (p. 93).

Students do not always initially see a viable solution pathway and sometimes will need multiple attempts to successfully solve the problem. This inherently means that problems can vary regarding topics, contexts, structure, and so on, and it means that teaching problem solving is not about teaching specific problems but about teaching students how to use their knowledge, skills, attitude, and resources to successfully respond to problems (Pölya, 1957).

A subsequent notion is this: *problem solving is one of the hallmarks of mathematics.* What allows problem solving to earn such a grand title is that problem solving is the essence of doing mathematics (NCTM, 1980). When students are engaged in problem solving, this means that students are drawing on their understanding of mathematical concepts and procedures with the goal to reach a successful response to the problem.

Although problem solving is a critical element of school mathematics, you may sometimes find that it is a source of frustration for your students. Problem solving is a unique experience for each student. As Lesh and Zawojewski (2007) note, "The problem solver's interpretation depends not only on external factors (i.e., task variables) but even more so on internal factors (i.e., how one interprets, or 'sees,' the mathematics problem)" (p. 766). Additionally, according to the results of the *TIMSS Videotape Classroom Study* (Stigler, Gonzales, Kawanaka, Knoll, & Serrano, 1999), teachers are often likely to "design lessons that remove obstacles and minimize confusion. Procedures for solving problems would be clearly demonstrated so students would not flounder or struggle" (p. 137). Lessons planned from this perspective, that students need protection from struggle, do not support the perseverance aspect of this CCSS Mathematical Practice, and they deny students the opportunity to develop meaningful mathematical understandings (Stein, et al., 2007).

There are two problem-solving issues that students must deal with: (1) the ability to make sense of problems and (2) the fortitude to participate or persevere in the problem-solving process toward a successful end. The latter is an important component of a *productive disposition,* which is addressed as one of the strands of mathematical proficiency defined in *Adding It Up* (NRC, 2001).

The Teacher's Role in Developing Mathematical Practice 1

You are instrumental in helping students develop skills and attitudes that build their ability to solve problems effectively. The tasks presented and the guidance provided enable students to gain confidence as they encounter a variety of problems that require them to employ a range of mathematical skills. To learn how to persevere in solving problems, students must be given opportunities to meet challenges, but not be overwhelmed by them.

Provide Good Problems

You play a critical role in supporting students' ability to make sense of problems and persevere in solving them. The first of these roles is the presentation of appropriate problems or tasks for students to solve. While it seems that *appropriate* is subjective, there are six questions you might discuss within your collaborative team when planning lessons to assess the quality of a problem-solving task.

1. **Is the problem interesting to students?** With information about students' lives (for example, their social interests or creative interests), you can create or select problems that will engage students by inviting them to be personally invested in the problem. Consider the problem in figure 2.2 related to the CCSS for mathematics grade 2 domain Measurement and Data (see 2.MD.8 in appendix E, page 174) that may capture students' interests.

Patti's mom gave Patti $2.50 for her birthday. What combination of bills and coins (for example, ones and quarters) could Patti's mom have given Patti?

Figure 2.2: Sample mathematics task.

2. **Does the problem involve meaningful mathematics?** Meaningful mathematics is mathematics that will propel students forward in their mathematical knowledge at an appropriate level. It is difficult for students to make sense of problems when the mathematics of the problem is not meaningful. Students will often get lost in or discouraged by the complex mathematics and miss the power of the problem. Problems can sometimes be distorted by the use of mathematics that does not add to students' understanding of the problem context. The choice of numbers used may simply complicate the process for students. For example, consider the previous problem (figure 2.2). Giving Patti an amount of $12.50 would unnecessarily complicate the problem and distract students from the purpose of the problem.

3. **Does the problem provide an opportunity for students to apply and extend mathematics?** Problems that support students in applying and extending mathematics they are learning or have learned help students understand the purposes of the problems and give students a starting point for solving the problem.

4. **Is the problem challenging for students?** The purpose of this challenge is not to frustrate students but to build within students the kind of attitudes and perseverance necessary to be a successful problem solver and to exercise students' mental mathematical thought. This is a good exercise for you to engage with in your collaborative team as well.

5. **Does the problem support the use of multiple strategies?** Two students can read the same problem and have two different ways of perceiving and approaching the problem. Consider the following example in figure 2.3 from the second-grade CCSS Mathematics domain Operations and Algebraic Thinking (see 2.OA.3 in appendix E, page 172).

Charlie's friend said Charlie had an even number of cars. Charlie wanted to make sure this was true. Charlie has 18 cars. What can Charlie do to prove that what his friend said is true?

Figure 2.3: Sample mathematics task.

6. **Will students' interactions with the problem reveal information about students' mathematics understanding?** Examining students' interactions with a problem (for example, students' work, discourse, and processes) should provide information about how students' thinking is hindered or evolving by interaction with the problem.

This list of questions is not exhaustive, but it is a beginning step toward examining problems that will potentially benefit students' mathematical learning.

Facilitate Student Engagement in the Problem-Solving Process

Successful problem solving does not mean that students will always conclude with the correct response to a problem but that students will undertake a genuine effort to engage in the problem-solving process, drawing on resources such as appropriate tools, prior knowledge, discussion with others, and questions to aid in the process. Successful problem solvers also recognize that powerful learning can be experienced even when an appropriate answer to a problem evades the student. Successful problem solvers exhibit a willingness to persevere.

Support Students to Unpack Problems, Check Reasonableness of Solutions, and Make Connections

To unpack a problem means to dissect it for the components (the information given, information needed, context, mathematical content, and so on) that might lead to an understanding of the problem and an appropriate response. This is where teachers should be cautioned against an overreliance on *key words* (such as *how many left, how many more, in each,* and *altogether*) and instead incorporate something more closely related to reading comprehension strategies (Clements, 2011). To comprehend problems effectively, students have to employ strategies they learn during reading instruction. These cognitive strategies include identifying relevant details, noting relationships, predicting, making inferences, synthesizing, visualizing, and distinguishing between mathematics terms and general vocabulary, as well as activating prior knowledge. You can remind students that the comprehension strategies they have learned during reading instruction can also be used to understand mathematics problems.

The thinking that is involved in unpacking a problem involves the student seeking information that gives insight on what strategies or ways of thinking might be helpful for solving the problem. It also requires students to flip through their mental files to determine if they have been previously confronted with a similar problem or with a problem that is someway connected to the present problem. Unpacking a problem also entails gathering data about the mathematics of the problem to determine what mathematical concepts are meaningful to the problem. For example, in figure 2.2 (page 28), unpacking the problem would involve the student reviewing the value of different coins and using mathematical concepts to determine that the same monetary amount can be made up of different combinations of coins and bills.

You can help students develop strengths of several processes that are important for the problem-solving experience. For instance, students benefit from knowing that as the problem solvers, they have the responsibility of organizing their thoughts about tackling the problem. These thoughts include a comparison of ways to represent the problem—Should it be with manipulatives? Should it be with drawings? Should it be with an algebraic expression? Teachers could read the questions in figure 2.4 to students to help them organize their thoughts about the problem.

The Problem in My Own Words	What Do I Know About the Problem?	What Do I Need to Know About the Problem?	Is There Any Other Information That Will Be Helpful to Me?

Figure 2.4: Problem-solving organizer.

Visit **go.solution-tree.com/commoncore** for a reproducible version of this figure.

Even after organizing thoughts about a problem and asking questions, students might still struggle with the problem-solving experience. However, healthy struggle is invaluable because it builds students' perseverance for long-term engagement with mathematics. Through perseverance, students come to expect that doing mathematics will often lead them to a need to try different routes of thinking.

You can also help students understand that the answer is not the final step in problem solving. A great deal of mathematical learning can happen when students are guided to explain and justify processes and check the reasonableness of the solution. In many instances, students can learn about other solutions for the problem and other ways of solving the problem, and mathematical connections can be made to other problems and content. Students can examine and change variables in the problem and hypothesize what might change in the process of solving the new problem and how the answer might change.

The Understanding Questions for Mathematical Practice 1

Discussions within the collaborative team are intended to extend your understanding of the Mathematical Practices and ways in which to plan instruction to provide learning experiences that will enable students to become successful in solving problems. Use these questions to guide the discussion.

1. **What is the intent of this Mathematical Practice?** A goal of CCSS Mathematical Practice 1 is for students to become successful problem solvers of word problems and operations.

2. **What teacher actions facilitate this Mathematical Practice?** To facilitate CCSS Mathematical Practice 1, you select appropriate problems and guide students in the problem-solving process (for example, engage students in discussions about problems, and ask questions that promote students' thinking about problems).

Reading problems aloud or selecting problems from children's literature may be particularly important for early (preK, kindergarten, and grade 1) learners.

3. **What evidence is there that students are demonstrating this CCSS Mathematical Practice?** When students are demonstrating Mathematical Practice 1, they are actively pursuing solutions to a variety of problems. They make decisions about strategies to use, showcase their thinking (show their work, respond to questions, and ask questions), and explain the outcomes of problem-solving experiences.

The following Collaborative Team Task is designed to guide the team to consider factors in developing instructional experiences that will contribute to students' skill in solving problems. This discussion will provide additional insight into what constitutes a *good* problem.

Collaborative Team Task: Mathematical Practice 1

Students' problem-solving experiences are grounded in the problems you provide them to discuss, explore, or solve. Your role in selecting good problems is very important because sometimes students work on "exercises" that do not extend their learning and only reinforce what they already know. Your task is to select a good problem and submit it to your collaborative team for exploration and discussion. The following questions will support this discussion.

1. What is the source of this problem? What are other fruitful sources for problems?

2. What is the grade level for this problem? (This is a valuable discussion for vertical collaborative teams.)

3. What CCSS Mathematics content is reflected in this problem?

4. Is the context of the problem generally familiar to students?

5. What piqued your interest in this problem when you first read it? Do you think it will capture students' attention in the same way?

6. What characteristic of this problem promotes mathematical discourse?

7. What type of learner will benefit from this problem?

8. Is there only one or more than one way to solve the problem?

9. Is there only one or more than one answer (or other type of appropriate response) for the problem?

10. Can this problem be used flexibly for assessment (formative or summative)?

11. How might you differentiate the problem (make it more or less challenging) to adjust to individual student learning needs?

12. How does engagement with the problem extend students' learning?

13. What is most challenging about selecting good problems for students?

Visit **go.solution-tree.com/commoncore** for a reproducible version of this feature box.

Mathematical Practice 2: Reason Abstractly and Quantitatively

Reasoning in mathematics is the means by which students try to make sense (by thinking through ideas carefully; considering examples, counterexamples, and alternatives; asking questions; hypothesizing; pondering; and so on) of mathematics so it is usable and useful (NCTM, 2000). Hence, the role of CCSS Mathematical Practice 2, "Reason abstractly and quantitatively," is critical to students' engagement in every area and at every level of the mathematics curriculum (NGA & CCSSO, 2010, p. 6). According to Ball and Bass (2003), "Mathematical reasoning is something that students can learn to do" (p. 33). In fact, these authors suggest two very important benefits of reasoning: it (1) aids students' mathematical understanding and ability to use concepts and procedures in meaningful ways and (2) helps students reconstruct *faded knowledge,* that is, knowledge that is forgotten but can be restored through reasoning with content.

Students can of course reason about many things including definitions, examples, and counterexamples. However, paramount in learning mathematics is the need for students to specifically reason about quantities, that is, the need to make sense of quantities and their meanings. Making sense of quantities and understanding their meaning involves addressing the numerical representation, either abstractly or in context. For example, the numeral 7 is an abstract representation of a quantity or a counting number. However, when a context is connected to 7, the number can take on a different meaning. For instance, 7 might be used in the context of order, such as the *seventh digit,* or in the context of identification, such as Team 7. Hence, on the surface, the concept of number may seem trivial, but actually, the concept of number is very complex when numbers are not learned in isolation but within various contexts. You cannot overlook the concept of number in students' learning procedures for the basic and advanced operations. In fact, "almost all the mathematics that children encounter in elementary school, and much of what they encounter beyond that level, is firmly based in number, [so] the importance of sound number sense cannot be overstated" (Perry & Dockett, 2002, p. 93).

The Teacher's Role in Developing Mathematical Practice 2

Although students may have the ability to use reasoning to address everyday occurrences, young learners are not likely to have had frequent opportunities to reason in the context of mathematics. Students' strategic use of reasoning is fostered through activities centered on numbers and their applications, along with conversations about the mathematical thinking involved.

Provide Distinct Opportunities for Students to Develop Number Sense

Students need to develop a deep number sense so they will have a strong foundation for reasoning. With a clear articulation of number sense, you can provide students with a variety of instructional supports to help develop theirs. Number sense can be viewed as an understanding of number that empowers students mathematically in at least six ways.

1. **Express interpretations about number:** Consider these numbers: 5, 7, 20, 9, and 13, and what would be involved in students making sense of them and their meanings. For example, the knowledge of *five-ness* affords students the ability to describe sets as equal to, greater than, or less than five. Students can also recognize when a set has five objects and when it does not. However, these same numbers can be considered further by exploring the addends that would make each number a sum. Different thinking and reasoning about the context would be involved in students making sense of the numbers and their meanings.

2. **Apply relationships between numbers:** Knowing how two or more numbers relate to each other supports students' engagement in mathematics in many ways. For example, in the CCSS for mathematics second-grade content domain Operations and Algebraic Thinking (see appendix D, page 172) knowing that 5 and 10 are related because $5 + 5 = 10$ supports students' fluency with addition.

3. **Recognize magnitude of numbers:** Students' understanding of the magnitude of numbers (including comparing quantities and sizes) is important to help students make sense of their world. Students also need to understand that though magnitude may be abstract, it is also contingent on the context. Simply asking students, "Is twenty a big number?" is not enough to support students' reasoning about magnitude of number because twenty may be big in one context— twenty eggs for breakfast—but not another—twenty stars in the night sky. Very young learners need opportunities to engage in discourse about magnitude of numbers in order to develop an understanding of number.

4. **Compute:** Computation using the basic operations depends on students' number sense. The stronger students' number sense, the more they are able to use strategies such as estimation and alternate representations of numbers—for example, viewing 16 as $5 + 5 + 6$, $10 + 6$, or $8 + 8$ (see first-grade CCSS domain Operations and Algebraic Thinking in appendix C, page 166) to facilitate computation. Moreover, in the realm of computation, students need to reason to make sense of operations. For instance, it is through reasoning, not mere memorization, that students come to truly understand that there are 12 tens in 125, not just 2. This supports the flexibility in computation that allows students to solve problems like $125 - 73$ by thinking "Subtract 3 ones from 5 ones to get 2 ones, and subtract 7 tens from 12 tens to get 5 tens, for a difference of 52" (see second-grade CCSS domain Number and Operations in Base Ten in appendix E, pages 172–173).

5. **Make decisions involving numbers:** One thing that makes the ability to reason abstractly and quantitatively crucial is that this is a very important life skill useful for making daily decisions. For example, consider a mathematical task from the CCSS for mathematics kindergarten domain Counting and Cardinality (see K.CC.1 in appendix C, page 162). Suppose a person is given instructions to walk north down Main Street and leave a package at the eighth house on the

left; the person would then need to be able to count to find the correct house. By exploring various real-life examples that involve decision making around real-life quantities, students come to realize the importance of being able to make sense of numbers in their own lives.

6. **Solve problems:** For students to be successful solving word problems, they need to be able to translate given information into an algebraic representation. Reasoning through given information in a word problem is what affords students with the numbers, variables, structures, and so on needed to develop algebraic representations that support efficient manipulations of numerals and symbols.

Draw Students' Attention to Numbers and Their Applications

There are several ways you can help students to reason about numbers. First, it is helpful to consider numbers to be a source of exploration for learners. Numbers are found everywhere, including on signs, license plates, room numbers, street addresses, and so on. Secondly, as the National Council of Teachers of Mathematics (2000) recommends, "regularly encourage students to demonstrate and deepen their understanding of numbers and operations by solving interesting, contextualized problems and by discussing the representations and strategies they [students] use" (p. 79). The benefit of problem solving can be strengthened by further supporting students' understanding and reasoning about responses to and extensions of the problem. For example, you could ask students, "How many classrooms are on our floor of the school?" Their thinking could be extended by asking, "Are there the same number of classrooms on the floor above or below ours?" With each of these questions, students should provide justifications for their answers. Asking, "How do you know?" requires students to justify their responses—whether numerically or otherwise—and helps them develop reasoning skills.

Encourage Discussion That Promotes Reasoning

Classroom discussion that promotes reasoning is discourse that involves teacher-to-student communication as well as student-to-student communication. Teacher-to-student communication might include questions from the teacher that probe students' thinking beyond the suggestions of an answer. You consider students' answers, whether right or wrong, as opportunities to stretch students' thinking beyond the answer realized. In addition, teacher-to-student communication can and should involve discussions emerging from students' hypotheses about a mathematical concept or procedure and students' conjectures on how mathematics works. This discussion can even stem from the presentation of student work samples, even work samples from fictitious students. Student-to-student communication is supported by peer-to-peer explanations and debates when students are required to provide justification for their thinking. Students working collaboratively to engage in mathematics can fuel student-to-student discourse by sharing their mathematical thought and decision making about the routes their thinking should take in order to arrive at sensible conclusions. Inferences about students' ability to reason can also be determined through the careful analysis of student work and performance in mathematics.

The Understanding Questions for Mathematical Practice 2

Being able to reason is central to students' success in learning mathematics as well as in other areas of the curriculum. These questions provide a framework for collaborative team discussions of Mathematical Practice 2.

1. **What is the intent of this Mathematical Practice?** A goal of CCSS Mathematical Practice 2 is for students to learn how to reason with and about mathematics.

2. **What teacher actions facilitate this Mathematical Practice?** To support students' development of reasoning, you should provide students space to think and reflect on mathematical content and support students in communicating and refining their thinking.

3. **What evidence is there that students are demonstrating this CCSS Mathematical Practice?** When students are demonstrating CCSS Mathematical Practice 2, they are sharing and justifying their mathematical conceptions and adjusting their thinking based on mathematical information gathered through discussions and responses to their questions.

The ability to reason is a learned skill, one that is nurtured and is essential to learning mathematics well. In the following Collaborative Team Task, you can explore ideas about how to help your students develop reasoning and engage in productive discussions that foster your own reasoning.

Collaborative Team Task: Mathematical Practice 2

This Collaborative Team Task is designed to focus the team's discussion on activities that promote the development of students' ability to reason. Articles from professional journals can be used to promote constructive discussions within the collaborative team. In the example that follows, two articles from *Teaching Children Mathematics* are used to support discussion and comparison of instructional practices within the collaborative team. If you do not have access to this journal, the team can select two other readings related to reasoning about number.

One-half of the collaborative team could read the following article:

Rathouz, M. (2011). 3 ways that promote student reasoning. *Teaching Children Mathematics, 18*(3), 182–189.

The other half of the collaborative team could read the following article:

Olson, J. (2007). Developing students' mathematical reasoning through games. *Teaching Children Mathematics, 13*(9), 464–471.

continued →

For the collaborative team meeting, each subteam should prepare to present a summary of the article and engage the other subteam in a discussion regarding the primary points of the article.

For example, Rathouz's article addresses the role of justifying solution methods in students' mathematics learning. What norms does your team have in place to ensure that students are learning how to justify their solution methods and how to determine if others' solution methods are valid?

Olson's article presents a variety of games that support students' mathematics learning and encourages the development of students' reasoning skills. What games are best for this role? What games do the collaborative team members currently use that support students' reasoning skills?

Visit **go.solution-tree.com/commoncore** for a reproducible version of this feature box.

Mathematical Practice 3: Construct Viable Arguments and Critique the Reasoning of Others

Students engaged in CCSS Mathematical Practice 3, "Construct viable arguments and critique the reasoning of others," are making conjectures based on their analysis of given situations (NGA & CCSSO, 2010, pp. 6–7). Students explain and justify their thinking as they communicate to other classmates and you. Classmates listen to explanations and justifications and judge the reasonableness of the claims. The successful facilitation of this standard is based on the social learning environment of the classroom. As Rasmussen, Yackel, and King (2003) state:

> Every class, from the most traditional to the most reform-oriented, has social norms that are operative for that particular class. What distinguishes one class from another is not the presence or absence of social norms but, rather, the nature of the norms that differ from class to class. (pp. 147–148)

Does your class have a norm that requires students to provide an explanation with their solution? This norm, if present, places importance on *how* students solved a problem rather than just *if* they solved the problem.

In a classroom in which students are expected to construct arguments and critique others' reasoning, students should:

1. Provide explanations and justifications as part of their solution processes

2. Attempt to make sense of their classmates' solutions by asking questions for clarification

3. Communicate when they don't understand or agree with solutions others present, spurring healthy debate between and among students

Eventually, these discussions become a natural part of the classroom discourse and can occur in an organized way without your direction. These norms are established through a process of negotiation in which you make your expectations clear but also involve students in the process of implementing the norms (Cobb, 2000). These negotiations often emerge when establishing classroom rules, such as "Be respectful" and "Listen when others are speaking." You need to discuss the importance of classroom rules, and the class can generate a reasonable number of rules and create a list that it agrees to follow at all times. These sorts of rules help to support what effective mathematics learners do. Mathematics learners make conjectures, test those conjectures, and discuss their implications within a community that is receptive to such discussions.

Dixon, Egendoerfer, and Clements (2009) describe a study in which an elementary school teacher encouraged students to participate in whole-class discussion during mathematics instruction without raising their hands to speak. While this was intimidating for the teacher at first, ultimately the students in this class provided more rich verbal and written mathematical explanations and justifications; students who were unsure of their solutions were more comfortable sharing them, and "students began to exhibit understanding that could be defined as more conceptual than procedural in nature" (p. 1074). The expectation isn't that all teachers should now eliminate the rule that students must raise their hands and be acknowledged before speaking, but rather, you should think about what sorts of expectations and behaviors support desired engagement during mathematics instruction and what might detract from it.

The Teacher's Role in Developing Mathematical Practice 3

A learning-centered classroom affords students opportunities to engage in conversations with their teacher and peers about their thoughts and actions as they solve problems. Such a classroom embodies a positive environment in which mutual respect flourishes because everyone is aware of the social norms and expectations. Teaching practices should foster a communicative atmosphere in which student voices are evident as they explore mathematics concepts, use mathematics vocabulary, and demonstrate their ability to use mathematical processes (Kinzer, Virag, & Morales, 2011).

Establish Supportive Social Norms

Once you determine desirable characteristics of classroom engagement that will support students making and testing conjectures and evaluating the reasoning of others, it is likely you will need to model these sorts of behaviors for your students. One way to do this is to share several correct solutions to the same problem. The solutions should vary in terms of the included explanations and justifications. You can share the solutions with the class as a whole-class discussion or have small groups evaluate the acceptability of the solutions. Discussion should focus on the completeness of the solutions and whether or not the explanations are limited to a list of steps followed to solve a problem or determine the *mathematical reasoning* involved. Emphasis should be placed on the need to include mathematical reasoning with solutions.

Similarly, you should share solutions that include adequate explanations and justifications and have students work in groups to critique the reasoning itself. This is different from determining if enough information was included. The focus here is on the mathematics. You can use think-aloud techniques with students as you make sense of the reasoning shared in the problem as a way to model what it means to critique the reasoning of others. In these instances, sample work that reflects common misconceptions provides a useful means for generating discussion around common errors.

Provide Opportunities for Students to Make and Evaluate Conjectures

Consider the following scenario in a second-grade classroom from the domain Number and Operations Base Ten (see 2.NBT.7, appendix E, page 173) in which students are engaged in exploring multidigit subtraction. Students work independently to solve 203 – 68 using strategies of their choice. Students share their solution strategies with the class. One student records the problem on the board and says, "I thought of 203 as 20 tens and 3 ones. I needed more ones to have enough to subtract 8 ones, so I exchanged 1 ten for 10 ones, leaving me with 19 tens and 13 ones. Then, I just subtracted 8 ones from 13 ones and 6 tens from 19 tens to get 135." (See figure 2.5.)

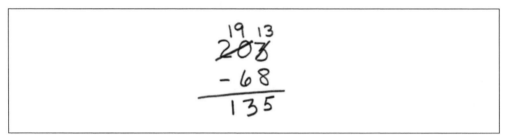

Figure 2.5: Sample student work.

Another student says, "You got the right answer, but I don't think you did it correctly. There aren't 20 tens in 203, there are 0 tens." The first student then goes on to explain that while there is a 0 in the tens place, the 2 in the hundreds place can be broken into 20 tens. Once the student made sense of this solution strategy, other students went on to share their strategies. Another student says, "I got a different answer. I added 2 to 68 to get 70, because 70 is easier to subtract than 68. But since I added 2 to 68, I needed to subtract 2 from 203, so I had 201 minus 70, which equals 131." In order for another student to make sense of this thinking, he draws a number line on the board. (See figure 2.6.)

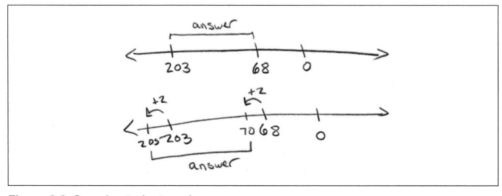

Figure 2.6: Sample student work.

By marking where 68 and 203 might be located, the student indicated that the difference between them would be the answer to the problem. Then, the student showed where 70 would be and noticed that the 203 would need to be changed to 205 rather than 201 to maintain the same distance. The student who shared this solution strategy was able to see the error and indicated his agreement with the correct solution.

Facilitate Meaningful Discussions of the Mathematics

During the discussion of the subtraction problem, the students were able to share their solutions with rich explanations and justifications so that others could make sense of their reasoning. Additionally, a member of the class was able to identify and address another student's misconception. If students did not provide enough information for a good discussion or were not able to identify the misconception, it would be necessary for the teacher to facilitate this process. This often occurs by asking challenging and probing questions (for example, "Where is the answer represented on the number line? When you shift from 68 to 70, what does that do to the answer to the subtraction problem?") that guide the sharing of information and critiquing of arguments. To do this effectively, you need a deep understanding of the mathematics you teach so you can support student engagement in this practice. Hill, Ball, and Shilling (2008) call this type of mathematics knowledge *specialized content knowledge*. With the two strategies discussed previously, you would need to be comfortable flexibly representing numbers (for example, 203 as 20 tens 3 ones, or 19 tens 13 ones) and using tools such as the number line to make sense of comparison subtraction. Your questions would then be based on bringing these concepts to the foreground during the discussion.

The Understanding Questions for Mathematical Practice 3

Purposeful talk is an essential component of an effective mathematics class. As students present their approaches to solving problems and listen to the comments of their peers, they acquire skill in engaging with ideas, thinking out loud with others, and working to co-construct those ideas. Similarly, as students work to make sense of the reasoning of others, they learn the very important skill of critical analysis.

1. **What is the intent of this Mathematical Practice?** A goal of CCSS Mathematical Practice 3 is for students to make and test conjectures and to communicate their mathematical thinking.

2. **What teacher actions facilitate this CCSS Mathematical Practice?** You establish social norms in the classroom that support communicating mathematical ideas and questioning the thinking of others. Your level of specialized content knowledge is such that you are able to provide rich problems to elicit conjectures and arguments, to identify common misconceptions, and to guide discussions around important mathematical ideas.

3. **What evidence is there that students are demonstrating this CCSS Mathematical Practice?** Students are presenting their solutions along with the

justifications for their choices. When there is disagreement regarding a solution, the student making the claim explains her thinking. The student critiquing the claim makes sense of the argument and then provides clarification, including examples or counterexamples and another justification.

Individually assessing interactions with the students is not an easy task even though it is likely that you routinely reflect on what happens to make some lessons successful and others not so successful. This Collaborative Team Task provides a framework for observing whole-class instruction with a colleague.

Collaborative Team Task: Mathematical Practice 3

Collaboration can support reflection on one's own practice. Work with a partner to set up a time to observe one another teach a mathematics lesson. The purpose of the observation will be to collect data regarding teacher-to-student and student-to-student interactions during whole-class instruction. Keep track of the following questions throughout the lesson.

1. What types of questions does the teacher ask students? Are they higher-order thinking questions, or are they questions that elicit rote responses?

2. How do students respond to question? Do they just give solutions, or is there an expectation that they will also explain their solution strategies?

3. How does the teacher react to the students' responses? Does the teacher ask for additional justifications and clarifications? Does the teacher ask other students to explain classmates' reasoning?

4. Do the students in the class listen to one another's contributions to the class discussion? If so, what data support this?

5. To whom does the teacher direct questions? Are only students who raise their hands called on? Does the teacher tend to call on students known to have the correct answers or students who will likely share misconceptions?

Discussion Questions

1. What trends do you notice in questioning techniques and social norms across the observed lessons of teachers within your collaborative team?

2. How might questioning help you improve the level of mathematics conversation in the classroom?

3. What action items do you have to establish social norms conducive to implementing CCSS Mathematical Practice 3?

Visit **go.solution-tree.com/commoncore** for a reproducible version of this feature box.

Mathematical Practice 4: Model With Mathematics

Students engaged in CCSS Mathematical Practice 4, "Model with mathematics," solve real-world problems by applying known mathematics (NGA & CCSSO, 2010, p. 7). This practice is often misinterpreted as representing mathematical concepts by using manipulatives exclusively because of the word *model*. While manipulatives and other representations can be used as instructional tools to make sense of real-world problems, that is just one element of this Mathematical Practice. Students might also use tools such as pictures or a hundreds chart to make sense of the mathematics. More generally, students use symbols and tools to represent real-world situations and move fluidly between different representations based on what questions they are trying to answer. The ways students model and represent situations will evolve as they learn more mathematics. For example, a preK–2 student might model a situation in which a student and two friends each have four friendship bracelets by writing 4 + 4 + 4 to determine how many bracelets they have in all, whereas a third-grade student might model the same situation with the expression 3 × 4. Both students have modeled the situation with mathematics using representations appropriate to their grade levels. A goal is for students to model mathematics to become more mathematically proficient.

The Teacher's Role in Developing Mathematical Practice 4

Students' learning in mathematics is enhanced when they have opportunities to use various modes to express their ideas. Although verbal communication is an important feature of mathematics instruction, students also need opportunities to use nonlinguistic representations like diagrams or mathematical models. Both verbal and nonverbal presentations can be used to facilitate students' ability to determine whether their thinking makes sense or is reasonable.

Provide Opportunities for Students to Solve Real-World Problems

This standard serves to connect CCSS Mathematical Practice 1 and CCSS Mathematical Practice 2 with its focus on *mathematizing* real-world problems. Students must first be given the opportunity to explore real-world problems or situations, and then they must be encouraged to represent those problems mathematically. Once students represent the problems with mathematics, they should solve the problems and interpret their results within the context of the problem. All of this depends on the students being provided the opportunity to solve problems that arise from everyday life.

Consider the following word problems in figure 2.7 related to the first-grade domain Operations and Algebraic Thinking (see 1.OA.1 in appendix D, page 166).

Jessica has 7 key chains. Alex has 8 key chains. How many key chains do they have altogether?

Jessica has 7 key chains. Alex has 8 key chains. How many more key chains does Alex have than Jessica?

Figure 2.7: Sample math tasks.

Frequently when teachers encounter these sorts of problems, it is common for them to focus on identifying the key words for their instruction (Clements, 2011). In these instances, students would be taught that *how many more* means *subtract,* and *altogether* means *add.* Now consider the following word problem in figure 2.8 (page 42).

> Jessica has 7 key chains. How many more key chains does she need to have 8 key chains altogether?

Figure 2.8: Sample math task.

Students whose instruction has overemphasized key words will likely see *altogether* and add 7 and 8 to get 15 key chains as their answer. These students are not engaged in modeling real-life situations with mathematics; they are just looking for key words, ignoring the situation, and moving directly to reasoning abstractly. It would be beneficial for you to provide students with opportunities to solve problems such as this one and to focus students' attention on making sense of the problem rather than looking for words to serve as cues devoid of context.

Focus Students' Attention on Sense Making and Reasonableness of Results

If instruction focuses on making sense of the problem, then students are more likely to act out the problem using their fingers, manipulatives, or drawings to represent the quantities in the problem. Once students choose a tool to represent the quantities, there is an opportunity to engage in CCSS Mathematical Practice 5, which is described in the next section. What is important here is that students make sense of the problem and then ensure that their solutions are *reasonable.* A student who used key words incorrectly and determined the solution to be 15 key chains would see that an answer of 15 key chains is not reasonable. If Jessica wants a total of 8 key chains, then adding more than 8 would not make sense. Focusing students' attention on making sense of problems and checking for reasonableness of results should begin as soon as students begin to solve problems. This is appropriate and important in the primary grades.

Have Students Develop Real-Life Contexts to Support Mathematical Expressions

In the first-grade CCSS for mathematics domain Operations and Algebraic Thinking (see 1.OA.8 in appendix D, page 167), students complete equations by determining the unknown whole number in equations such as $8 + ? = 11$. A useful strategy to help students make sense of modeling real-world contexts with mathematics is to provide them with equations such as this and challenge them to develop a corresponding real-world context. Consider a task from the first-grade CCSS for mathematics domain Operations and Algebraic Thinking (see 1.OA.1 in appendix D, page 166), in which students are challenged to add to solve word problems. If a student provides a context that represents adding both given quantities, such as, "Jessica has 8 key chains. Alex gives her 11 more. How many key chains does Alex have now?" we can assume that this student needs additional support making sense of the equation $8 + ? = 11$. This student might think that when there are numbers and an addition symbol, the goal is to add whatever is provided. By affording opportunities for students to develop real-world contexts to correspond to mathematics expressions, and then to check to make sure the correspondence is accurate, you are facilitating students' sense making relative to modeling mathematics. In order for you to be comfortable in this role, you should spend time exploring such representations with your colleagues in your collaborative team.

The Understanding Questions for Mathematical Practice 4

Many situations that students encounter in their daily lives involve the use of mathematics—counting change from a purchase, sharing pieces of birthday cake, figuring out how much material is needed to make a puppet, choosing menu items that match the money they have in hand, and so on. Presenting students with problems that reflect everyday experiences ensures that students recognize the practicality and value of learning mathematics.

1. **What is the intent of this Mathematical Practice?** A goal of CCSS Mathematical Practice 4 is for students to model real-world situations with mathematics in order to solve problems in everyday life in reasonable ways.

2. **What teacher actions facilitate this Mathematical Practice?** You focus students' attention on mathematizing real-life situations, and then question students to remind them to be sure that the solutions to these problems are reasonable relative to the context in which they arose.

3. **What evidence is there that students are demonstrating this CCSS Mathematical Practice?** Students are active participants in using mathematics to make sense of daily life. They use symbols and tools to help them make sense of and solve naturally arising problems in reasonable ways.

Learning to use various forms of representation is central to helping students extend their thinking in mathematics and other subjects as well. As your team explores multiple representations in mathematics for students, you might want to reflect on the ways in which you can use different forms of expression to develop and convey your ideas about instructional practice.

Collaborative Team Task: Mathematical Practice 4

Modeling in mathematics is very much related to the concept of *multiple representations*, as well as students' ability to interpret visual and verbal presentations symbolically. Being equipped to guide students to develop or expose students to multiple representations is particularly important for diverse primary-grade classrooms in which different students will certainly have different learning strengths, background knowledge, and learning styles. Multiple representations, such as text, numerical representations, pictorial representations, concrete representations, and so on, provide powerful opportunities for students to develop conceptual understanding—particularly in grades preK–2.

Your collaborative team should select a mathematical concept, particularly one that students often struggle with, and discuss the mathematical concept in regards to

continued →

its multiple representations and the benefit that each representation might afford learners. The following chart might be used to record your team's discussion to share with others.

Mathematical concept:			
Text Representation	Numerical Representation	Pictorial Representation	Concrete Representation

Visit **go.solution-tree.com/commoncore** for a reproducible version of this feature box.

Mathematical Practice 5: Use Appropriate Tools Strategically

The nature of mathematics facilitates the use of a variety of tools for teaching and learning. Every mathematics classroom should be equipped to accommodate CCSS Mathematical Practice 5, "Use appropriate tools strategically" (NGA & CCSSO, 2010, p. 7). Hands-on, active, and concrete learning support this CCSS Mathematical Practice. For students, particularly at the preK–2 levels, this standard is *not* about watching the teacher demonstrating various tools. Specifically, this practice is about students *experiencing* the opportunity to develop an understanding by engaging in applications involving mathematics. In fact, some mathematics content domains, such as Measurement and Data, cannot be sufficiently explored unless students have access to appropriate tools that aid them in literally doing this mathematics.

The Teacher's Role in Developing Mathematical Practice 5

In far too many classrooms, the teacher does most of the talking and demonstrating while students play a spectator role. Although this depiction might not be so characteristic of preK–2 classrooms, an over-emphasis on telling and showing, rather than engaging, in these early years has the potential to detract from the interactive involvement with learning critical concepts and skills so important in early childhood settings. The CCSS for mathematics have established conditions for instructional practice that require students' active participation in the learning tasks. Consequently, classrooms need to be equipped with resources that enable students to use various sensory modes as they explore solutions to mathematical problems.

Provide Students With Access to Appropriate Tools

In order for students to select appropriate tools, those tools first have to be made available to them. You should have an effective plan for acquiring or providing access to tools and an effective system for students to use those tools (for example, having tools organized in plastic bins on students' tables). In a nutshell, a variety of tools should be readily available to students to support their mathematical explorations. Table 2.1 lists ten common mathematics teaching and learning manipulatives for grades K–2 and the corresponding CCSS for mathematics content domain (the manipulatives may be used for other domains as well). You also need to make sure that a variety of other practical tools are available to students—for example, two-column mats for work with tens and ones and early recording of two-digit numbers, part-part-whole grids for representing addition and subtraction situations, hundreds charts for counting and early mental-math activities, and grid paper, tape, scissors, and rulers, as appropriate to the grade.

Table 2.1: Common Mathematics Teaching and Learning Manipulatives

Manipulative	CCSS Content Domain
Two-color counters	Number and Operations in Base Ten
Number cubes	Measurement and Data; Number and Operations in Base Ten
Square color tiles	Measurement and Data
Pattern blocks	Operations and Algebraic Thinking
Tangrams	Geometry
Colored cubes	Number and Operations in Base Ten
Beads on a string	Number and Operations in Base Ten
Cuisenaire® rods	Number and Operations in Base Ten
Various countable objects	Number and Operations in Base Ten
Fraction circles	Geometry

Facilitate Students' Selection of Tools

Once you have ensured that a variety of tools are available to students, you can provide them with support in selecting appropriate tools for a particular mathematics exploration. It is important to keep in mind that often a mathematical tool (manipulative) can be used for study in multiple areas of mathematics. For instance, a set of pattern blocks is useful for studying numerical and visual patterns but also for composing and partitioning shapes. Sometimes students may be uncertain about which tool to select for a particular mathematics task. By providing students with options, you can gather information about students' learning preferences, their thinking as related to a particular tool, and which tools work most effectively for which students. In addition, by providing guidance instead of selecting tools for students, you provide space for students to make hypotheses, try new ways of studying mathematics, and have a context for comparing how different tools can either be useful or a hindrance for studying the specific mathematics. Here are five questions for use in the collection of tools made available to students:

1. Does the tool provide a meaningful model to support the mathematics?

2. Does the tool extend students' thinking and support their learning of the given mathematical topic?

3. Is the tool necessary?

4. Is the tool easy to use?

5. Does the tool provide support for students to engage in and solve a problem?

Help Students Become Aware of the Power of Tools

You may find that it is very engaging (and even enjoyable) to teach mathematics with a variety of tools. However, the real issue is whether student learning was supported by the use of tools—tools should not be used for the sake of using tools. If students use tools to engage in mathematics and walk away from the experience with little or no understanding of the mathematics, then the use of the tools was ineffective. You will want to continually ask challenging questions and probe students' thinking before, during, and after students use tools to study mathematics. Figure 2.9 has questions you can use to probe students' thinking regarding tool usage.

Questions Before Tool Usage

What tool do you think you need for your task?

Why did you select this tool?

Questions During Tool Usage

Show me how you are using the tool. Is it helpful to you?

How is using the tool helping you learn?

Questions After Tool Usage

What did you learn by using this tool?

Will you use a different tool next time?

Figure 2.9: Tool-usage questions.

The Understanding Questions for Mathematical Practice 5

Effective instruction achieves the goal of successful learning and achievement for all students. Such instruction takes into account activities that appeal to the visual, auditory, and tactile kinesthetic learning modes (Erwin, 2004). Appropriately using tools in mathematics lessons is another component in ensuring that all students are successful.

1. **What is the intent of this Mathematical Practice?** A goal of CCSS Mathematical Practice 5 is for students to make proper decisions about which tools (if any) they will use to learn the mathematics.

2. **What teacher actions facilitate this CCSS Mathematical Practice?** You can facilitate this practice by making appropriate tools accessible to students and guiding students in their selection and use of these tools.

3. **What evidence is there that students are demonstrating this CCSS Mathematical Practice?** Students engaged in this CCSS Mathematical Practice are actively using manipulatives and other practical learning tools when needed to develop their mathematics understanding.

Access to a cumulative list of learning tools is a great time-saver for busy teachers. In this Collaborative Team Task, you have the opportunity to assemble a catalog of learning tools.

Collaborative Team Task: Mathematical Practice 5

Each member of your collaborative team likely has access to a variety of learning tools to support students' mathematics learning. The results of this task will be a team members' catalog of learning tools that may be shared for students' benefit.

Create a chart similar to the following, and provide it to each team member to complete. The information on this chart can be collapsed into one chart to be shared with and discussed by all team members.

	Manipulative Tool	General Tool	Technology Tool
Connecting cubes	✓		
Virtual manipulatives			✓
Place-value mat		✓	

Visit **go.solution-tree.com/commoncore** for a reproducible version of this feature box.

Mathematical Practice 6: Attend to Precision

CCSS Mathematical Practice 6, "Attend to precision," refers to the need for students (and teachers) to communicate precisely and correctly (NGA & CCSSO, 2010, p. 7). Such *precision* is established at the earliest levels as young children encounter mathematics activities. Student communication might involve developing and using mathematical vocabulary properly; using symbols appropriately, most notably the equal sign; specifying units along with the associated quantities; and including clear and concise explanations when describing solutions. Additionally, an expectation of CCSS Mathematical Practice 6 is that students will be accurate and appropriate with procedures and calculations. Accuracy is self-explanatory, but appropriateness as it relates to precision is a bit more elusive. Part of solving problems provided in context involves determining the level of precision that is necessary. Sometimes an estimate is sufficient. If that is the case, how close of an estimate is warranted or acceptable? The same is true with measurement. The level of accuracy for measurements is often determined by the context of the problem. Consider, for example, the following mathematical task for the first-grade CCSS for mathematics domain Measurement and Data (see 1.MD.1 and 1.MD.2 in appendix D, page 168):

> Ms. Albright's class is trying to determine the fastest route to take from the class to the playground so that students can get the most time possible playing outside. The class has mapped out 3 different ways to go. Which is the best choice?

This problem also supports CCSS Mathematical Practice 4 as students are making sense of a real-world problem and finding ways to represent it with mathematics. The problem solver is left with determining appropriate ways to address this problem. One aspect of the problem-solving process is to determine the level of precision necessary to answer the problem. Students could use snap cubes to measure the routes so that they could determine the length of the routes to the nearest snap cube. Would meter sticks be appropriate? What about similar-length strides? Students engaged in solving this problem might develop justifications that support variation in acceptable accuracy. These aspects of solving problems and making sense of mathematics are explicated through CCSS Mathematical Practice 6.

The Teacher's Role in Developing Mathematical Practice 6

Acquiring, using, and understanding the language of mathematics is essential to students' success in the subject and in applications of mathematics within other subject areas. This means that students must be exposed to mathematical vocabulary and symbols in meaningful contexts and given tasks that enable them to use the terms purposefully in both oral and written activities. Because many words in English have more than one meaning, students need experiences that help them recognize that familiar words have specialized meanings when used in mathematics.

Model Appropriate Use of Mathematics Vocabulary, Symbols, and Explanation

Students often emulate their teachers when they are not precise with vocabulary and definitions, general language, and ideas related to mathematics. For example, when teaching the second-grade CCSS for mathematics domain Geometry (see 2.G.1 in appendix E, page 174), if you describe rectangles as having two long sides and two short sides in order to support students' efforts to identify rectangles, you are likely doing so to help provide students with an accessible visual. However, in the process, they are also inadvertently excluding the square as a special case of the rectangle. You might *describe* a given rectangle as having two long sides and two short sides. While *some* rectangles can be described like this, the *definition* of a rectangle must not be so limiting as to exclude the square. You want to be careful of the messages you send your students at all times during mathematics instruction. Reaching agreement on the use of mathematics language is an appropriate use of your time in your collaborative team.

The CCSS for mathematics promotes the use of properties of operations to add in the first-grade domain Operations and Algebraic Thinking (see 1.OA in appendix D, page 167). When you model such practices or record the thinking of your students, you must be careful to honor the meaning of the equal sign. Consider 8 + 7. A student might use the associative property of addition to solve this problem by first breaking apart the 7 into 2 and 5 and then adding 8 + 2 to get 10 and 10 + 5 to get 15. The student might say, "I thought of 7 as 2 plus 5. I know that 8 plus 2 is 10, and 5 more is 15." When recording this student's thinking, you must be careful to not string the equal signs together and write 8 + 2 = 10 + 5 = 15. While this represents the student's spoken explanation, it also indicates that 8 + 2 = 15. That is not a precise or accurate use of the equal sign and must be avoided. Instead, represent the student's explanation as follows:

8 + 2 = 10

10 + 5 = 15

This representation models the appropriate use of symbols while simultaneously representing the student's thinking related to the problem. You must attend to precision with the vocabulary, symbols, and explanations you use in the classroom so that students do not learn unintended and inaccurate mathematics but rather are provided a model of attending to precision.

Provide Opportunities for Students to Share Their Thinking

When students are given opportunities to explain and justify their mathematical ideas, they can become engaged in Mathematical Practice 6. For example, when students are asked to describe how they solved an addition problem, they should be expected to perform the calculations accurately and to use language to describe the procedures they used precisely. Revisiting 203 − 68 (2.NBT.7, appendix E, page 173), a student might describe how he or she used a standard algorithm to find the difference. The student might say, "I had to borrow, but I couldn't borrow from the 0, so I borrowed from the 2. I crossed out the 2 and made it a 1; then I added a 1 to the 0 to make it a 10. I crossed out the 10 and made it a 9 and made the 3 a 13. Then I subtracted 13 minus 8 to get 5, 9 minus 6 to get 3, and 1 minus nothing to get 1." This student has not used proper place-value language in his explanation. By providing the opportunity for the student to share his thinking, you can now ask questions of this student and the class to develop the proper language to describe the subtraction process. You might ask, "When you crossed out the 2 and made it a 1, was that really a 2, and did you really just cross it out and make it a 1? What were you actually doing to the number 203?" In this way, the teacher is helping the students focus on the precision of the vocabulary used and the explanations provided and thereby emphasizing students' conceptual understanding of mathematics. The students will be led to see that what they were actually doing is exchanging 1 hundred for 10 tens and so on. Similarly, in the grade 2 CCSS for mathematics domain Measurement and Data (see 2.MD in appendix E, page 174), you should expect students to include appropriate units with quantities when sharing solutions to problems involving linear measurements as well as other solutions to problems provided in context.

Prepare Students for Further Study

How often is "you can't subtract a big number from a small number" heard in elementary classrooms? This overgeneralization causes problems later when students learn that when working with integers they *can* subtract this way, and the result is a negative number. By communicating ideas that do not support the mathematics to come later in the curriculum, you are setting students up for confusion as they encounter mathematics in later grades. This confusion is avoidable when you model the CCSS Mathematical Practice 6.

The Understanding Questions for Mathematical Practice 6

To think and act like a mathematician, students need to be able to use the language of mathematics accurately and appropriately. Helping students become lovers of words—logophiles—should not be limited to reading and writing instruction. Many opportunities exist in mathematics class to help students become word conscious and, at the same time, build their knowledge of mathematics.

1. **What is the intent of this Mathematical Practice?** A goal of CCSS Mathematical Practice 6 is for students to attend to precision in all aspects of communication related to mathematics.

2. **What teacher actions facilitate this CCSS Mathematical Practice?** When you model the appropriate use of vocabulary, symbols, and explanations for current grade-level content, you prepare students for the mathematics to come in future grades. It is important to provide opportunities for students to share their mathematical ideas and for you to attend to what they share for accuracy.

3. **What evidence is there that students are demonstrating this CCSS Mathematical Practice?** Evidence of this CCSS Mathematical Practice must be grounded in communication, whether written or oral. Students engaged in this CCSS Mathematical Practice are using careful, accurate definitions; they are including units with quantities as necessary; and they are performing computations carefully and appropriately and accurately describing the procedures they used. Sharing of ideas for this aspect of student learning should be an ongoing part of the work in your collaborative team.

The following Collaborative Team Task centers on precision in using mathematical language. Through discussion of the activity, you may discover that occasionally you need to be more precise in how you use mathematics vocabulary, as well as general terms that have specialized meanings in mathematics. If you have videos of lessons from the observations accompanying the Collaborative Team Task for CCSS Mathematics Practice 3 (page 40), use the videos to examine how precisely language is used in those lessons.

Collaborative Team Task: Mathematical Practice 6

Work as a collaborative team to brainstorm ways in which students might be using imprecise vocabulary in their mathematics talk. Topics might include language associated with place value, addition, subtraction, and measurement. Identify a topic that is closely related with the students' current focus of instruction. Keep a journal of students' imprecise use of the identified terms during mathematics instruction over the next one to two weeks. Share your journal with the team and discuss ways of supporting students' attention to precision. Use a chart similar to the following.

Topic:		
Term	**Use of Term**	**Description of Inaccuracy**
Borrow	Regrouping during subtraction	The term *borrow* implies that the digits are not part of the same number.

Visit **go.solution-tree.com/commoncore** for a reproducible version of this feature box.

Mathematical Practice 7: Look For and Make Use of Structure

A major contribution to the beauty of mathematics is its structure. There's structure all across the mathematics curriculum. Consider structure in geometry (every square is a rhombus), basic operations (an even number plus an even number always results in a sum that is an even number), and numerical patterns, in the case involving doubling (1, 2, 4, 8, and so on). Structure helps students determine what to expect in mathematics. If students learn how and why mathematics works and why it works the way it does, they then begin to notice, look for, and even anticipate how to use the structure within mathematics to solve problems—they become engaged in what it means to do mathematics. There are several ways to support students in their development of looking for and making use of structure in mathematics.

The Teacher's Role in Developing Mathematical Practice 7

Students are familiar with school and classroom routines, which provide structure for the time and activities they experience. Consequently, they develop an understanding of structure in their lives. They know it's early when they wake up, a bit later when they go to school, almost lunchtime when they start feeling hungry, and time to go home a little after lunch—all the while not knowing how to tell time. The structure of these routines allows them to approximate times using daily benchmarks. Thus, students informally learn that structure is an important component of mathematics learning.

Draw Students' Attention to Structure in Mathematics

Students may or may not recognize structure in mathematics. For those students who do not readily recognize structure in mathematics, it is important that they be encouraged to attend to structure. You can do this by presenting examples that are conducive to exploring structure (see figure 2.10, page 52) and then providing students with opportunities to create their own examples of structure to share and discuss with one another.

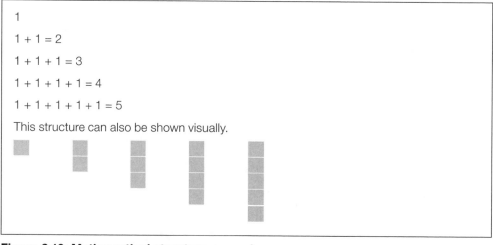

1

1 + 1 = 2

1 + 1 + 1 = 3

1 + 1 + 1 + 1 = 4

1 + 1 + 1 + 1 + 1 = 5

This structure can also be shown visually.

Figure 2.10: Mathematical structure examples.

Engage Students in Exploring Patterns in Numbers

Patterns provide a very productive context for helping students recognize and use structure in mathematics. For example, in the kindergarten CCSS for mathematics domain Counting and Cardinality (see K.CC.1, appendix C, page 162), when counting to 100 by ones and tens, students can explore where repetitions take place, such as in "thirty"-one, "thirty"-two, "thirty"-three, and so on.

The more students have an opportunity to explore structure and the more frequently you point out and discuss structure, the more confident students will become in looking for and recognizing structure on their own. For example, have preK students identify numbers using collections of one to ten counters. Then, work backward starting with ten counters, and remove a counter for each number. A second step may be to provide random collections of counters up to ten (three, five, nine, and so on) and have students identify the number of counters, and then ask how many one more or one less would be.

Help Students Make Use of Structure

Students can benefit from acknowledging structure when studying across the mathematics curriculum. After students are confident in recognizing structure, you can model for students the mathematical power that comes from using structure in mathematics. For example, there are many instances in which students can learn through a problem and develop an understanding that no matter the context, problems of a certain structure are worked exactly the same way. Consider the following addition task from the second-grade CCSS for mathematics domain Operations and Algebraic Thinking (see 2.OA.1 in appendix E, page 172).

Joan is going camping and needs to carry everything she brings in her backpack. Her tent and sleeping bag weigh 13 pounds, her food and water weigh 15 pounds, and her clothes weigh 6 pounds. How much will Joan's pack weigh?

Last week, Ms. Shey went shopping for supplies for her classroom. She bought 28 pencils, 7 boxes of tissues, and 14 bottles of glue. How many items did she buy?

If students understand the structure of the problem, they can be successful with this problem type, even if the context changes. In these sample problems, students *add* collections of similar units—pounds or items—in the same way.

The Understanding Questions for Mathematical Practice 7

When students understand the structure of problems, they observe patterns, which help in solving problems. Providing students with different opportunities to understand structure will help early mathematics learners recognize familiar structures in problems—these structures are particularly helpful when learning how to add and subtract as they may include joining, separating, comparing, and understanding part-whole relationships.

1. **What is the intent of this CCSS Mathematical Practice?** A goal of CCSS Mathematical Practice 7 is for students to recognize structure and to use mathematical structure to learn mathematics with understanding.

2. **What teacher actions facilitate this CCSS Mathematical Practice?** Your actions that facilitate CCSS Mathematical Practice 7 showcase various patterns for students to explore and provide students the opportunity to describe the structure they see.

3. **What evidence is there that students are demonstrating this CCSS Mathematical Practice?** Students engaged in this CCSS Mathematical Practice demonstrate awareness of structure in mathematics by identifying instances of structure, discussing structure, and using structure in advantageous ways to solve problems and learn other mathematics. For example, some students will see $9 + 8$ as a doubles plus 1 fact ($8 + 8 = 16$ plus one more for 17). More formally, they might see it this way: $9 + 8 = (8 + 1) + 8 = (8 + 8) + 1 = 16 + 1 = 17$. This use of the fact strategy *doubles plus one* is essentially applying the commutative and associative properties of addition.

Looking for and making use of structure as a Mathematical Practice is a developmental challenge for preK, K, and grade 1 students in particular. However, students at the preK–2 levels are exposed to structure informally as they engage in work with patterns, use strategies to develop fluency when adding and subtracting within 20, and develop other critical standards at these instructional levels. In the following Collaborative Team Task, you have an opportunity to discuss how you have approached Mathematical Practice 7 with your students.

Collaborative Team Task: Mathematical Practice 7

One opportunity for grade 1 and 2 students to consider structure is in determining related sums and differences. For instance, ask students, "What are different ways to make 27?"

Possible student answers may be:

$20 + 7$

$30 - 3$

continued →

10 + 10 + 7

Teachers can then ask probing questions like, "How do you know your responses are correct?" "What is another way you can use 20 and 7 together to make 27?" "Can you make 27 with 4 addends?"

In your collaborative team, discuss the variety of ways each of you might address these examples of structure. How could they be connected to properties for addition, such as the commutative or associative properties?

Discuss other areas of the mathematics curriculum in which structure is important though perhaps initially hidden from learners. Share ways you have addressed this phenomenon in your collaborative team.

Visit **go.solution-tree.com/commoncore** for a reproducible version of this feature box.

Mathematical Practice 8: Look For and Express Regularity in Repeated Reasoning

When engaged in CCSS Mathematical Practice 8, "Look for and express regularity in repeated reasoning," students move beyond simply solving problems to finding ways to generalize the methods they use and to determine shortcuts for those procedures (NGA & CCSSO, 2010, p. 8). Consider the process of making sense of number pairs that make 8 and support the CCSS kindergarten domain Operations and Algebraic Thinking (see K.OA.3 in appendix C, page 163). Students first need to determine that there is more than one way to combine pairs of numbers for a sum of 8. They might explore using connecting cubes to see that one yellow cube and seven white cubes make eight, and similarly, seven yellow cubes and one white cube make eight. They can record these results in the equations 1 + 7 = 8 and 7 + 1 = 8. Students look for repeated reasoning when they begin to record their equations in an organized list such as the following.

8 + 0 = 8

7 + 1 = 8

6 + 2 = 8

5 + 3 = 8

Students express regularity in repeated reasoning when they see that by reducing the first addend by one and increasing the second addend by one, the sum is still 8. Students develop shortcuts when they realize that because 6 + 2 = 8, for example, then they can change 6 to 5 and 2 to 3 and they know that 5 + 3 = 8 without counting. Eventually, students generalize this result to pairs of numbers to make other sums like 7 or 9. This process of first noticing repeated calculations and making sense of them to determine general methods and ultimately shortcuts for computing is the intent of CCSS Mathematical Practice 8.

The Teacher's Role in Developing Mathematical Practice 8

Being able to acknowledge regularity in reasoning is important in mathematics, as it is in everyday life. Think how complicated life would be if every individual experience had to be recalled in isolation without the benefit of appreciating similarities and differences. Understanding relationships and forming generalizations in mathematics develops over time as students learn to identify regularity in reasoned responses and recognize the value of structure in their learning.

Avoid Teaching Shortcuts Before Students Develop Understanding of Important Concepts

With their desire to simplify students' learning pathways and minimize confusion (Stigler et al., 1999), teachers are often tempted to provide students with efficient computational procedures too early. When this occurs, students miss the opportunity to look for and express regularity in repeated reasoning. Instead, you should provide students with opportunities to make sense of problems and to look for the regularity in the calculations. This practice interacts with CCSS Mathematical Practice 1 (page 26), as this will require that students develop perseverance to make sense of the repeated reasoning.

Scaffold Examples to Highlight Regularity in Repeated Reasoning

The examples you provide and the questioning techniques you employ help students notice if calculations repeat. Asking students to describe the processes they use and look for repetition in those processes provides the scaffolding necessary for primary-grade students to begin to make sense of the process of determining general methods for calculations. You will need to consider multiple examples—as well as their progression—to help students move from seeing the repeated reasoning of a single example to being able to build a general method.

Establish Expectations for Students and Share Conjectures About General Methods

The classroom environment and expectations established that relate to classroom mathematics interactions set the stage for students to engage in this practice. If there is an expectation that students will make conjectures related to what they notice in the mathematics they experience, students are more likely to look for and make sense of such generalizations. Your role is to create and maintain these norms in your classroom. In classrooms that expect students to create generalizations and then defend them, as well as consider potential counterexamples, students will have the opportunity to create general methods for repeated reasoning. In a classroom such as this, students might explore computations and record those computations in a table. The whole class might then discuss the generalizations that can be made from the table to form and test conjectures. Thus, CCSS Mathematical Practice 8 is closely linked to CCSS Mathematical Practice 3 (page 36).

The Understanding Questions for Mathematical Practice 8

Developing proficiency with this CCSS Mathematical Practice might be considered in the context of these adages: *haste makes waste* and *slow and steady wins the race*. You can help students learn to appreciate that slowing down, having patience, and persevering are valuable behaviors in achieving success in mathematics.

1. **What is the intent of this CCSS Mathematical Practice?** A goal of CCSS Mathematical Practice 8 is for students to look for repetition in the calculations they complete with the goal of determining general methods and related shortcuts.

2. **What teacher actions facilitate this CCSS Mathematical Practice?** You should be careful to avoid oversimplifying instructions or making sense of shortcuts in calculations for students. Instead, you want to provide examples for students to complete, highlighting regularity for students to identify, by questioning students regarding the processes they use. As an example, students could think about 38 – 17 as three ten blocks and eight ones and then remove seven ones and one ten to show a difference of twenty-one. Using these representations helps build students' conceptual understanding by relating *removing a group from a larger group* to the procedural shortcut of 38 – 17. This will require instructional time to develop. Additionally, you will create an environment that supports students in making and sharing conjectures about general methods they notice.

3. **What evidence is there that students are demonstrating this CCSS Mathematical Practice?** Evidence that students are demonstrating Mathematical Practice 8 takes the form of classroom discussions or written descriptions in which students describe the conjectures they make regarding what they notice about repeated calculations, as well as define their general methods.

Repetition is a key element in determining patterns and in allowing one to develop conjectures. The following Collaborative Team Task provides an opportunity for you to examine mathematics content that is suitable for repeated reasoning and to consider the instructional strategies you will use to teach such concepts.

Collaborative Team Task: Mathematical Practice 8

As you begin to make plans to engage students in this CCSS Mathematical Practice, it is helpful to think of opportunities for students to use repeated reasoning. This sort of reasoning can be promoted with a variety of mathematical tasks such as with the *doubles plus one* or *doubles minus one* strategies when exploring sums for basic facts. For example, to solve 6 + 7 using doubles plus one, students would add 6 + 6 to get 12, which is a known fact to the young learner, and then add 1 to get 13.

Work as a collaborative team to examine mathematics concepts and related skills that lend themselves to an emphasis on looking for and making sense of repeated reasoning. Make plans to engage students in this practice during instruction of those topics and write reflections on the results. Discuss the reflections at the next collaborative team meeting.

Visit **go.solution-tree.com/commoncore** for a reproducible version of this feature box.

Mathematical Practices Implementation

As discussed in chapter 1, effective mathematics instruction rests in part on careful planning (Morris et al., 2009). Ensuring that the CCSS Mathematical Practices are an important component of each day's mathematics lesson will require significant and careful planning by your collaborative team. The lesson-planning tool in figure 2.11 will support your collaborative development of daily lessons to embed the Standards for Mathematical Practice. This tool is intended to support the vision of instruction for your school or district, and teams can use it to discuss daily lesson construction that will include the Standards for Mathematical Practice.

Unit: Date: Lesson:		
Learning target: As a result of today's class, students will be able to ＿＿＿＿＿＿＿		
Formative assessment: How will students be expected to demonstrate mastery of the learning target during in-class checks for understanding?		
Probing Questions for Differentiation on Mathematical Tasks		
Assessing Questions (Create questions to scaffold instruction for students who are "stuck" during the lesson or the lesson tasks.)	**Advancing Questions** (Create questions to further learning for students who are ready to advance beyond the learning target.)	
Targeted Standard for Mathematical Practice: (Describe the intent of this Mathematical Practice and how it relates to the learning target.)		
Tasks (The number of tasks may vary from lesson to lesson.)	**What Will the Teacher Be Doing?**	**What Will the Students Be Doing?** (How will students be actively engaged in each part of the lesson?)
Beginning-of-Class Routines How does the warm-up activity connect to students' prior knowledge?		
Task 1 How will the learning target be introduced?		

Figure 2.11: CCSS Mathematical Practices lesson-planning tool.   continued →

Task 2 How will the task develop student sense making and reasoning?		
Task 3 How will the task require student conjectures and communication?		
Closure How will student questions and reflections be elicited in the summary of the lesson? How will students' understanding of the learning target be determined?		

Visit **go.solution-tree.com/commoncore** for a reproducible version of this figure.

It might be useful to categorize the CCSS Mathematical Practices in ways that are meaningful to the team. The conversation regarding best ways to group the practices will likely lead to useful discussions related to ways to engage students meaningfully in mathematics. Collaborative teams are uniquely structured to provide you the time and support you need to interpret the CCSS Mathematical Practices, focus on their intent for students, embed the Mathematical Practices into daily mathematics lessons and plans for assessment, and reflect together on the effectiveness of implementation. The questions provided and the unpacking or understanding for these practices in this chapter can serve as a guide to your collaborative team as you work together to develop a shared understanding of the CCSS Mathematical Practices. Use table 2.2 to support your efforts to develop shared understanding in your collaborative team.

Although the CCSS Mathematical Practices are not content per se but rather ways of interacting with the content, they cannot exist without the CCSS for mathematics content standards (see appendices C, D, and E, pages 161, 165, and 171). Planning for instruction, therefore, must simultaneously involve careful consideration of the mathematical content goals and how the CCSS Mathematical Practices can be implemented during the lesson to aid students in developing deep understanding of the content standards. Chapter 3 will examine the unique characteristics and essential features of the CCSS for mathematics content standards.

Table 2.2: Developing Shared Understanding of the Mathematical Practices

	Describe the Intent of This CCSS Mathematical Practice	Describe One Teacher Action That Might Facilitate This CCSS Mathematical Practice	Describe Evidence of Students Engaged in This CCSS Mathematical Practice
CCSS Mathematical Practice 1			
CCSS Mathematical Practice 2			
CCSS Mathematical Practice 3			
CCSS Mathematical Practice 4			
CCSS Mathematical Practice 5			
CCSS Mathematical Practice 6			
CCSS Mathematical Practice 7			
CCSS Mathematical Practice 8			

Visit **go.solution-tree.com/commoncore** for a reproducible version of this table.

Chapter 2 Extending My Understanding

1. Examine the Process Standards (NCTM, 2000) and the Strands of Mathematics Proficiency in *Adding It Up* (NRC, 2001) in detail. How are each related to the CCSS Mathematical Practices? How might you and your collaborative teams explain these relationships to other stakeholders, including parents or guardians?

2. Design a plan for building student awareness (or deepening student understanding) of the Mathematical Practices. What initial tasks or activities will you use? How do you plan to continue to reinforce these practices? What is

your plan for developing parent/guardian and family awareness of the practices? Initial tasks? Ongoing reinforcement?

3. Develop a list of student behaviors as defined in the Mathematical Practices. Record the teacher actions that might promote student implementation of the practices. Then, schedule informal peer observations or video record mathematics classes in action. Spend time as a collaborative team debriefing these observations.

   ○ Did collaborative teams observe these dispositions? How, when, and under what conditions did they see students exhibit the Mathematical Practices?

   ○ What surprised you?

Online Resources

Visit **go.solution-tree.com/commoncore** for links to these resources.

- **Common Core Implementation Videos (NGA & CCSSO, 2011; www.ccsso .org/Resources/Digital_Resources/Common_Core_Implementation _Video_Series.html):** To assist states with CCSS implementation, this series of video vignettes examines the standards in greater depth. Be sure to check out "Mathematical Practices, Focus and Coherence in the Classroom" and "The Importance of Mathematical Practices." You can also visit the Hunt Institute's YouTube channel (www.youtube.com/user/TheHuntInstitute#g/u) to access these videos.

- **Common Core Look-fors (CCL4s)—Mathematics iPad/iPhone App (http://splaysoft.com/CCL4s/Welcome.html):** CCL4s is a comprehensive tool designed to help teacher learning teams deepen their awareness and understanding of the actions and conditions that promote student engagement with the CCSS for Mathematical Practice, with connections to the content standards. An exciting blend of creativity, innovation, and strategic technology use, this app supports purposeful classroom observation though effective staff collaboration.

- **Mathematical Practices Learning Community Templates (www.schools.utah .gov/CURR/mathsec/Common-Core/MathematicalPracticesLearning CommunityTemplates.aspx):** These resources include nine templates for use by teacher learning teams that are seeking to understand the Mathematical Practices and their connections to the NCTM Process Standards and Standards of Mathematics Proficiency.

- **Video Illustrations of the Common Core Standards for Mathematical Practice (Inside Mathematics, 2010; http://insidemathematics.org/index .php/common-core-standards):** This site provides classroom videos and lesson samples designed to illustrate the Mathematical Practices in action.

- **Standards for Mathematical Practice (Common Core State Standards Initiative, 2011; www.corestandards.org/the-standards/mathematics/introduction/standards-for-mathematical-practice):** This site links the text of the eight Mathematical Practices and the selection on "Connecting the Standards for Mathematical Practice to the Standards for Mathematical Content."

- **Common Core State Standards Resources (NCSM, 2011; www.mathedleadership.org/ccss/materials.html):** These professional development files are ready to use and designed to help teachers understand how to implement the Mathematical Practices in their classrooms.

CHAPTER 3

Implementing the Common Core Mathematics Content in Your Curriculum

Chapter 2 presented a strong argument for designing the transition to the CCSS through the window of teacher and student engagement in the Mathematical Practices (see appendix B, page 157). This makes a lot of sense as you consider the mathematics content of the CCSS. What's the content? How does this mathematics differ from what you are now teaching or have previously taught? Are there particular standards that require additional focus? What about topics that appeared to be a struggle for your students last year or throughout your career? These "in my room with my kids" concerns are legitimate at every grade level.

This chapter provides a number of analysis tools for examining your classroom, school, or district implementation of the content domains and expectations of the Common Core State Standards. As you work collaboratively with colleagues, you will be able to address and become conversant with the paradigm shift *less is more*. The Common Core standards require you to shift to *less* (fewer standards) is *more* (opportunity to dig deeper with understanding) at each grade level in your school.

The CCSS at the elementary level (K–5) outline a clearly defined and coherent set of grade-level standards calling for a deep student understanding of those standards. Knowing how to read the CCSS grade-level standards is an important first step in developing a common vocabulary within the collaborative team. Recall figure 1.1 (page 11) and the key terms for Common Core mathematics grades K–2. Three key terms from figure 1.1 are used throughout this chapter—*standards, clusters,* and *domains.*

The focused nature of the CCSS, and the careful attention paid to students' developmental learning progressions, means that some of the topics you traditionally taught in certain grades have been moved to other grade levels, and some topics have simply been eliminated from the elementary school curriculum. The purpose of the more focused CCSS curriculum is to provide you more time to teach fewer critical topics with greater depth and student understanding. As you use the analysis tools in this chapter, be sure to also plan for the amount of time (days) you will need for teaching the various content standards and subsequent mathematics units.

One of the primary purposes for taking time to discuss the CCSS content standards in your grade-level collaborative team is to develop shared teacher ownership and understanding of the CCSS content standards and the Mathematical Practices. By discussing each domain and the corresponding content standard cluster, your team will better understand the meaning of each standard. Your collaborative team discussions will also allow your team to design expectations for student demonstrations of understanding and proficiency for each standard.

But first, your team should spend some time to explore the historical and policy-related underpinnings of the mathematics curriculum for the CCSS.

Collaborative Content Analysis

Helping students use their prior knowledge to enable them to recognize what is new and different in their learning is a key element of scaffolding instruction. Similarly, as you explore the CCSS for mathematics, it will be helpful to compare aspects of the different mathematics standards that have framed your prior knowledge for the grade-level curriculum you teach. Taking a look at the historical documents that have influenced the CCSS content allows you and your colleagues to identify what is familiar, what is new, and what is challenging. And, it will allow for team discussions about the changes required in the CCSS you will deliver to your students.

Before you examine the CCSS for mathematics for your grade level, you may find it helpful to use appendix F (page 175) and refer to the history of mathematics curriculum standards development that framed previous standards and provides the foundation for the CCSS. In all likelihood, the standards you have been using were based on three landmark documents that have influenced preK–8 mathematics instruction since 1989, when the National Council of Teachers of Mathematics published *Curriculum and Evaluation Standards for School Mathematics* (NCTM, 1989).

1. In 2000, NCTM updated the curriculum standards in *Principles and Standards for School Mathematics* (PSSM), which has served as the blueprint for revised state standards throughout 2000–2010.

2. In 2006, NCTM released the *Curriculum Focal Points*. The *Curriculum Focal Points* were intended to serve as a discussion document for states and school districts as they began a conversation around the more important or *focus* topics at particular grades for preK–8. The CCSS *critical areas* presented at the beginning of each grade level's discussion (see appendix C, page 161, for example) are, in essence, the *Curriculum Focal Points*. See table F.2 (page 177) to get a sense of these critical areas for grades preK–2.

3. In 2008, the National Mathematics Advisory Panel (NMAP) identified the Critical Foundations of Algebra. These clusters of concepts and skills are considered essentials for all students prior to formal coursework in algebra and include major content topics, with suggested grade-level benchmarks for grades 3–5 as outlined in appendix F. The work of NMAP has strongly influenced the conceptual understanding and skill proficiency needed in grades preK–2 for students to be ready for the grades 3–5 expectations.

As we have noted previously, preK standards are not a component of the CCSS. The main reason for this omission is that preK is not a state requirement. Several states have created their own preK standards as a part of the 15 percent of additional mathematics that states may add to the CCSS. Consider Maryland and New York if you are contemplating the establishment of your own preK standards (see appendix A, page 153, for a summary of the New York and Maryland efforts and links to the work of these two states). As a beginning, look at the mathematical content expectations in these preK standards. An analysis of the domain or topic headings for grades K–2 (see table F.1, page 176) provides a starting point in thinking about what's important at and across particular grade levels. Using table F.1 may provide an opportunity for your collaborative team to discuss and determine professional development needs and your comfort with the content domains

As you consider and analyze mathematics standards at the preK (see appendix A, page 153) and kindergarten levels (see appendix C, page 161), an initial analysis involving the Focal Points may be the best first step. The following deeper levels of analysis are a *backmapping* of what the Common Core State Standards provide as considerations for the kindergarten level as well as considerations for prerequisite experiences at the preK level. This appears to have been the tactic Maryland employed in creating its preK standards. The Maryland preK standards relate very closely to the CCSS in several ways, including the domain and standard language employed as well as links to forthcoming work at the kindergarten level.

The CCSS provide a second-level professional development opportunity for your collaborative team on the important mathematics for grades K–2. By reading through appendix F (page 175) and responding to the questions provided, your collaborative team will be better prepared to engage in meaningful discussions about what's important, mathematically, across each of these three grade levels. Additionally, the documents presented in appendix F provide a resource that eliminates any major surprises regarding actual content topics as experienced teachers review the CCSS domains, standards, and clusters for grades K–2.

You and your team can use the following Collaborative Team Task to help you summarize your observations about the changes in mathematics standards and what you can look forward to as you learn more about the CCSS content expectations. Use appendix F as needed to help you respond to these questions.

Collaborative Team Task: What Do the Changes in Mathematics Standards Mean for Our Grade Level and Our School?

Your team needs to focus on changes that will be required with implementation of the CCSS for mathematics at your grade level. The following questions will help your team expand on your thinking about the impact of the CCSS for your work and planning.

1. Which aspect of the CCSS content is of most concern to you?

continued →

2. What kind of support do you anticipate you will need to make the transition from what you do now to what you will be required to do with implementation of the CCSS?

3. In what ways has the information about the CCSS Mathematical Practices (chapter 2) helped to provide you with new insights relative to how you will approach your instruction with the expectations of the CCSS content standards?

4. What do you think should be the priorities for your team during the school year as you reflect on the changes in mathematics standards for your grade level?

As discussed in chapter 1, it is critical that you develop a shared understanding with your colleagues of the content to be taught because it helps develop consistent curricular expectations, serves equity goals, and creates ownership among all teachers (DuFour et al., 2010). As you examine the content domains within grades K–2 to develop this shared understanding, you can use these understanding questions for the content standard clusters in each of the five domains to guide your work.

1. What's familiar in the CCSS for each grade level?

2. What appears to be new content to this particular grade level based on prior standards (*Principles and Standards for School Mathematics* [NCTM, 2000], state standards, and so on)? What's challenging for students and teachers (this may include common misconceptions)?

3. What needs unpacking? What topics need emphasizing?

Additional considerations will include how your team may want to unpack the standards within a content standard cluster in order to highlight areas of emphasis, which may be distributed throughout the year or emphasized at a particular time—for example, a two- to four-day lesson on the content standard cluster and where this mathematics may occur within the instructional year: first half of the year, early in the year, and so on, and how this standard might be revisited throughout the year. Your role in implementing the standards is developed through the Collaborative Team Task, a model of which comes at the end of the first domain section for each grade level. This task provides an opportunity for your team to participate in an in-depth examination of selected standards, those that present the greatest challenge for you and your students. This activity will enable your team to think about what needs to be unpacked and what topics need to be emphasized. The task also asks you to identify relevant Mathematical Practices and resources and to identify indicators for student demonstrations of learning the standard.

While a separate analysis beyond the Focal Points analysis (see table F.2, page 177) is not possible for preK, this K–2 analysis should provide the prerequisite background thinking for any preK discussion, which may then be influenced by a review of state efforts at the preK level (for example, Maryland, New York, Ohio, Wisconsin, and others). The K–2-level analysis will be an unpacking of the CCSS for these levels.

The following sections provide an in-depth view of each content domain and standard within grades K–2 based on the teacher's role for implementing the standards. You should view this analysis as a beginning point for the ongoing discussions in your collaborative team. This analysis and related discussion with your team is critical to developing mutual understanding of and support for consistent curricular priorities, pacing, lesson design, and the development of grade-level common assessments (see chapter 4). This analysis, because of its depth, should follow the *Curriculum Focal Points'* (NCTM, 2006) connection to the critical areas of the CCSS (see table F.1 in appendix F, page 176).

As you participate in the professional development linked to this analysis, you and your collaborative team members should continuously examine and discuss your grade-level content reactions as a grade-level team. However, from time to time, you should also examine the other grade-level content expectations for the K–2 cluster in order to discuss transition issues noted across grades.

Finally, you and your colleagues at each grade level should use tables 3.1 (page 68), 3.2 (page 78), and 3.3 (page 89) as you review a particular grade's standards and provide your own response to the analysis questions for each standard. The activities in these tables are designed to help you analyze the CCSS for mathematics in relation to your experience in working with other standards. The understanding questions in the tables represent a continuum from known (What's familiar?) to the unfamiliar and challenging (What's new? What's challenging?) to accommodation (What needs unpacking? What topics need emphasizing?). These understanding questions for the content standard clusters can be used to frame your team's discussion of the standards.

This chapter provides a sequenced response to these questions for the content standard clusters in each domain for each K–2 grade level. You can use the responses as benchmarks against which to compare those that result from your team discussions.

As we begin to analyze the CCSS for levels K–2, you should consider use of *Mathematics Learning in Early Childhood: Paths Toward Excellence and Equity* (NRC, 2009). This excellent resource is all about mathematics learning at the early childhood level and could guide discussion, professional development efforts, and curriculum implementation at these levels, including the preK level.

Kindergarten: What's the Mathematics?

The CCSS content at the kindergarten level is similar to what you may expect at this grade level. The major emphasis for you and your students will be to involve beginning work with the Counting and Cardinality domain. This is then extended to related activities within the Operations and Algebraic Thinking and Number and Operations in Base Ten domains. Student work with numbers at this level begins the framing of number-sense related activities.

The CCSS for mathematics specify two critical areas for the kindergarten level:

> (1) representing, relating, and operating on whole numbers, initially with sets of objects; (2) describing shapes and space. More learning time in Kindergarten should be devoted to number than to other topics. (NGA & CCSSO, 2010, p. 9)

Table 3.1 provides an analysis tool you and your collaborative team can use as you think about the understanding questions for the content standard clusters in each domain for kindergarten. The Common Core Mathematics Content Domains and Standards for Kindergarten are provided in appendix C (page 161).

Table 3.1: Grade-by-Grade Analysis Tool—Kindergarten

Content Standard Cluster	Which Standards in the Cluster Are Familiar?	What's New or Challenging in These Standards?	Which Standards in the Cluster Need Unpacking or Emphasis?
Counting and Cardinality (K.CC)			
Know number names and the count sequence.			
Count to tell the number of objects.			
Compare numbers.			
Operations and Algebraic Thinking (K.OA)			
Understand addition as putting together and adding to, and understand subtraction as taking apart and taking from.			
Number and Operations in Base Ten (K.NBT)			
Work with numbers 11–19 to gain foundations for place value.			
Measurement and Data (K.MD)			
Describe and compare measurable attributes.			
Classify objects and count the number of objects in categories.			
Geometry (K.G)			
Identify and describe shapes.			

Content Standard Cluster	Which Standards in the Cluster Are Familiar?	What's New or Challenging in These Standards?	Which Standards in the Cluster Need Unpacking or Emphasis?
Analyze, compare, create, and compose shapes.			
General Comments			

Visit **go.solution-tree.com/commoncore** for a reproducible version of this table.

Counting and Cardinality (K.CC)

Counting and Cardinality is a kindergarten-only domain within the Common Core State Standards. The emphasis on counting, writing, and comparing numbers is foundational to later student work involving counting and place value. See appendix C, page 162, to review all standards within the domain.

The K.CC Content Standard Clusters

The Counting and Cardinality (K.CC) domain has three content standard clusters, which contain seven standards (see appendix C, page 162).

1. Know number names and the count sequence.

2. Count to tell the number of objects.

3. Compare numbers.

The Understanding Questions for the K.CC Content Standard Clusters

The three questions in table 3.1 provide a framework for you and your team to use to develop greater understanding of the intent of each content standard cluster for the Counting and Cardinality (K.CC) domain.

Know number names and the count sequence is the first content standard cluster for the K.CC domain and involves counting to 100 and counting forward from a given number.

- **What's familiar?** What's expected within this standard is typical of kindergarten state and school district standards regarding the importance of counting and writing numbers. Children come to school with informal mathematics knowledge, in particular the ability to count and think about numbers in a variety of experience-based contexts (Baroody, 1992; Fuson, 1988; NCTM, 2000).

- **What's new? What's challenging?** There is nothing particularly new here with regard to mathematical content expectations at this level. However, for some young children, beginning a counting sequence from a given number (such as starting at 8 and counting to 19) may be challenging.

- **What needs unpacking? What topics need emphasizing?** There is an opportunity to link and extend the standards, which focus primarily on counting, to the next standard, which develops rational counting and a true connection between the name of a number and its value. Such presentations should be very related—counting orally and representing amounts related to a number (count starting at 5 and ending at 11). For example, "Show me the number of counters that represent your starting number, and then add a counter each time you name a number, making sure to stop at 11."

  This standard also provides a preassessment opportunity for you regarding counting. As noted, many children will come to kindergarten with proficiency in the noted counting objectives. An oral preassessment may help you identify beginning needs related to counting and also experiential backgrounds relating counting to objects identified.

Count to tell the number of objects is the second content standard cluster for the K.CC domain. This standard connects counting to cardinality.

- **What's familiar?** The related standards here are very familiar as appropriate expectations at the kindergarten level. These standards are at the beginning of the preK–2 number and operations core necessary for the development of a number sense.

- **What's new? What's challenging?** For some learners, actually stopping with the last number name in a sequence of relating number names to representations is a challenge. Similarly, a nice informal assessment of a child's ability to literally see a number is through evaluating a child's comfort level in creating and identifying a collection of x (number from 1 to 20) objects in a variety of configurations. For example, the child could make six objects and count them. A related activity would be for a teacher to use dot cards. Using 3" × 5" or 4" × 6" index cards, place stick-on dots in a variety of configurations. Flash the cards (like flash cards), and ask students how many there are (later on you can extend the activity and ask how many plus one and so on).

- **What needs unpacking? What topic needs emphasizing?** As noted earlier, connecting these standards to counting is a way for students to make sense of the relationship between numbers and quantities and begin to develop a number sense. Start with smaller numbers first, but create opportunities with numbers through 20. Also, include discussions of numbers that are *more* and *less* as well as comparisons of group sizes, which relate to the next standard.

Compare numbers is the third content standard cluster for the Counting and Cardinality (K.CC) domain. While comparing sets of objects is experiential, it is extended within the Counting and Cardinality domain.

- **What's familiar?** Once again, if you are a kindergarten teacher, you should be comfortable with extending counting activities to have students compare objects in groups using the terms *greater than, less than,* or *equal to.*

- **What's new? What's challenging?** While comparing and even informal ordering by group size will be a natural extension of counting and representing collections of objects, the actual term *equal* or the phrase *equal to* and the concept of *sameness*—balancing the size of groups—is a challenge for some students and a very important concept (Carpenter, Franke, & Levi, 2003) due to its connection to work with operations and equations.

- **What needs unpacking? What topics need emphasizing?** You could argue that all of the standards in this cluster develop collectively. Yes, as children learn to count orally, they should validate a particular number through a representation (physical materials or drawings). Students should be able to see amounts in various configurations and also compare the size of groups and identify numbers that are greater than or more, or less than or smaller than. Work with counting, representing numbers, and comparing will continue throughout kindergarten (and preK as well) and be informally assessed in activities, which range from lining children up for an event to discussing the date emphasized in a class calendar activity. Counting and cardinality activities should help younger students become flexible in number use, which is the bedrock of developing a number sense.

The three-part analysis of each content standard cluster will enable you and your team to build understanding and extend insights into how to most effectively teach Common Core mathematics. The following Collaborative Team Task is a model that you can use to plan implementation of the selected domain standards. The template for the model is shown for the K.CC domain. This template is available as a reproducible for each of the five content domains in kindergarten. You can use these guides to support your team's discussion and planning for the CCSS standards implementation at your school.

Collaborative Team Task:
Planning Implementation of Domain K.CC

Based on your analysis of the content standard clusters for Counting and Cardinality, select a content standard cluster that you know will be challenging for your students (and possibly for you, too). Use the questions in the table to guide development of your unit design plans. Ask one of your team members to be video recorded while teaching the lesson you design. You could also share a digital version of your notes in an interactive document (such as a pencast; see page 105) of the mathematics within the lesson that is developed in this activity. Use your video or pencast for discussion in a subsequent team meeting as you provide formative feedback to your team about

continued →

student progress toward proficiency in the chosen content standard cluster and the K.CC standards in that cluster.

Content standard cluster (see appendix C, page 162): _____

Reason for selecting the content standard cluster: _____

What Content Needs to Be Unpacked for Lesson Design Around This Cluster?	Which Topics Need to Be Emphasized?	How Will Students Be Engaged in the Mathematical Practices as They Learn This Content?	What Resources Will Be Needed?	How Will Students Demonstrate Learning of This Content Standard Cluster?

Visit **go.solution-tree.com/commoncore** for a reproducible version of this feature box.

Operations and Algebraic Thinking (K.OA)

The Operations and Algebraic Thinking domain focuses on counting, place value, and addition and subtraction of whole numbers. At this level, the emphasis is on understanding addition as *putting together* and *adding to* and understanding subtraction *as taking apart* and *taking from*. See appendix C, page 163, for a full discussion of this domain.

The K.OA Content Standard Cluster

The Operations and Algebraic Thinking (K.OA) domain has one content standard cluster, which contains five standards (see appendix C, page 163).

1. Understand additions as putting together and adding to, and understand subtraction as taking apart and taking from.

The Understanding Questions for the K.OA Content Standard Cluster

The three questions in table 3.1 (page 68) provide a framework for you and your team to use to develop greater understanding of the intent of the content standard cluster for the Operations and Algebraic Thinking (K.OA) domain.

Understand addition as putting together and adding to, and understand subtraction as taking apart and taking from is the single content standard cluster for the K.OA domain. The focus of these standards is on building understanding relative to addition and subtraction, with particular attention to decomposing numbers and using representations.

- **What's familiar?** Much of what is expected in these standards is related to the beginnings of conceptual understanding of the whole-number operations of addition and subtraction, with a focus on composing and decomposing numbers. These expectations will be very familiar for those who are used to regularly provided time for mathematics within the kindergarten curriculum.

- **What's new? What's challenging?** You should not interpret the expectation, which calls for fluency with addition and related subtraction combinations to and from 5, as a step toward recall and abstractness. While cognitive demand should make this standard very attainable, use of manipulative and pictured representations should help your kindergarteners place their focus squarely on understanding. Additionally, solving problems involving beginning work with addition and subtraction and finding number pairs for numbers less than or equal to 10 are excellent foundational activities for work with equations, but may not be within current or former curricular expectations.

- **What needs unpacking? What topics need emphasizing?** Much of the work with numbers at the kindergarten level extends naturally from counting and will be an important part of your emphasis on mathematical thinking at this level throughout the instructional year. Formal and informal settings in which students combine and compare numbers and build number pairs to solve problems will be important for emphasis. You should pay particular attention to concepts like *greater than, less than,* and *equal.* The common addition and subtraction situations from the CCSS, presented as tables 5.2 (page 142) and 5.3 (page 143) and adapted from a similar table within the *Mathematics Learning in Early Childhood: Paths Toward Excellence and Equity* (NRC, 2009), provide a viable professional development opportunity for your collaborative team at this level. Framing contexts and problems that are appropriate for kindergarten students using the situations suggested would be a valuable kindergarten collaborative team activity.

Number and Operations in Base Ten (K.NBT)

The Number and Operations in Base Ten domain extends counting, begins and extends work with place value, introduces the properties of operations and mental mathematics, and moves students to achieving fluency with addition and subtraction of whole numbers. The emphasis at this level is on composing and decomposing the numbers 11–19 to gain a foundation for place value with tens and ones.

The K.NBT Content Standard Cluster

The Number and Operations in Base Ten (K.NBT) domain has one content standard cluster, which contains one standard (see appendix C, page 163).

1. Work with numbers 11–19 to gain foundations for place value.

The Understanding Questions for the K.NBT Content Standard Cluster

The three questions in table 3.1 (page 68) provide a framework for you and your team to use to develop a greater understanding of the intent of the content standard cluster for the Number and Operations in Base Ten (K.NBT) domain.

Work with numbers 11–19 to gain foundations for place value is the single content standard cluster for the K.NBT domain. The emphasis in this content standard cluster is on beginning work with tens and ones.

- **What's familiar?** The extension of prior work in counting and representing numbers less than 20, with an emphasis on building place-value concepts, is important at this level. Most kindergarten teachers will be comfortable with extending the representation of numbers to tens and ones representations and with the composing and decomposing activities suggested in this standard.

- **What's new? What's challenging?** Language around tens and ones and access and comfort with using base-ten manipulative materials are important elements of this work. While never perceived to be *the* quick fix toward understanding, appropriate use and comfort with representation tools are important at this level.

- **What needs unpacking? What topics need emphasizing?** While the work with tens and ones suggested in this standard extend prior understandings with counting, number, and comparing, the composing and decomposing activities (for example, thinking about 13 as one ten and three ones or 17 as one ten and seven ones) will take time and will also occur in the second half of or later in the instructional year. Important discussions around how many lessons, extending the work to problems, and access to materials should be part of the kindergarten-level professional development activities within your collaborative team.

Measurement and Data (K.MD)

The Measurement and Data domain considers the measurement process, representing and interpreting data, and time and money as measurement-related contexts. The emphasis at this grade level is on measurable attributes (length).

The K.MD Content Standard Clusters

The Measurement and Data (K.MD) domain has two content standard clusters, which contain three standards (see appendix C, page 163).

1. Describe and compare measurable attributes.

2. Classify objects and count the number of objects in each category.

The Understanding Questions for the K.MD Content Standard Cluster

The three questions in table 3.1 (page 68) provide a framework for you and your team to develop greater understanding of the intent of each content standard cluster in the Measurement and Data (K.MD) domain.

Describe and compare measurable attributes is the first content standard cluster for the K.MD domain. Measurable attributes include length or weight for this grade level.

- **What's familiar?** Both standards should be familiar as a context for applying the work kindergartners do with numbers at this grade level.

- **What's new? What's challenging?** While nothing is new here, some students may be challenged by activities comparing particular attributes. Such comparisons will range in level of challenge primarily due to the experiential background of students. Students who have not held objects in their hands and been asked which is heavier may wonder a bit about such activities at first, but the expectations here should be very attainable by most students.

- **What needs unpacking? What topics need emphasizing?** The learning activities here will most likely serve as valuable contexts for linking the ongoing work with number. It is very important for these young learners to be engaged in the process of measurement. This is all about these students literally seeing and discussing measureable attributes and comparing measures. Work with measurement attributes could occur throughout the instructional year, with some prerequisite background needed regarding counting.

Classify objects and count the number of objects in each category is the second content standard cluster for the K.MD domain. This cluster connects classification to counting.

- **What's familiar?** This expectation is very much related to the prior work with describing measureable attributes and comparing objects and is also related to ongoing work with number.

- **What's new? What's challenging?** Engaging your students in the measurement process, as noted with the other standards aligned with Measurement and Data, is critical to the number-related responses expected here. Some learners will need help organizing their responses related to particular classifications (which essentially involve comparing and ordering). Access to actual objects for the classification work will be important.

- **What needs unpacking? What topics need emphasizing?** The student work with this content standard cluster will most likely take place after your instruction that engages students in comparing and sorting by number amounts. This student work may be an extension activity early in the year, but it is certainly expected for all students by the end of the year.

Geometry (K.G)

Geometry is the mathematics dedicated to space and spatial learning. K–2 geometry emphasis topics include identifying, describing, and reasoning about shapes, and analyzing, comparing, creating, and composing shapes.

The K.G Content Standard Clusters

The Geometry (K.G) domain has two content standard clusters, which contain six standards (see appendix C, page 164).

1. Identify and describe shapes (squares, circles, triangles, rectangles, hexagons, cubes, cones, cylinders, and spheres).

2. Analyze, compare, create, and compose shapes.

The Understanding Questions for the K.G Content Standard Clusters

The three questions in table 3.1 (page 68) provide a framework for you and your team to use to develop greater understanding on the intent of each content standard cluster for the Geometry (K.G) domain.

Identify and describe shapes (squares, circles, triangles, rectangles, hexagons, cubes, cones, cylinders, and spheres is the first content standard cluster for the K.G domain. These standards engage students in early experiences with the identification of shapes.

- **What's familiar?** Young children are usually very comfortable when working with two- and three-dimensional shapes. The first two geometry standards will extend students' experiences with shape from informal experiences at home or within preK settings.

- **What's new? What's challenging?** While not overly challenging, the actual identification of shapes as either two-dimensional (flat) or three-dimensional (solid) shapes may be a somewhat new expectation for this level. Relating two-dimensional shapes to flat figures and three-dimensional shapes to solids, using varied exemplars, and providing many opportunities for children to be engaged in working with and describing 2-D and 3-D shapes will support acquisition of this and the related standards in this cluster.

- **What needs unpacking? What topics need emphasizing?** Geometry should unfold throughout the kindergarten year. Your work with differences between two-dimensional and three-dimensional shapes may include one to two lessons with that particular emphasis but could then be extended and contextualized through regular discussions of shape.

Analyze, compare, create, and compose shapes is the second content standard cluster for the K.G domain. Students analyze, compare, model, and compose shapes in their work with these standards.

- **What's familiar?** Activities involving shapes and working with two-dimensional and three-dimensional shapes will be familiar for kindergarten teachers and their students.

- **What's new? What's challenging?** Composing shapes to form other shapes and using specific geometry-related language (like *vertices* or *corners*) may be new at this level. While not overly challenging, specific activities and lessons that focus on composition of shapes by joining other shapes will be important, and the use of materials for such activities will be an important consideration for your collaborative planning.

- **What needs unpacking? What topics need emphasizing?** This cluster is essentially all about geometric investigations. You and your team may consider regular access to centers, which would include geometric investigations (for example, comparing shapes, composing shapes, and so on), and also consider a two-dimensional and three-dimensional shape unit for those concepts that may need directed activity.

Kindergarten Analysis: Concluding Comment

Kindergarten is the formal school-based first step mathematically for many learners. At this level, foundations involving counting and comparing, place value, and early conceptual experiences with addition and subtraction are critically important. Such experiences and others, which also involve measurement and geometry, begin each student's mathematical journey.

Grade 1: What's the Mathematics?

If you are an experienced first-grade teacher, you will likely view the Common Core State Standards at this level as a collection of important standards that, for the most part, will look and feel familiar to you. Challenges will be for you and your collaborative team to become more comfortable with the common addition and subtraction situations, which will frame work with these operations at this grade level and the second-grade level. Collaborative team discussions about the use of representations, including concrete models and drawings, to help develop student understanding of place value and then extend these understandings to addition and subtraction will be time well spent. Finally, Measurement and Data standards at this grade level provide excellent opportunities for you to not only engage your students but also to provide a context for their work with number.

The structure and language of the CCSS for mathematics domains and standards include an emphasis on understanding and regular use of a variety of representations. The goal is to ensure the depth of understanding needed regarding important mathematics concepts. This takes time—time to teach and time for your children to learn. This less-is-more opportunity of fewer standards with a greater level of depth and understanding expected amplifies the opportunity for your students to engage in the corresponding Standards for Mathematical Practice—every day. It will depend on, however, the ability of your collaborative team to plan effectively and intentionally for these student opportunities.

The CCSS for mathematics specify four critical areas for the first grade:

> (1) developing understanding of addition, subtraction, and strategies for addition and subtraction within 20; (2) developing understanding of whole number relationships and place value, including grouping in tens and ones;

(3) developing understanding of linear measurement and measuring lengths as iterating length units; and (4) reasoning about attributes of, and composing and decomposing geometric shapes. (NGA & CCSSO, 2010, p. 13)

Table 3.2 provides an analysis tool you can use as you think about the understanding questions for the content standard clusters in each domain for first grade. The Common Core Mathematics Content Domains and Standards for Grade 1 are provided in appendix D (page 165).

Table 3.2: Grade-by-Grade Analysis Tool—Grade 1

Content Standard Cluster	Which Standards in the Cluster Are Familiar?	What's New or Challenging in These Standards?	Which Standards in the Cluster Need Unpacking or Emphasis?
Operations and Algebraic Thinking (1.OA)			
Represent and solve problems involving addition and subtraction.			
Understand and apply properties of operations and the relationship between addition and subtraction.			
Add and subtract within 20.			
Work with addition and subtraction equations.			
Number and Operations in Base Ten (1.NBT)			
Extend the counting sequence.			
Understand place value.			
Use place-value understanding and properties of operations to add and subtract.			
Measurement and Data (1.MD)			
Measure lengths indirectly and by iterating length units.			
Tell and write time.			

Content Standard Cluster	Which Standards in the Cluster Are Familiar?	What's New or Challenging in These Standards?	Which Standards in the Cluster Need Unpacking or Emphasis?
Represent and interpret data.			
Geometry (1.G)			
Reason with shapes and their attributes.			
General Comments			

Visit **go.solution-tree.com/commoncore** for a reproducible version of this table.

Operations and Algebraic Thinking (1.OA)

The Operations and Algebraic Thinking domain focuses on counting, place value, and addition and subtraction of whole numbers. At this level, the emphasis involves addition and subtraction within 20 and properties and equations involving addition and subtraction. See appendix D, pages 166–167, for a full discussion of this domain.

The 1.OA Content Standard Clusters

The Operations and Algebraic Thinking (1.OA) domain has four content standard clusters, which contain eight standards (see appendix D, pages 166–167).

1. Represent and solve problems involving addition and subtraction.

2. Understand and apply properties of operations and the relationship between addition and subtraction.

3. Add and subtract within 20.

4. Work with addition and subtraction equations.

The Understanding Questions for the 1.OA Content Standard Clusters

The three questions in table 3.2 provide a framework for you and your team to use to develop greater understanding of the intent of each content standard cluster in the Operations and Algebraic Thinking (1.OA) domain.

Represent and solve problems involving addition and subtraction is the first content standard cluster for the 1.OA domain. The implication is that your students have regular opportunities through the year to solve problems involving addition and subtraction, thus regularly engaging students in Mathematical Practice 1—Make sense of problems and persevere in solving them, as described in chapter 2.

- **What's familiar?** Significant work with addition and subtraction of whole numbers is a very familiar expectation for you at this grade level.

- **What's new? What's challenging?** While work with addition and subtraction is a major emphasis topic at the first-grade level, you may be unaware of the common addition and subtraction situations presented in tables 5.2 (page 142) and 5.3 (page 143) from the CCSS appendix. These common addition and subtraction situations are adapted from *Mathematics Learning in Early Childhood: Paths Toward Excellence and Equity* (NRC, 2009). Professional development opportunities within your collaborative team should consider these addition and subtraction situations. Another challenge will be for you to ensure that your students engage in work involving addition and subtraction and an approach to instruction that is problem based; that is, students regularly encounter and solve problems involving addition and subtraction.

- **What needs unpacking? What topics need emphasizing?** As noted, addition and subtraction of whole numbers is a critical foundation topic at this grade level, and lessons involving understanding of these operations will occur throughout much of the instructional year. Problem-solving-related activities should occur daily; however, specific lessons will be dedicated to problem types that involve more than two addends.

Understand and apply properties of operations and the relationship between addition and subtraction is the second content standard cluster for the 1.OA domain. Students will apply the commutative and associative properties for addition and subtraction as they encounter this content standard cluster.

- **What's familiar?** Extending conceptual development and related understandings regarding addition and subtraction have been expectations, which most first-grade teachers know as important elements of their curriculum.

- **What's new? What's challenging?** What will be new, but not necessarily challenging, will be for you to think about subtraction as an *unknown addend* problem, thus relating subtraction to addition so that 11 – 3 can be thought of as 3 + ? = 11. Far too many young learners see subtraction as very different from addition and are challenged when asked to think about subtraction as finding the unknown addend. Work on such understandings will be supported with professional development around the common addition and subtraction situations mentioned earlier in this chapter (see NGA & CCSSO, 2010, p. 88).

- **What needs unpacking? What topics need emphasizing?** Your work here involving the commutative and associative properties will need to include specific lessons as students work with addition. However, building a sense of number by, for instance, finding all number pairs that add to 10, will help your students in actual application of the associative property as they add, for instance, 8 + 4 + 2, by seeing and knowing that 8 + 2 is 10 and then adding just 4 more. Actual use of the commutative and associative properties is the goal here—beyond initial lessons. Lessons involving subtraction as take away (for example, "I had 7 doughnuts, and we ate 5; how many are left?"), subtraction as comparing (for example, "I have 7 doughnuts; and Mia has 4 doughnuts, how many more doughnuts do I have?"), and subtraction as finding the unknown addend (for example, "I want 7 cards and have 3; how many more cards do I need?") are important lessons or lesson activities to engage your students in using physical models and pictured renderings or drawings to literally show how the subtractions work and how addition and subtraction are related operations. The emphasis on using the properties and extending the meaning of addition and subtraction will occur over many days or weeks of instruction as work with these operations commences at this grade level.

Add and subtract within 20 is the third content standard cluster in the 1.OA domain. This content standard cluster focuses on strategies for acquiring fluency with the addition and related subtraction facts.

- **What's familiar?** These expectations are about addition and the related subtraction facts and will be very familiar to you as typical first-grade expectations.

- **What's new? What's challenging?** The challenges for you here are finding the time needed to develop a child's ability to demonstrate fluency with the facts to 10 and exposuring him or her to all facts within 20. Importantly, these standards build fact acquisition not solely on memory but on relating facts to counting (for example, counting on 2 to add 2), counting on and counting back, making 10, composing and decomposing numbers, and using relationships between addition and subtraction, essentially fact strategies. Some of your students will be able to acquire the quick recall of the addition and related subtraction facts earlier and seemingly easier than others. Regardless, building understanding of addition and subtraction within 10 and 20 is very important.

- **What needs unpacking? What topics need emphasizing**? As noted earlier, the emphasis on addition and subtraction at this grade level is historic and expected. Adding and subtracting within 20 and achieving fluency with addition and subtraction within 10 will take time. Time will be needed for you to help your students develop strategies like counting on, making 10, becoming comfortable decomposing numbers, and relating addition to subtraction. Such lessons, and the time needed for additional practice and maintenance activities with various addition and subtraction combinations, will occur during the time spent on addition and subtraction throughout the year, which will begin in the early weeks of the year and continue through the third quarter.

Work with addition and subtraction equations is the fourth content standard cluster for the 1.OA domain and reflects a prealgebra standard related to equality and equations.

- **What's familiar?** These expectations extend student work with addition and subtraction.

- **What's new? What's challenging?** The prealgebra approach these standards allude to will be new for many of you. These expectations extend previous and ongoing work with addition and subtraction to considering equations and working with missing numbers using a placeholder (for example, ? or ☐) as a variable.

- **What needs unpacking? What topics need emphasizing?** The emphasis on beginning concepts of algebra through equations and missing numbers (? or ☐ representing a variable) will be in the form of specific lessons highlighting the meaning of the equal sign and how to represent a missing number in an addition or subtraction equation. These lessons should be presented as your students gain comfort and confidence with addition and subtraction. The concepts here may also be maintained through your explanation, or student explanations, of solutions to problems (for example, "I have 7 tennis balls. Heather had 8 and lost 1 tennis ball. Do we have the same? Who has more?").

The three-part analysis of each content standard cluster will enable you and your team to build understanding and extend insights into how to most effectively teach the Common Core mathematics. The Collaborative Team Task is a model that you can use to plan implementation of the selected domain standards. The template for the model is shown for the 1.OA domain. This template is available as a reproducible for each of the four content domains in first grade. You can use these guides to support your team's discussion and planning for CCSS implementation at your school.

Collaborative Team Task:
Planning Implementation of Domain 1.OA

Based on your analysis of the content standard clusters for Operations and Algebraic Thinking, select a content standard cluster that you know will be challenging for your students (and possibly for you, too). Use the questions in the table to guide development of your unit design plans. Ask one of your team members to be video recorded while teaching the lesson you design. You could also share a digital version of your notes in an interactive document such as a pencast (see page 105) of the mathematics within the lesson that is developed in this activity. Use your video or pencast for discussion in a subsequent team meeting as you provide formative feedback to your team about student progress toward proficiency in the chosen content standard cluster and the 1.OA standards in that cluster.

Content standard cluster (see appendix D, page 166): _____

Reason for selecting the content standard cluster: _____

What Content Needs to Be Unpacked for Lesson Design Around This Cluster?	Which Topics Need to Be Emphasized as Parts of the Lesson?	How Will Students Be Engaged in the Mathematical Practices as They Learn This Content?	What Resources Will Be Needed?	How Will Students Demonstrate Learning of This Content Standard Cluster?

Visit **go.solution-tree.com/commoncore** for a reproducible version of this feature box.

Number and Operations in Base Ten (1.NBT)

The Number and Operations in Base Ten domain for the K–2 grade levels extends counting, begins and extends work with place value, introduces the properties of operations and mental mathematics, and moves students to achieving fluency with addition and subtraction of whole numbers. The emphasis at this grade level is on extending counting and place value as related to addition and subtraction.

The 1.NBT Content Standard Clusters

The Number and Operations in Base Ten (1.NBT) domain has three content standard clusters, which contain six standards (see appendix D, pages 167–168).

1. Extend the counting sequence.

2. Understand place value.

3. Use place-value understanding and properties of operations to add and subtract.

The Understanding Questions for the 1.NBT Content Standard Clusters

The three questions in table 3.2 (page 78) provide a framework for you and your team to use to develop greater understanding of the intent of each content standard cluster in the Operations and Algebraic Thinking (1.OA) domain.

Extend the counting sequence is the first content standard cluster for the 1.NBT domain. This content standard cluster extends counting beyond 100.

- **What's familiar?** This work extends counting from the kindergarten level, which involves students in counting to 100 by ones and tens. This will be a familiar first-grade expectation.

- **What's new? What's challenging?** The only real challenge with counting to 120 for some students will be beginning the counting sequence from a given number (for example, starting with 34 and counting to 79). However, actually reading, writing, and representing a number, including use of the written numeral, will be challenging for some of your students.

- **What needs unpacking? What topics need emphasizing?** Counting certainly continues beyond the Counting and Cardinality domain at the kindergarten level, and this standard extends kindergarten-level counting experiences. Your students will need time to represent a particular number, say the number, and then write the number (for example, "Show me the number 136 using base-ten blocks, say the number, and then write the number"). Such work may be approached by the size of the number, but validation of student proficiency with counting from a particular number, representing a number, and writing the number are all related and important indicators of understanding of the counting process. Some of these related experiences will occur in the first half of the instructional year, and then be extended toward the end of first grade.

Understand place value is the second content standard cluster in the 1.NBT domain with a focus on understanding two-digit numbers.

- **What's familiar?** This beginning work with place value will be expected at this grade level. The time spent with numbers 11 to 19 is important at this grade level because their naming is different. However, the real import here is serious work with place value and tens and ones, which most of you will acknowledge as typical for this grade level.

- **What's new? What's challenging?** The challenge and a common misunderstanding for many of your students will be actual use of the symbols >, =, or <. Of greater importance is the conceptual understanding of such comparisons of two-digit numbers. While comparing, as a concept, is not new, actual introduction of the >, =, and < symbols will be considered new for some at this level.

- **What needs unpacking? What topics need emphasizing?** The place-value emphasis here is very important. You will need materials or tools (Mathematical Practice 5) to help with student representations of two-digit numbers. Time will be needed to create, discuss, and write numbers. Specific lesson time will be needed for lessons involving the preteen (11 and 12) and teen (13 to 19) numbers. Discussions along the lines of "Why are these number names different?" and "What's different about the sequence of counting by tens that would go thirteen, twenty-three, thirty-three, forty-three, and so on?" should help build understandings here. First grade is a two-digit—tens and ones—year. You'll need to provide many opportunities for your students to create and write such numbers throughout the year. This is not a block of lessons to be completed and never addressed again. Although some specific focus lessons on representations will be necessary, the place-value impact here needs to be maintained throughout the year.

Use place-value understanding and properties of operations to add and subtract is the third content standard cluster in the 1.NBT domain. The focus here is adding and subtracting within 100.

- **What's familiar?** Addition and subtraction of two-digit numbers will be a familiar, end-of-year topic for you at this grade level.

- **What's new? What's challenging?** What may be new for you will be the number-sense focus here as your students are encouraged to do mental math by finding ten more or ten less. Your students should also be encouraged to use concrete models and pictured representations as they add and subtract, which is certainly not a new idea or expectation, but far too many teachers do not have access to or use such representational models and tools (Mathematical Practice 5). If you don't have access to such tools, you and your collaborative team members should work together to obtain them.

- **What needs unpacking? What topics need emphasizing?** Work with two-digit addition and subtraction will occur toward the end of the first-grade year. Your emphasis must be on the conceptual basis for these procedures with two-digit numbers. Consideration must also be given to relating the similarities between the addition and subtraction procedures. Finally, time to consistently maintain the mental mathematics ideas of ten more or ten less and generally becoming fluent with tens is important here as a critical element of number sense.

Measurement and Data (1.MD)

The Measurement and Data domain considers the measurement process, representing and interpreting data, and time and money as measurement-related contexts at the preK–2 levels. The emphasis at this grade level is on linear measure, time, and representing and interpreting data with up to three categories.

The 1.MD Content Standard Clusters

The Measurement and Data (1.MD) domain has three content standard clusters, which contain four standards (see appendix D, page 168).

1. Measure lengths indirectly and by iterating length units.

2. Tell and write time.

3. Represent and interpret data.

The Understanding Questions for the 1.MD Content Standard Clusters

The three questions in table 3.2 (page 78) provide a framework for you and your team to use to develop greater understanding of the intent of each content standard cluster for the Measurement and Data (1.MD) domain.

Measure lengths indirectly and by iterating length units is the first content standard cluster in the 1.MD domain. The focus in these standards is on iteration and its importance to linear measurement.

- **What's familiar?** Measuring activities that involve length will be a familiar topic for you at this level.

- **What's new? What's challenging?** The level of specificity suggested within these expectations will be new and perhaps challenging. Comparing and ordering lengths is an excellent measurement in context activity (for example, "This belt is longer than Cooper's belt") and should be accessible for most of your students. Thinking of the measurement process through iteration of smaller objects, which is the actual process of measuring length, is not a measurement experience students have traditionally had. Getting your young learners to actually measure in this way is important (for example, "How many pencils long is this cane?").

- **What needs unpacking? What topics need emphasizing?** Measurement provides an excellent context for doing mathematics. It helps you develop student proficiency in the Mathematical Practices as well. You and your collaborative team can create specific lessons that guide your students in ordering and comparing objects using a third object as the *ruler* in this context. Similarly, assistance with iterating smaller units to determine a length (for example, using *x* paper clips to measure the length of a desk) will be important—initially. However, while one to three particular lessons will be focused lessons on the actual measuring, additional activities to engage students in this early work with linear measure should occur throughout the year—perhaps as center activities or a problem-of-the-day activity.

Tell and write time is the second content standard cluster in the 1.MD domain. The emphasis for this cluster will be the student telling and writing time to the nearest hour and half-hour.

- **What's familiar?** You expect to teach time at this grade level. Time is one of those historic conventions within the mathematics curriculum.

- **What's new? What's challenging?** While nothing is new, the potential for working with both analog and digital clocks is important. Additionally, telling time to the half-hour provides you and your students a context for beginning work with fractions, which will be introduced through partitioning regions in the geometry domain.

- **What needs unpacking? What topics need emphasizing?** Instructional time will be needed for specific lessons on telling time to the nearest hour and half-hour. Access to visual models for both digital and analog timepieces will be important. Beyond conducting one to three specific lessons on these topics, you should maintain telling time throughout the year with daily schedules and particular times of the day with significant importance—time for specials, lunchtime, end of the school day, and so on.

Represent and interpret data is the third content standard cluster in 1.MD domain and includes student learning experiences with up to three categories of data.

- **What's familiar?** Data analysis at this grade level is relatively familiar. First graders typically interpret real graphs (for example, number of those wearing shoes with laces compared to number of those wearing shoes without laces— use actual shoes to create the real graph), tables, and specific graphs—typically, bar graphs.

- **What's new? What's challenging?** The challenge is for you to provide opportunities for students to organize, represent, and interpret data with up to three categories, which means initial activities may be to organize one set of data (for example, number of students in the class each day for a school week), which can then be extended to multiple categories (such as favorite books or favorite lunches).

- **What needs unpacking? What topic needs emphasizing?** Time for your students to become engaged in data analysis can certainly occur early in the instructional year, but such opportunities should be extended with a variety of contexts throughout the year. Analyzing data provides an excellent opportunity for engaging your students in Mathematical Practices around problem solving, reasoning, and using tools and provides a context for the CCSS domains of Operations and Algebraic Thinking and Number and Operations in Base Ten.

Geometry (1.G)

Geometry is the mathematics dedicated to space and spatial learning. Emphasis topics include identifying, describing, and reasoning about shapes, and analyzing, comparing, creating, and composing shapes. The focus at this level is on reasoning about shapes and their attributes.

The 1.G Content Standard Cluster

The Geometry (1.G) domain has one content standard cluster, which contains three standards (see appendix D, page 169).

1. Reason with shapes and their attributes.

The Understanding Questions for the 1.G Content Standard Clusters

The three questions in table 3.2 (page 78) provide a framework for you and your team to use to develop greater understanding of the intent the content standard cluster for the Geometry (1.G) domain.

Reason with shapes and their attributes is the single content standard cluster for the 1.G domain. Students are involved with activities related to composing and partitioning shapes.

- **What's familiar?** Engaging first-grade students in activities related to attributes of two- and three-dimensional shapes is a familiar topic for you at this grade level.

- **What's new? What's challenging?** There is a lot of mathematics in this content standard cluster. Expectations include defining attributes and nondefining attributes of shapes, composing two-dimensional and three-dimensional shapes, and partitioning circles and rectangles, which is essentially beginning work with fractions. While not challenging with regard to the mathematics, the challenge for you will be considering placement within the instructional year for each of these related but different standards. Access to instructional tools (Mathematical Practice 5) including, but not limited to, two- and three-dimensional models of common shapes will be important, as will access to virtual shape renderings. Finally, partitioning regions into halves and fourths will not be recognized as a typical grade 1 experience. All too often, children at this level merely name fractional parts of a region without attending to the sharing of equal-sized parts so important in the partitioning definition for fractions. The Institute of Education Sciences (Siegler et al., 2010) recommends emphasizing *sharing* (which students understand experientially) or *partitioning* to prepare students for work with fractions. Emphasizing sharing and partitioning also draws on a child's informal understandings and informal experiences with division.

- **What needs unpacking? What topics need emphasizing?** As noted, the expectations within this domain are related but different. Activities that engage children in defining attributes of and nondefining attributes of shapes should occur early in the year. You can also extend the instruction to composing two-dimensional and three-dimensional shapes, which will build on your student work with attributes later in the year. Closer to the end of the year, you should emphasize activities related to partitioning shapes to represent halves and fourths. These are critically important as beginning conceptual experiences for future student work with fractions in grades 3–5.

Grade 1 Analysis: Concluding Comment

First grade is foundational. Standards and topics of emphasis include counting and place value. Understanding place value serves as the pathway to understanding the operations of addition and subtraction. Students will be expected to acquire fluency with addition and related subtraction combinations through 20 and will experience linear measure through iteration, telling time, and beginning work with fractions through partitioning geometric shapes. Daily opportunities to engage the Mathematical Practices, particularly through problem-solving and reasoning practices, will serve to guide and nurture student understanding of place value, addition, and subtraction at this grade level.

Grade 2: What's the Mathematics?

Grade 2 is important. This is, for the most part, the capstone grade for addition and subtraction of two-digit numbers. As you know, this will be a challenge for some learners. It will be very important for you to engage the Mathematical Practices (chapter 2) throughout the many lessons, which focus on place value and addition and subtraction, at this grade level.

Student flexibility with addition and subtraction situations will also be important. Other content domains, which will be particularly important and somewhat challenging at this level, include the emphasis on Measurement and Data related to time and money, measurement involving the use of a number line and making a line plot, and the Geometry domain's work with identifying a number of shapes, partitioning rectangles into rows and columns of same-size squares, and partitioning circles and rectangles into halves, thirds, and fourths. Consider that fourteen of this grade level's twenty-seven expectations are within the Operations and Algebraic Thinking and Number and Operations in Base Ten domains. While this is a surface analysis, it still speaks to the importance of developing number sense as related to addition and subtraction at this grade level.

The CCSS for mathematics specify that instructional time in grade 2 should be spent on four critical areas:

(1) extending understanding of base-ten notation; (2) building fluency with addition and subtraction; (3) using standard units of measure; and (4) describing and analyzing shapes. (NGA & CCSSO, 2010, p. 17)

Table 3.3 provides an analysis tool you can use as you think about the understanding questions for the content standard clusters in each domain for grade 2. The Common Core Content Domains and Standards for grade 2 are provided in appendix E (page 171).

Table 3.3: Grade-by-Grade Analysis Tool—Grade 2

Content Standard Cluster	Which Standards in the Cluster Are Familiar?	What's New or Challenging in These Standards?	Which Standards in the Cluster Need Unpacking or Emphasis?
Operations and Algebraic Thinking (2.OA)			
Represent and solve problems involving addition and subtraction.			
Add and subtract within 20.			
Work with equal groups of objects to gain foundations for multiplication.			
Number and Operations in Base Ten (2.NBT)			
Understand place value.			
Use place value understanding and properties of operations to add and subtract.			
Measurement and Data (2.MD)			
Measure and estimate lengths in standard units.			
Relate addition and subtraction to length.			
Work with time and money.			
Geometry (2.G)			
Reason with shapes and their attributes.			
General Comments			

Visit **go.solution-tree.com/commoncore** for a reproducible version of this table.

Operations and Algebraic Thinking (2.OA)

The Operations and Algebraic Thinking domain is a K–5 domain. At levels K–2, it focuses on counting, place value, and addition and subtraction of whole numbers. At this level, the emphasis is solving problems involving addition and subtraction, adding and subtracting within 20, and developing conceptual foundations related to multiplication of whole numbers.

The 2.OA Content Standard Clusters

The Operations and Algebraic Thinking (2.OA) domain has three content standard clusters, which contain four standards (see appendix E, page 172).

1. Represent and solve problems involving addition and subtraction.

2. Add and subtract within 20.

3. Work with equal groups of objects to gain foundations for multiplication.

The Understanding Questions for the 2.OA Content Standard Clusters

The three questions in table 3.3 (page 89) provide a framework for you and your team to use to develop greater understanding of the intent of each content standard cluster for the Operations and Algebraic Thinking (2.OA) domain.

Represent and solve problems involving addition and subtraction is the first content standard cluster for the 2.OA domain. Problem-solving opportunities will include one-step and two-step problems.

- **What's familiar?** Students at this grade level should solve problems involving addition and subtraction—lots of them. This familiar expectation should include solving word problems, interpreting data sets using addition and subtraction, and more.

- **What's new? What's challenging?** Nothing's new regarding the need for your second-grade students to have lots of experience solving problems involving addition and subtraction. However, your collaborative team discussions may focus on the common addition and subtraction situations for addition and subtraction (see table 5.2, page 143, and table 5.3, page 143). As mentioned earlier, these situations, adapted from the National Research Council (2009) report on early childhood mathematics, may not be familiar, and time ensuring your comfort with such problem types would be well spent (for example, within your collaborative team develop *adding to* and *taking from* problems within a context related to the school or a favorite sport).

- **What needs unpacking? What topics need emphasizing?** This expectation is one that extends throughout the year; fluency with addition and subtraction involving whole numbers is an expectation at this grade level, and your students should encounter problems involving these operations—lots of them!

Add and subtract within 20 is the second content standard cluster in the 2.OA domain. The focus in this content standard cluster is related to addition and subtraction facts or combinations.

- **What's familiar?** Fact acquisition related to the basic addition and related subtraction facts will be a very familiar expectation of you at this grade level.

- **What's new? What's challenging?** While fact acquisition will be expected at this grade level, being able to recall facts, as you know, is easier for some of your students than others. In addition, use of mental math and fact strategies—such as counting on, making a ten, decomposing a number leading to a ten (for example, $14 - 5$ can be thought of as $14 - 4 = 10$ and then $10 - 1 = 9$), using the relationship between addition and subtraction (for example, "If I know $7 + 5 = 12$, then I know $12 - 5 = 7$"), and creating equivalent but easier or known sums (for example, adding $8 + 7$ by creating the known or easier equivalent [a double] $7 + 7 + 1 = 15$)—will be an important element of your students' understanding of sums and differences to 20.

- **What needs unpacking? What topics need emphasizing?** What's really important at this level is for your students to develop fluency and comfort with the mental math and fact strategies discussed previously. Providing your students direct work with the strategies, using manipulative materials or drawings, and including plenty of opportunity to use them will be important. Time will be needed for specific review of the mental math and fact strategies and to check for and maintain fact acquisition.

Work with equal groups of objects to gain foundations for multiplication is the third content standard cluster in the 2.OA domain. This standard is a conceptual building block for multiplication of whole numbers.

- **What's familiar?** Beginning work with multiplication is a familiar, typically end-of-year topic at this grade level.

- **What's new? What's challenging?** The standards here both focus on a conceptual understanding of multiplication and include lessons that would involve organizing equal groups of objects (such as two groups of six objects) and then determining the number of objects and writing an equation as a sum of equal addends ($6 + 6 = 12$) as one conceptual model (groups of objects) for multiplication. The second conceptual model for multiplication (standard 2.OA.4, page 172) engages learners in using a rectangular array or area model to represent up to five rows and five columns; then write an equation to express the total as a sum of equal addends (for example, $5 + 5 + 5 + 5 + 5 = 25$). The challenge here will be for you to provide opportunities for both of these conceptual models to be developed. Such opportunities will engage your students in activities in which they will develop equal groups and rectangular arrays or area models using physical materials or drawings.

- **What needs unpacking? What topics need emphasizing?** These standards will require several lessons, which will occur toward the end of the instructional year. Time will need to be spent on *seeing* multiplication as groups of objects and as represented by a rectangular array or area model. These lessons represent the initial conceptual seeding for multiplication of whole numbers. Your students will benefit from many activities in which they create equal-sized groups and rectangular arrays to determine the total amount.

The three-part analysis of each content standard cluster will enable you and your team to build understanding and extend insights into how to most effectively teach the CCSS for mathematics. The following Collaborative Team Task is a model that you can use to plan implementation of the selected domain standards. The template for the model is shown for the 2.OA domain. This template is available as a reproducible for each of the four content domains in second grade. You can use these guides to support your team's discussion and planning for CCSS implementation at your school.

Collaborative Team Task: Planning Implementation of Domain 2.OA

Based on your analysis of the content standard clusters for Operations and Algebraic Thinking, select a content standard cluster that you know will be challenging for your students (and possibly for you, too). Use the questions in the table to guide development of your unit design plans. Ask one of your team members to be video recorded while teaching the lesson you design. You could also share a digital version of your notes in an interactive document such as a pencast (see page 105) of the mathematics within the lesson that is developed in this activity. Use your video or pencast for discussion in a subsequent team meeting as you provide formative feedback to your team about student progress toward proficiency in the chosen content standard cluster and the 2.OA standards in that cluster.

Content standard cluster (see appendix E, page 172): _____

Reason for selecting the content standard cluster: _____

What Content Needs to Be Unpacked for Lesson Design Around This Cluster?	Which Topics Need to Be Emphasized as Parts of the Lesson?	How Will Students Be Engaged in the Mathematical Practices as They Learn This Content?	What Resources Will Be Needed?	How Will Students Demonstrate Learning of This Content Standard Cluster?

Visit **go.solution-tree.com/commoncore** for a reproducible version of this feature box.

Number and Operations in Base Ten (2.NBT)

The Number and Operations in Base Ten domain for levels K–2 extends counting, begins and extends student work with place value, introduces the properties of operations and mental mathematics, and moves students to achieving fluency with addition and subtraction of whole numbers. The emphasis topics at this level include understanding place value, using properties of operations, and developing fluency with addition and subtraction within 100.

The 2.NBT Content Standard Clusters

The Number and Operations in Base Ten (2.NBT) domain has two content standard clusters, which contain nine standards (see appendix E, pages 172–173).

1. Understand place value.

2. Use place-value understanding and properties of operations to add and subtract.

The Understanding Questions for the 2.NBT Content Standard Clusters

The three questions in table 3.3 (page 89) provide a framework for you and your team to use to develop greater understanding of the intent of each content standard cluster for the Number and Operations in Base Ten (2.NBT) domain.

Understand place value is the first content standard cluster in the 2.NBT domain. The emphasis for this content standard cluster includes students working with three-digit numbers, and counting, reading, and writing numbers to 1,000.

- **What's familiar?** These standards extend prior work with place value through three-digit numbers and should be very familiar to you.

- **What's new? What's challenging?** As noted, these standards extend place value to three-digit numbers. While the standards are not unique to this grade level, time will be needed to ensure that your students are comfortable with tens and ones or two-digit numbers before they expand to all aspects of the work with three-digit numbers—including counting by hundreds, number names, and expanded form. In addition, you and your students should have access to manipulative models or tools (Mathematical Practice 5) for representing two- and three-digit numbers.

- **What needs unpacking? What topics need emphasizing?** Your work with this topic will need to be distributed. Early-in-the-year work with two-digit numbers should reinforce first-grade expectations. Work with place value to two digits will precede addition and subtraction with three-digit numbers and will occur toward the end of the instructional year. As fluency with addition and subtraction is expected with two-digit numbers and the operations are then extended to three-digit numbers, you will see that work with understanding and developing proficiency with addition and subtraction is clearly a critical area at this grade level.

Use place-value understanding and properties of operations to add and subtract is the second content standard cluster in the 2.NBT domain. The emphasis in this content standard cluster is acquiring fluency with addition and subtraction of two-digit numbers and extending this work to three-digit numbers, with a particular focus on the use of addition and subtraction strategies.

- **What's familiar?** Developing fluency with addition and subtraction within 100 is clearly a topic of import within curricular guidelines and standards in most curricula at this grade level. Extending the work to three-digit numbers is also a typical textbook and curricular opportunity.

- **What's new? What's challenging?** While the expectations within this standard cluster, essentially fluency with adding and subtracting up to four two-digit numbers and beginning work with adding and subtracting within 1,000, are typical for many schools and school districts, the challenge is for you to consider the developmental readiness of your students for this work. One might suggest that as you and your students become more and more comfortable with truly developing a sense of number and the understanding and readiness for these standards, more and more students will truly develop fluency with adding and subtracting two-digit numbers. These expectations and the readiness for them are great topics for collaborative team discussions. Additionally, your comfort with using concrete models and drawings and strategies based on place value, properties of operations, and the relationship between addition and subtraction and composing and decomposing tens or hundreds are also potential emphasis points for collaborative team meetings and planning. Finally, encouraging students to explain why strategies work engages multiple Mathematical Practices and deepens understanding. This is very important for establishing computational proficiency at this grade level.

- **What needs unpacking? What topics need emphasizing?** These standards will require a lot of instructional time. Toward the end of the first half of the year and perhaps into the third quarter of the year, you'll emphasize the standards related to adding and subtracting two-digit numbers (2.NBT.5 and 2.NBT.6, page 173). Later-in-the-year work with three-digit numbers, involving concrete models or drawings and the strategies noted earlier in this section, will be emphasized. The work here with addition and subtraction algorithms builds on student understandings related to place value. In addition, these standards also involve mental mathematics and ensuring that students are able to explain the strategies they employ for adding and subtracting. The standards in this cluster represent the computational foundation for addition and subtraction of whole numbers. Making sure that you have the time to do this well is important. How to do this will be an important collaborative team discussion with lots of sharing between first-, second-, and third-grade teachers, particularly when considering students who will be challenged to meet the fluency expectation at this grade level.

Measurement and Data (2.MD)

The Measurement and Data domain considers the measurement process, representing and interpreting data, and time and money as measurement-related contexts at the preK–2 levels. The emphasis at this grade level includes learning linear measure, understanding time and money, and representing and interpreting data using line plots, picture graphs, and bar graphs.

The 2.MD Content Standard Clusters

The Measurement and Data (2.MD) domain has four content standard clusters, which contain four standards (see appendix E, pages 173–174).

1. Measure and estimate lengths in standard units.

2. Relate addition and subtraction to length.

3. Work with time and money.

4. Represent and interpret data.

The Understanding Questions for the 2.MD Content Standard Clusters

The three questions in table 3.3 (page 89) provide a framework for you and your team to use to develop greater understanding of the intent of each content standard cluster for the Measurement and Data (2.MD) domain.

Measure and estimate lengths in standard units is the first content standard cluster in the 2.MD domain. Students will estimate and measure lengths to the nearest inch, foot, centimeter, or meter.

- **What's familiar?** While measurement is an important context for using number, how measurement actually plays out in state and school district curriculum materials differs quite a bit, so for some, these standards may be familiar, while this will not be the case for others.

- **What's new? What's challenging?** The focus of these standards is essentially linear measurement. You may consider these standards less than typical if you are used to measuring length, capacity, and mass at this grade level. Another difference is that these standards call for the use of appropriate tools, expressing the length of an object in two equivalent measures (2 ft. and 24 in.), which suggests the use of a ruler. Finally, your students will be engaged in estimating lengths to the nearest centimeter, meter, inch, or foot, which will be new.

- **What needs unpacking? What topics need emphasizing?** Measurement is doing mathematics. These standards will require specific instruction relative to using appropriate measuring tools, measuring twice using different units of length, estimating, and measuring to determine how much longer one object is than another. These lesson-specific activities can then be extended through center activities, which will reinforce and apply these important linear measurement ideas. Engaging your students at this level in estimating measures, comparing measurements, and using standard measurement tools will be points of emphasis within this linear measurement focus.

Relate addition and subtraction to length is the second content standard cluster for the 2.MD domain. In learning related to this standard, students will solve measurement-related problems that will apply concepts and skills involving addition and subtraction within 100.

- **What's familiar?** The emphasis in this cluster is on using measurement as a context for addition and subtraction of whole numbers. While such a context may not be familiar to you, it does provide an obvious window of application for the significant work with addition and subtraction at this grade level.

- **What's new? What's challenging?** While using measurement as a context for addition and subtraction is not a major surprise at this level, using a number line for such addition and subtraction may be a new context for your lesson design. That said, remember that a ruler is essentially a physical or manipulative model of a number line, so the number line makes sense as a ruler-like tool. A challenge may be finding time to actually provide your students activities related to these standards.

- **What needs unpacking? What topics need emphasizing?** It makes sense to present these standards (2.MD.5 and 2.MD.6, appendix E, page 174) as problem-based contexts for maintaining addition and subtraction skills at this grade level. You may also consider center activities involving problems designed to address these standards. A specific lesson related to use of the number-line diagram (connecting the number line to a ruler) as a context for adding and subtracting will be needed, with practice activities related to this standard provided within various lessons or as a center.

Work with time and money is the third content standard cluster in the 2.MD domain. Learning activities will include telling and writing times to the nearest five minutes and solving problems involving money.

- **What's familiar?** Time and money are standard and very familiar mathematics topics at this grade level.

- **What's new? What's challenging?** While neither the time nor money standard in this cluster represent a new or different content-topic emphasis, each continues to be challenging for some students. It will be important for collaborative teams at grades 1–3 to discuss and then determine how they address time and money across these grade levels. These are admittedly quirky topics, which some would argue are actually cultural topics rather than mathematics. After all, our clock is a modulo 12 system, and adding and subtracting money engages decimals, which students have yet to encounter mathematically. Part of the challenge will be when and how to address these topics. It should also be noted that the money standard (2.MD.8, appendix E, page 174) does not address making change, which is certainly achievable for students at this grade level.

- **What needs unpacking? What topics need emphasizing?** Of these two standards, the money standard will be easier to address because while one to three specific lessons may be needed in reviewing and extending prior work with monetary amounts and counting money and making change, much of the emphasis will be just considering money as a context for problem solving that will engage addition and subtraction. Time is another story. You will need to provide lessons involving digital and analog time and telling time to the nearest five minutes. Beyond a few specific lessons for both the time and money standards, this work should be maintained throughout the instructional year in problem-based activities within lessons or as center activities.

Represent and interpret data is the fourth content standard cluster in the 2.MD domain. The emphasis includes representing and interpreting data using line plots and picture and bar graphs.

- **What's familiar?** Generating and analyzing data using graphs at this level, particularly picture and bar graphs are familiar expectations.

- **What's new? What's challenging?** The specificity of these two standards will likely be new to you and students at the second-grade level, particularly creating a line plot. (See figure 3.1 for an example.) Note that a line plot represents the frequency of particular events.

  Once again, your familiarity with the common addition and subtraction situations, mentioned frequently in this chapter, will be important as you consider such problems using information in a bar graph. First- to third-grade teachers in collaborative teams may benefit from discussion related to creating and using line plots and interpreting data from line plots during data collection.

Favorite School Lunches

Figure 3.1: **Sample line plot.**

- **What needs unpacking? What topics need emphasizing?** You may consider specific lessons targeted to each of these standards with additional activities provided as centers or as a problem context within lessons involving measurement or work with whole numbers (2.MD.9, appendix E, page 174). These lessons would probably occur within a cluster of specific measurement or data lessons. Their placement will depend on the content applied, but the lessons would most likely occur along with the work with linear measure.

Geometry (2.G)

Geometry is the mathematics dedicated to space and spatial learning. Geometry emphasis topics at this level include reasoning about and partitioning shapes. The focus at this grade level also extends the partitioning of circular and rectangular regions.

The 2.G Content Standard Cluster

The Geometry (2.G) domain has one content standard cluster, which contains three standards (see appendix E, page 174).

1.   Reason with shapes and their attributes.

The Understanding Questions for the 2.G Content Standard Clusters

The three questions in table 3.3 (page 89) provide a framework for you and your team to use to develop greater understanding of the intent of each content standard cluster for the Geometry (2.G) domain.

Reason with shapes and their attributes is the single content standard cluster for the 2.G domain. Students will recognize and draw shapes with specific attributes and partition shapes.

- **What's familiar?** The geometric concepts expected in this cluster are not likely to be familiar to you and your students at this level beyond the recognition of shapes with specific attributes, which began at the kindergarten level.

- **What's new? What's challenging?** There is a lot that is different in this domain at this grade level. The emphases are quite different. They include drawing shapes based on particular attributes; partitioning shapes into rows and columns of same-size squares, which is a precursor to work with area; and partitioning shapes into two, three, or four equal shares, which continues the beginning work with fractions started in grade 1. While these geometry standards range from drawing to preliminary work with area and fractions, they should be attainable by your students at this grade level.

- **What needs unpacking? What topics need emphasizing?** Grades 1–3 collaborative team discussions and planning related to these three standards will be an important professional development focus. Actual lessons will be needed regarding the language specificity of the shapes to be recognized (for example, pentagons and hexagons) and then drawn. Similarly, a specific lesson on partitioning rectangles into rows and columns and then determining the total square will be needed. This is a nice precursor to area, which is a third-grade topic. Finally, one to two lessons on partitioning circles and rectangles into two, three, or four equal shares and discussing the shares using the fractions halves, fourths, and thirds will also need to be planned and implemented. Follow-up activities for each of these standards can be center based or used as maintenance or extension activities in other lessons. This collection of shape-related lessons may occur as a geometry unit of approximately one week or inserted as specific focus lessons where appropriate.

Grade 2 Analysis: Concluding Comment

Second grade culminates the early childhood (preK–2) level. Second graders develop understandings related to place value, become fluent with addition and subtraction of two-digit whole numbers, and develop a foundation for multiplication. Time and money are important contexts for using mathematics and problem solving at this grade level. You and your collaborative team should give special consideration to professional development opportunities related to place value—as it is critically important at this level. Collaborative planning time to sort out the necessary time for work with the critical areas at this grade level—extending understanding of base-ten notation, building fluency with addition and subtraction, using standard units of measure, and describing and analyzing shapes—will be important.

Mathematics Content: A Different Look at Emphasis

Table 3.4 (page 100) emphasizes the number of K–5 standards within a domain and the number of standards per grade level. One of the conclusions may be a *less is more* argument indicating fewer standards per grade level as compared with existing state, provincial, or school district standards. Such a distinction implies more time provided to *drill down* and truly engage students in activities designed to develop understanding and proficiency. Use the data in table 3.4 and the reflection questions in figure 3.2 (page 100) to guide your collaborative team discussions for content focus and emphasis throughout the year.

Table 3.4: CCSS—Content Analysis, Grades K–5

Domains	K	1	2	3	4	5	Totals
Counting and Cardinality	9						5%
Operations and Algebraic Thinking	5	8	4	9	5	3	19%
Number and Operations in Base Ten	1	8	10	3	6	8	21% (K–5); 26% (K–2)
Number and Operations—Fractions				7	12	11	31% (3–5)
Measurement and Data	3	4	10	12	8	8	26%
Geometry	6	3	3	2	3	4	12%
Totals*	24	23	27	30	34	34	

Note: Please consider this table for discussion only as to the impact of the CCSS. The totals are only a count of the standards (including substandards: a, b, c, and so on) within a content standard cluster. This is not an attempt to consider weight, emphasis, or time needed for particular standards, which is another factor for your consideration. Standards is defined here as the full content standard cluster of expectations under a particular domain (such as Geometry).

Visit **go.solution-tree.com/commoncore** for a reproducible version of this table.

---

1. Counting and Cardinality, Operations and Algebraic Thinking, and Number and Operations in Base Ten—61 percent of grades K–2

2. Number-related domain emphasis (Counting and Cardinality, Operations and Algebraic Thinking, Number and Operations in Base Ten):

   - 63 percent in kindergarten

   - 70 percent in grade 1

   - 52 percent in grade 2

3. Does the number emphasis at these grades make sense to you? Would you do things differently? What to you wonder or worry about here?

4. Note the emphasis on measurement and data in grade 2. Does this make sense to you?

Figure 3.2: Content analysis reflection considerations and questions.

Content Analysis by Domain

As collaborative teams become more comfortable considering the mathematical prerequisites leading into particular grade levels, a logical next step will be to examine the hierarchical nature of the mathematics across the grades. Clements and Sarama (2009) and others have written about the importance of learning trajectories as students encounter mathematics concepts and develop understandings. Table 3.5 provides a domain-by-domain analysis of the mathematics within the CCSS for grades K–2. Note that the Counting and Cardinality domain appears only at the kindergarten level. We have included standards from grade 3 to illustrate the coherence of standards across grade levels. As professional development opportunities are expanded to consider growth across the domains in the CCSS, collaborative teams should be able to track, for instance, the importance of addition and subtraction as they are developed and extended across grades K–2. Using table 3.5 will also allow your collaborative teams to review specific standards—beyond the general standard statements provided in table 3.5—to consider growth and gaps from grade to grade. This across-domain analysis will also help your collaborative teams to again recognize the concentration and focus on particular topics at these grade levels.

Table 3.5: Domain-by-Domain Cross-Grade Analysis

Grade K	Grade 1	Grade 2	Grade 3
Counting and Cardinality (K only)			
Know number names and the count sequence.			
Count to tell the number of objects.			
Compare numbers.			
Operations and Algebraic Thinking			
Understand addition as *putting together* and *adding to,* and understand subtraction as *taking apart* and *taking from.*	Represent and solve problems involving addition and subtraction.	Represent and solve problems involving addition and subtraction.	Represent and solve problems involving multiplication and division.
	Understand and apply properties of operations and the relationship between addition and subtraction.	Add and subtract within 20.	Understand properties of multiplication and the relationship between multiplication and division.
	Add and subtract within 20.	Work with equal groups of objects to gain foundations for multiplication.	Multiply and divide within 100.

continued →

Grade K	Grade 1	Grade 2	Grade 3
.	Work with addition and subtraction equations.		Solve problems involving the four operations, and identify and explain patterns in arithmetic.
Number and Operations in Base Ten			
Work with numbers 11 to 19 to gain foundations for place value.	Extend the counting sequence.		
	Understand place value.	Understand place value.	
	Use place-value understanding and properties of operations to add and subtract.	Use place-value understanding and properties of operations to add and subtract.	Use place-value understanding and properties of operations to perform multidigit arithmetic.
Number and Operations—Fractions			
			Develop understanding of fractions as numbers.
Measurement and Data			
Describe and compare measurable attributes.	Measure lengths indirectly and by iterating length units.	Measure and estimate lengths in standard units.	Solve problems involving measurement and estimation of intervals of time, liquid volumes, and masses of objects.
Classify objects and count the number of objects in categories.	Tell and write time.	Relate addition and subtraction to length.	Represent and interpret data.
	Represent and interpret data.	Work with time and money.	Geometric measurement: Understand concepts of area, and relate area to multiplication and to addition.

Grade K	Grade 1	Grade 2	Grade 3
		Represent and interpret data.	Geometric measurement: Recognize perimeter as an attribute of plane figures, and distinguish between linear and area measures.
Geometry			
Identify and describe shapes.	Reason with shapes and their attributes.	Reason with shapes and their attributes.	Reason with shapes and their attributes.
Analyze, compare, create, and compose shapes.			
General Comments			

Source: Adapted from NGA & CCSSO, 2010.

Visit **go.solution-tree.com/commoncore** for a reproducible version of this table.

Content Considerations

This chapter has provided a number of tools to support you as you work in your collaborative team to determine and analyze the CCSS mathematics content. The chapter's tables support the discussion of the mathematics content you must now teach in grades K–2. You can then determine the depth desired for your analysis of the content and when and how collaborative teams will engage in the analysis suggested. The ultimate goal will be for each member of your collaborative team to have a clear understanding of the important mathematics that impacts his or her grade—to realize that what's provided within the CCSS is not all that different contentwise from what you have experienced, but to recognize the differences and understand that the CCSS do provide opportunities to dig deep and to really make less (fewer expectations) become more (provide a depth of understanding).

Finally, the questions you will need to ask within your collaborative team and then address as part of your CCSS content professional development efforts will help you determine the next steps to take in the coming months and next school year. These questions are shown in figure 3.3.

- Which grade levels will implement the CCSS next year?
- How many of the CCSS standards will you address at your grade level?
- What is your plan for the amount of instructional time you will spend on each standard?

Figure 3.3: Anticipation questions for future planning.   continued →

- Do you have the instructional tools (Mathematics Practice 5) to accomplish your proposed plan? If not, what materials are needed?

- How will your students be engaged in the CCSS Mathematical Practices through their experiences in Counting and Cardinality, Operations and Algebraic Thinking, Number and Operations in Base Ten, Measurement and Data, and Geometry?

Visit **go.solution-tree.com/commoncore** for a reproducible version of this figure.

This chapter should guide your school's professional development efforts in thinking about, analyzing, and unpacking the content domains and standards of the CCSS as your collaborative team takes responsibility for implementing and assessing the expectations of the Common Core State Standards.

Chapter 3 Extending My Understanding

1. Examine the CCSS domains, clusters, and standards at a particular grade level (or grade band).

   ○ Which are considered critical areas for instructional emphasis—at each grade level (K–2)?

   ○ Conduct a side-by-side comparison with your current mathematics curriculum standards, spending time unpacking and looking for emphasis.

   ○ As a collaborative team identify the familiar, new, or challenging content. How might this impact your implementation plan?

2. Examine a specific CCSS content standard. Discuss the meaning of the standard, analyze and interpret new or unfamiliar language, and describe student understandings and proficiency expected.

3. Examine a CCSS content standard cluster that is new or challenging for a selected group of your students. Determine which Mathematical Practices you will use to help students achieve this standard.

4. Examine the instructional materials currently used to support your mathematics program. Determine the extent to which these materials are aligned with the CCSS by using the Mathematics Curriculum Materials Analysis Project tools discussed in the following online resources. How will you use this information to guide planning, delivery of instruction, and effective assessment?

Online Resources

Visit **go.solution-tree.com/commoncore** for links to these resources.

- **CCSS Mathematics Curriculum Materials Analysis Project (Bush et al., 2011; www.mathedleadership.org/ccss/materials.html):** The CCSS Mathematics Curriculum Analysis Project provides a set of tools to assist K–12 textbook selection committees, school administrators, and teachers in the analysis and selection of curriculum materials that support implementation of the CCSS for mathematics.

- **Illustrative Math Project (http://illustrativemathematics.org):** The main goal for this project is to provide guidance to states, assessment consortia, testing companies, and curriculum developers by illustrating the range and types of mathematical work that students will experience in implementing the Common Core State Standards for mathematics.

- **Progressions Documents for the Common Core Math Standards (http://math.arizona.edu/~ime/progressions):** The CCSS for mathematics were built on progressions—narrative documents describing the progression of a topic across a number of grade levels, informed both by research on children's cognitive development and by the logical structure of mathematics. The progressions detail why standards are sequenced the way they are, point out cognitive difficulties and provide pedagogical solutions, and provide more detail on particularly difficult areas of mathematics. The progressions documents found on this site are useful in teacher preparation, professional development, and curriculum organization, and they provide a link between mathematics education research and the standards.

- **Recommendations for CCSS Professional Development (http://common coretools.files.wordpress.com/2011/05/2011_04_27_gearing_up.pdf):** These initial recommendations are from the Gearing Up for the Common Core State Standards in Mathematics conference. They can serve as guidelines for K–8 mathematics professional development for states transitioning to the CCSS.

- **Livescribe Pencasts (www.livescribe.com):** As one way to engage your colleagues, you may want to consider using pencasts of student work to help drive collaborative discussions related to student understanding of important standards within each of the content domains for grades K–2.

CHAPTER 4

Implementing the Teaching-Assessing-Learning Cycle

The vision of the Common Core State Standards for mathematics (NGA & CCSSO, 2010) is one that interprets the learning of important mathematics as consisting of both mathematics content and mathematical practices—a vision the National Council of Teachers of Mathematics (2010) shares in *Making It Happen*. Much of your implementation effort surrounding the CCSS will focus on making sure your instruction is aligned with the more coherent and focused CCSS content standards and that the Mathematical Practices are interpreted as both essential mathematics to be learned and as ways in which your students should engage in learning the mathematics content. These are crucial steps in implementing the CCSS. Ensuring that these interpretations are well understood and implemented in your classroom, however, is just the beginning work necessary to ensure student attainment of the CCSS.

A Major Shift in the Function of Grades K–2 Mathematics Assessment

This chapter examines the paradigm shift from the traditional use of summative assessment instruments (strictly to grade and evaluate student learning) to the use of collaboratively developed formative assessment processes to guide your instruction. When implemented effectively, your assessment practices are a critical instructional tool to improve teaching and student learning. Since the enactment of the No Child Left Behind Act of 2001 (NCLB, 2002), most of the assessment focus has been directed at preparing all students to perform well on state accountability tests. In many states, this led to tests and instruction, which essentially narrowed the curriculum to focus on lower-level procedural skills—skills that make up but one component of the more balanced vision of the CCSS, which states that "mathematical understanding and procedural skill are equally important" (NGA & CCSSO, 2010, p. 4). Consequently, past improvements on state accountability tests may not reflect actual improved student learning in the broader set of skills and concepts called for in the CCSS. Think about the process of assessment teachers in your school often use at your grade level. For student mathematics learning to improve according to the CCSS, you will need to shift your assessment work to using *formative assessment* as a collaboratively developed process for improving your instruction and student learning.

Popham (2008) points out that it is important to be clear on the definition of formative assessment: "Formative assessment is a planned process in which assessment-elicited evidence of students' status is used by teachers to adjust their ongoing instructional procedures or by students to adjust their current learning tactics" (p. 6). Wiliam (2011) offers a similar definition:

> An assessment functions formatively to the extent that evidence about student achievement is elicited, interpreted, and used by teachers, learners, or their peers to make decisions about the next steps in instruction that are likely to be better, or better founded, than the decisions they would have made in the absence of that evidence. (p. 43)

According to both Popham (2008) and Wiliam (2011), formative assessment isn't just an assessment instrument but rather a planned process whose defining characteristic is its use to improve student learning. Formative assessment only takes place when you use the results of assessments to advance student learning. As William (2007a) concludes:

> So the big idea of formative assessment is that evidence about student learning is used to adjust instruction to better meet student needs; in other words, teaching is adaptive to the student learning needs and assessment is done in real time. (p. 191)

According to Popham (2008), at the highest levels of implementation, formative assessment "consists of schoolwide adoption . . . chiefly through the use of professional development and teacher learning communities" (p. ix). Therefore, your collaborative team is the primary mechanism to shift your schoolwide culture toward an emphasis on using formative assessment as the process to improve mathematics instruction and student learning. This is often referred to as assessment *for* student learning. When this is accomplished, assessment becomes the critical *feedback bridge* between improved instruction and student learning (Wiliam, 2011).

According to Wiliam (2011):

> When formative assessment practices are integrated into the minute-to-minute and day-by-day classroom activities of teachers, substantial increases in student achievement—of the order of a 70 to 80% increase in the speed of learning are possible. . . . Moreover, these changes are not expensive to produce. . . . There is nothing else remotely affordable that is likely to have such a large effect. (p. 161)

The National Mathematics Advisory Panel (2008) in its final report, *Foundations for Success,* under its strict standard for scientific research, made this definitive recommendation to improve mathematics achievement at the K–8 level: "Teachers' regular use of formative assessment improves their students' learning. . . . The results are sufficiently promising that the Panel recommends regular use of formative assessment for students in the elementary grades" (p. xxiii).

Because formative assessment can be such a powerful instructional tool, highly effective assessment practices in grades K–2 mathematics should integrate formative assessment *for* learning with summative assessment instruments *of* learning. Formative assessment *for* learning is used to adapt, modify, and direct instruction. Summative assessment *of* learning is used to evaluate students' achievement, assign grades, and evaluate the overall effectiveness of the mathematics program based on school, district, state, province, or consortia assessments. In other words, *every* assessment instrument whether or not it is used for grading or evaluation purposes can and should serve a formative function and become an essential aspect of your work in collaborative teams.

The PLC Teaching-Assessing-Learning Cycle

Assessment can no longer solely serve a summative function—that of assigning grades and providing accountability—if the goal is to improve student learning and successfully implement the CCSS. For mathematics teaching and learning to improve, the formative assessment process must become the assessment focus of collaborative teams.

Figure 4.1 lists the critical questions you need to ask in your collaborative team in order to begin the process of implementing formative assessment in a planned way. When you address these questions in your collaborative team, it supports growth toward assessment practices that bridge the gap between teaching and learning in order to improve student learning.

---

1. In advance of teaching the lesson, chapter, and unit of study (all three levels of planning), how well does each member of your grade-level collaborative team understand the student learning targets (the content standard, depth of knowledge, and Mathematical Practices) and the assessments aligned with those learning targets?

2. Has your team collaboratively developed and agreed on scoring rubrics and procedures for both formative and summative assessment instruments that will accurately reflect student achievement of the learning targets?

3. To what degree do your collaborative team's assessments build student confidence and encourage students to take responsibility for what they know and still have to learn?

4. How well does your collaborative team provide timely formative (and summative) assessment feedback that is both frequent and descriptive (versus evaluative), providing students with specific information regarding their strengths as well as strategies to improve?

5. How well does each member of your collaborative team, and the team as a collective group, modify instruction or provide additional instructional supports for students as necessary, based on the results of both formative and summative classroom assessment to improve student learning and future instruction?

Source: Adapted from Kanold, Briars, & Fennell, 2012.

Figure 4.1: Key assessment questions for grade-level collaborative teams.

Visit **go.solution-tree.com/commoncore** for a reproducible version of this figure.

When collaborative teams address these key questions, they support you in shifting the assessment emphasis from one that views assessment as primarily something that occurs at the end of instruction to determine if learning has occurred to an ongoing process that is used to improve teaching and learning. Wiliam and Thompson (2007) argue that teacher learning teams can play a key role in supporting this shift to assessment *for* learning because their sustained nature allows "change to occur developmentally, which

. . . increases the likelihood of the change 'sticking' at both the individual and school level" (p. 17).

The teaching-assessing-learning cycle described in figure 4.2 outlines a process that not only includes the planned development of formative assessments within collaborative teams but also provides a framework you can use to review your current use of summative assessments, such as chapter or unit tests. The process turns these summative assessments, which teachers use in collaborative teams as assessments *of* student learning for grading purposes, into formative learning opportunities—"the formative use of summative tests" (Wiliam, 2011, p. 38). Every student assessment opportunity, whether it is used for grading purposes or not, serves a formative function in the cycle and provides an opportunity for your collaborative team to monitor, adapt, and guide instruction.

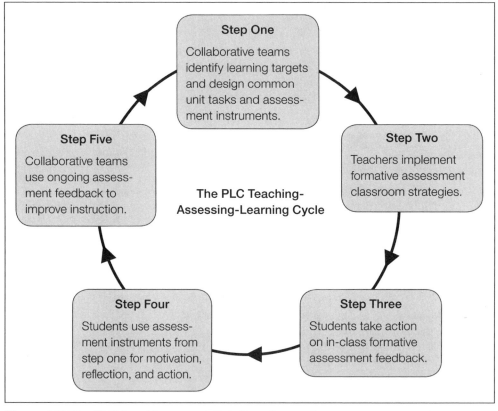

Figure 4.2: The PLC teaching-assessing-learning cycle.

Visit **go.solution-tree.com/commoncore** for a reproducible version of this figure.

This teaching-assessing-learning cycle—the PLC assessment cycle—requires you to work together within your grade-level collaborative team to design both common summative assessment instruments and formative assessment strategies in advance of beginning each one- to three-week period of mathematics instruction. The one- to three-week cycle is intentionally recommended because research suggests that formative assessment is only effective—results in improved student achievement—if done in short (within and between lessons) or medium cycles (one to four weeks) (Wiliam & Thompson, 2007). During the process of creating a unit of summative and formative assessments, you and other collaborative team members clearly define and develop a shared expectation for student performance. Your collaborative team must also determine how to communicate your learning expectations to students, which is done in part through the instructional tasks you select to use during the unit of instruction and the ongoing formative assessment tasks and strategies you design and implement (see step two in figure 4.2).

The assessment cycle begins with implementing a one- to three-week instructional unit of collaboratively developed lesson plans and the assessment tasks and tools designed to focus on the critical mathematics during that period of instruction. It is important to note that you do not have to move clockwise through the steps. That is, you can and should make adjustments, moving back and forth to different steps in the cycle as needed, based on results of formative assessment processes. This may mean your lesson plans and instructional time allocations have to be adjusted due to differences in student achievement within your class.

During instruction you need to help students focus on their performance and support them in making their own adjustments with respect to their learning strategies (see question three in figure 4.1, page 109; Popham, 2008). You need to remain reflective concerning the effectiveness of your lesson plans and keep notes throughout the unit of instruction so that your collaborative team can discuss successes and challenges and make appropriate adjustments for the following year. The cycle then repeats itself for the next one to three weeks of instruction.

It is important to note that effective formative assessment during a unit of instruction, which appears as a step in figure 4.2, is not an isolated event but rather an ongoing process embedded within instruction that is carried out continuously as lessons unfold (Wiliam, 2007a, 2011). This is possible to do because there are levels of *formality* with respect to formative assessment that are described more fully in step two (Ginsburg & Dolan, 2011; Marzano, 2007).

Step One: Collaborative Teams Identify Learning Targets And Design Common Unit Tasks and Assessment Instruments

In a professional learning community culture, before the first lesson of the next unit of mathematics instruction begins, your collaborative team reaches agreement on the design and proper use of high-quality, rigorous common assessment instruments for all students in your grade level. When grade-level collaborative teams create these common assessment instruments together, they enhance the coherence and fidelity to the student learning expectations. The wide variance in student task performance expectations (an inequity creator) from teacher to teacher is minimized when you work collaboratively with your colleagues to design assessments and tasks appropriate to the identified learning targets for the unit.

You can use figure 4.3 as a resource to guide your collaborative team discussions and evaluate your collaborative team readiness to teach, assess, and learn before the unit begins.

---

1. **Student opportunity to learn:** Do all teachers at your grade level have access to the same content? By the end of the unit will every teacher have covered the same content with the same rigor?

2. **Depth of knowledge:** Are cognitive requirements between the formative assessment tasks and the learning targets in the unit consistent for each teacher? Is the same complexity of knowledge (and skill) sought and required by all teachers for the mathematics unit?

3. **Range of knowledge:** Is the range of content covered under each of the content clusters for the unit of knowledge similar from teacher to teacher in the grade level? Do all teachers of the course include daily tasks that prepare students for procedural fluency as well as the conceptual understanding tasks that will be part of the common assessment instruments that all teachers in the grade level use?

4. **Balance of representation:** Are learning targets for a particular cluster of standards given the same emphasis on the common assessment instruments that all teachers on the teacher team use?

5. **Source of challenge:** Does student assessment (test) performance actually depend on mastering the learning targets and not on irrelevant knowledge or skills?

Figure 4.3: Aligning learning targets with assessment instruments and tasks.

Visit **go.solution-tree.com/commoncore** for a reproducible version of this figure.

As each one- to three-week period of instruction approaches, your collaborative team meets to design lessons based on three essential assessment issues for the one- to three-week unit of instruction (Kanold et al., 2012; Stiggins, Arter, Chappuis, & Chappuis, 2006):

What Are the Identified Learning Standards?

One of the advantages of the CCSS is the more clearly defined standards for each grade level. The number of standards per grade level is reduced in the CCSS compared to most traditional state standards to allow an instructional emphasis on developing student understanding, in part by engaging students in using the Mathematical Practices. This in turn creates an expectation that assessment of student learning will include assessing students' *understanding* of the conceptual knowledge necessary for developing procedural fluency through the Mathematical Practices. Consider the following questions to help identify learning standards.

- What are the mathematical skill- and concept-level CCSS learning standards for proficiency?

- What does proficiency look like?

- What are the mathematical understanding-level learning standards for proficiency?

- What does understanding look like for this unit of study?

- What are the Mathematical Practices that will be emphasized within this unit of instruction?

Figure 4.4 shows grade 2 standards from the CCSS for mathematics under the domain Number and Operations in Base Ten and the content standard cluster *Use place-value understanding and properties of operations to add and subtract* (see appendix E, page 173).

Use Place-Value Understanding and Properties of Operations to Add and Subtract

5. Fluently add and subtract within 100 using strategies based on place value, properties of operations, or the relationship between addition and subtraction.

6. Add up to four two-digit numbers using strategies based on place value and properties of operations.

7. Add and subtract within 1,000, using concrete models or drawings and strategies based on place value, properties of operations, or the relationship between addition and subtraction; relate the strategy to a written method. Understand that in adding or subtracting three-digit numbers, one adds or subtracts hundreds and hundreds, tens and tens, and ones and ones; and sometimes it is necessary to compose or decompose tens or hundreds.

8. Mentally add 10 or 100 to a given number 100–900, and mentally subtract 10 or 100 from a given number 100–900.

9. Explain why addition and subtraction strategies work, using place value and the properties of operations.

Source: Adapted from NGA & CCSSO, 2010, p. 19.

Figure 4.4: CCSS grade 2 Number and Operations in Base Ten (2.NBT).

As these second-grade standards from the CCSS illustrate, there is an emphasis on both skills and understanding as students are expected to *use strategies, explain, understand,* and *use understanding.* Expecting a student to understand implies that you will assess whether a student has understood. According to the CCSS (NGA & CCSSO, 2010):

> Asking a student to understand something means asking a teacher to assess whether the student has understood it. But what does mathematical understanding look like? One hallmark of mathematical understanding is the ability to justify, in a way appropriate to the student's mathematical maturity, why a particular mathematical statement is true or where a mathematical rule comes from. Mathematical understanding and procedural skill are equally important, and both are assessable using mathematical tasks of sufficient richness. (p. 4)

Determining whether or not a student is developing conceptual understanding requires continuous formative assessment during a lesson (informal) and across the span of a one- to three-week unit of instruction. The second-grade standards in figure 4.4 illustrate the connection between the CCSS content standards and the Mathematical Practices. The emphasis on explaining why addition and subtraction strategies work, using place value and the properties of operations, provides you the opportunity to instructionally emphasize and also assess Mathematical Practice 3—Construct viable arguments and critique the reasoning of others—and Mathematical Practice 7—Look for and make use of structure (see appendix B, pages 158 and 159). The formative assessment component during a unit of instruction provides your collaborative team the opportunity to discuss the Common Core vision of mathematics instruction and learning, emphasizing both content and student processes for learning the content.

What Are the Identified Common Assessment Instruments?

Based on the standards for the one- to three-week unit of instruction, collaborative teams have to develop the *common* assessment instruments that each collaborative team member will use during the unit of instruction. What are the quizzes, tests, or performance assessment instruments that will be used for the purpose of determining a student's grade or mastery level? In addition, the collaborative team must agree on the common *scoring rubrics* used for grading student work on the established performance targets. How will these rubrics, which define student performance expectation levels, be shared with your students during instruction to communicate the expectation level? How will students be provided descriptive feedback on their progress so they can make appropriate adjustments to their own learning strategies to advance their mastery on the summative assessment instruments?

Figure 4.5 highlights an adapted five-stage summative assessment development process (Kanold et al., 2012) that you can use to develop more effective summative assessment tools.

What Are the Identified Daily Formative Mathematical Tasks?

Working backward from the collaboratively designed summative assessment instruments that will be used for the one- to three-week unit of instruction, what are the common mathematical tasks that need to be part of each grade-level teachers' daily lessons in order to ensure students are prepared for the rigor and expectations of the assessment instrument tasks? Collaboratively designing lessons as a grade-level team allows you and your collaborative team to discuss and share effective instructional approaches. More importantly, it provides you the support you need to help ensure that your lessons address skills and conceptual understanding, as well as problem-solving tasks with an emphasis on the Mathematical Practices appropriate to the mathematics content standards.

Preparing to develop the conceptual understanding that underlies the CCSS content standards requires that students learn mathematics by engaging in the CCSS Mathematical Practices as described in chapter 2. You should spend significant time during your collaborative team lesson-planning sessions to determine how you will connect Mathematical Practices to the mathematics content. For example, if your collaborative team's lesson plan calls for a consistent depth of knowledge (see figure 4.3, page 112), you should include preplanned questions to engage students in describing the relationship

1. **Plan:** Assess what and how. How important is this topic? Is this one of the CCSS grade-level areas for critical focus? What is the breadth and depth of the learning targets for the topic? Are the learning targets—skill level and understanding level—clear to everyone on the collaborative team? How will they be made clear to the students? What role will the CCSS Mathematical Practices have in the assessment?

2. **Develop:** Determine the sample questions and tasks for the assessment. Select, create, or modify assessment items or tasks and scoring rubrics as needed to meet student needs. What will be the format and methods used for student demonstrations of proficiency? Are there tasks that assess both the CCSS content standards and Mathematical Practices?

3. **Critique:** Evaluate the assessment for quality. How does the collaborative team know it has written a high-quality assessment? Does the school have well-defined and understood criteria for high-quality assessment development?

4. **Administer and score:** A unit assessment is given to the students and immediately scored using the collaboratively developed scoring rubric, and students receive timely descriptive feedback concerning their performance. Ideally, grade-level collaborative teams grade unit assessments together to improve the accuracy of feedback students receive. Students receive results immediately—ideally, the next day, but at most within two class days (Reeves, 2011).

5. **Revise:** Evaluate assessment quality based on results, and revise as needed for the following year. The results should also be used to identify learning targets and assessment questions that may need to be repeated as part of the next unit of study to build student retention—for example, areas identified in the CCSS Frameworks for a more critical focus and emphasis.

Source: Adapted from Stiggins et al., 2006, pp. 106–117.

Figure 4.5: Common assessment planning process.

Visit **go.solution-tree.com/commoncore** for a reproducible version of this figure.

between addition and subtraction and prompts to encourage student responses, and then the lesson plan will embed instructional strategies to engage students in the Mathematical Practices (see appendix B, page 157). Implementing the CCSS Mathematical Practices during *planning* increases the opportunity for formative learning to take place and increase student achievement.

Step one is the critical place that potentially manufactures inequities in student mathematics learning. If your collaborative team does not reach agreement on the mathematical tasks and the rigor of the tasks you plan to include in a unit's lessons and assessments, then the students' learning outcomes will vary. This point cannot be overstated. Differences in teacher effectiveness within schools are at least four times the size of differences between schools (Wiliam, 2011). Equity in mathematics education requires that your grade-level collaborative teams ensure the use of common mathematical tasks of sufficient richness to engage students in observable mathematical discussions that can simultaneously serve as a form of ongoing formative assessment (Kanold et al., 2012).

Step Two: Collaborative Teams Implement Formative Assessment Classroom Strategies

In step two of the assessment cycle, grade-level collaborative teams select formative assessment strategies to determine if students are making progress developing skills and mathematical understandings. Formative assessments, particularly at the lesson level, do not have to be and should not always be formal pencil-and-paper tests or quizzes. Creating and implementing written or formal assessments during each lesson will both take time away from instruction and decrease the likelihood that team members will implement formative assessment strategies (Popham, 2008). Popham (2008) and others (Ginsburg & Dolan, 2011; Wiliam, 2011) have suggested several "informal" strategies of assessment *for* learning that can provide you valuable insight into the level of student understanding as a lesson unfolds. Some of these strategies are included in figure 4.6.

An additional advantage of these formative assessment strategies is that they increase the level of student engagement, a key characteristic of classroom environments that promote high student achievement (Wiliam, 2011). You should spend time in your collaborative team reflecting on the formative assessment strategies you use and their impact on student engagement, particularly with respect to the use of strategy one (see figure 4.6). Effective questioning is a high-leverage strategy used not only to increase student engagement but also to maintain the cognitive demand of mathematics tasks as a lesson unfolds (Stein et al., 2007). Devoting collaborative team time to preplanning these formative assessment questions is critical (Boaler & Staples, 2008). During the middle of instruction, as a lesson unfolds, you simply don't have the time to generate on-the-spot questions that effectively assess emerging student understanding you can use to guide your instruction (Popham, 2008; Smith & Stein, 2011). Formulating questions prior to a lesson that are *interpretable*—that is, that lead to incorrect answers that reveal student progress toward developing understanding—is a particularly valuable use of planning time (Wiliam, 2011). The use of effective questioning during instruction embeds formative assessment processes in instruction in nonintrusive ways. This strategy's potential to increase student learning, if you listen carefully to student responses for the level of student understanding and respond accordingly, is significant (Wiliam, 2007b; see Mathematical Practice 2, pages 157–158).

More formalized formative assessment strategies include sampling one or two homework items daily and giving quick quizzes with immediate feedback every two to three lessons. Faced with teaching multiple subjects to thirty or more students, you likely do not have time to grade every practice problem on every assignment. However, it is important you collect and use student homework results to modify and guide future instruction, but don't spend class time grading homework. Spot-checking three to five critical problems (item sampling) can provide you with valuable daily formative assessment evidence that can be used to modify and adjust your instruction to meet individual student needs.

Strategy One: Key Questioning During Whole-Class Discussion

You use preplanned questions during critical points of the lesson to assess student understanding. "These pivotal adjustment-influencing questions must be carefully conceptualized before the class session in which the discussion will take place. . . . Teachers can't expect to come up with excellent adjustment-influencing questions on the spur of the moment" (Popham, 2008, p. 60). It is important to monitor who is called on to respond to questions to ensure that all class members have an equal chance.

Strategy Two: Miniwhiteboard Responses

Supply every student with a miniwhiteboard. You ask a preplanned question or provide the students with a critical problem to solve. The students then hold up their responses on whiteboards, and you scan the responses to make a decision concerning the students' mastery levels and needed instructional modifications.

Strategy Three: Traffic Lights or Red and Green Disks

You supply students with colored plastic cups—green, yellow, and red—or a CD-sized disk that is red on one side and green on the other. At critical points during the lesson, ask students to display the color of cup or disk that corresponds to their level of understanding (green means that the student understands, while the red—or yellow—cup indicates the student does not understand and that instructional adjustments are necessary).

Strategy Four: All-Student Response Systems

If you have access to SMART Boards and clicker systems in your classroom, you can design key multiple-choice questions that students can work on at critical points in the lesson and send their answers to you using the clickers. This displays a real-time chart indicating the class's response to the question and immediately lets you know the level of the class's understanding or common misconceptions (if the multiple-choice options are keyed to common misconceptions).

Strategy Five: Diagnostic Interview Questions

Ask individual students questions to reflect on, articulate, and uncover how they are thinking while working individually or in small groups. The key is for you to engage in evaluative listening—listening to assess the student's understanding in order to modify instruction.

Figure 4.6: Formative assessment strategies.

Visit **go.solution-tree.com/commoncore** for a reproducible version of this figure.

Every two to three lessons, your collaborative team should administer a relatively short, quick screening assessment that you designed together to assess the content of the immediate two to three previous lessons. These quick assessments need not be long in length. Ten or fewer items that take no more than ten to fifteen minutes to complete are sufficient to provide you with more formal evidence concerning the current level of your students' understanding and can be used to trigger instructional adjustments as necessary. It is recommended that these more formal formative assessments are administered every two to three lessons because research indicates that more frequent assessment, assuming the results are used to target and tailor instruction, is related to greater student learning gains (Marzano, 2007).

Part of the process of developing formative assessments, whether informal or formal, includes determining in advance the level of student performance that will signal your need to make instructional adjustments (Popham, 2008). For example, what is the minimum class performance necessary on a quick screening assessment that will indicate that no instructional adjustment is necessary? You may decide as a collaborative team that if the class average on a common assessment is 90 percent or better, then no instructional adjustment is necessary. To be effective, your feedback on a student's response to a preplanned question during a lesson or a student's work on a practice assignment must be specific and descriptive. Providing students with descriptive feedback on formative assignments, including strengths, weaknesses, and next steps, with respect to how to make progress toward learning targets, is more effective than simply marking the work correct or incorrect, or even marking it correct or incorrect *with* comments (Davies, 2007; Marzano, 2006; Wiliam, 2011).

According to Wiliam (2007b), in order to "improve the quality of learning within the system, to be formative, feedback needs to contain an implicit or explicit recipe for future action" (p. 1062). Feedback that provides students with a *recipe* they can use to improve their level of understanding can motivate students to continue to persevere in making sense of problems—Mathematical Practice 1. For example, suppose a first-grade student is struggling to solve addition equations like 6 + 2. Classroom instruction may have emphasized *counting on* as the solution strategy. If a student struggles with this approach, then the *recipe* a student could follow to improve his understanding may be to use two-color counters, with six red counters and two yellow counters representing the addends. The student could then count all the counters. The physical representation may make it easier for the student to understand counting on.

Step Three: Students Take Action on Formative Assessment Feedback

Effective formative assessment is not only about you using evidence to modify and adjust your instruction but also about students using the data to make their own adjustments in the processes they use to achieve the learning targets (Popham, 2008; Wiliam, 2011). Do your students learn to take more responsibility for their learning by using the feedback you provide them? This is the goal of step three in the assessment cycle. In order for students to use formative assessment data to make adjustments to their own learning strategies, it is necessary that you make curricular expectations clear to students. Figure 4.7 describes three curricular clarifications you need to make so students can effectively use formative assessment data to self-monitor and adjust their learning strategies.

Stiggins et al. (2006) suggest strategies you can use to support students in taking more responsibility for their own learning. Several of these strategies are adapted in figure 4.8. They provide insight into the nature of teacher-designed but *student-led* formative assessment *actions*.

Clarification One: Provide a Clear and Understandable Vision of the Standard

At the beginning of every lesson, subset of lessons, or unit, you need to provide students with the curricular aim in language they can understand. For example, the kindergarten CCSS for mathematics domain Operations and Algebraic Thinking includes the standard "Decompose numbers less than or equal to 10 into pairs in more than one" (NGA & CCSSO, 2010, p. 11). Kindergarten students need to understand that *decompose* means they can *break apart* numbers in multiple ways—a number can be viewed as having pairs of other numbers embedded within it. For example, the *break-aparts* of 7 would be 6 and 1, 5 and 2, 4 and 3, 3 and 4, 2 and 5, and 1 and 6.

Clarification Two: Clarify Evaluative Criteria

It is important to clarify the criteria that will be used to determine the quality of their work. If the scoring rubric for assessments will assess students' understanding, then the scoring criteria and rubrics that reflect this should be shared with students. This can be facilitated by sharing with students anonymous student examples and models of strong and weak work to help students better visualize the nature of targeted level of understanding.

Clarification Three: Share the Building Blocks

You need to share with students the major building blocks (subskills) they must master in order to reach the standard. The content standard clusters in the CCSS often represent these building blocks. Unless students know what the building blocks are, it is difficult for them to assess their progress. A function of grade-level collaborative learning teams is to unpack the CCSS content standards and identify the necessary essential understandings, both for you and your students.

Source: Adapted from Popham, 2008, pp. 76–81.

Figure 4.7: Necessary curricular clarifications.

Strategy One: Provide a Clear and Understandable Vision of the Learning Target

Share with your students the CCSS cluster, learning targets, and prior-knowledge understanding expectations in advance of teaching the lesson or unit, giving the assignment, or doing the activity. Provide students with scoring guides written so they can understand them. More importantly, develop and design scoring criteria and rubrics with them.

Strategy Two: Use Examples and Models of Strong and Weak Work

Use models of strong and weak work—anonymous student work, work from life beyond school, and your own work. Begin with work that demonstrates strengths and weaknesses related to problems students will commonly experience, especially the problems or tasks that require student demonstrations of understanding. Ask students to discuss with peers the strengths and weaknesses of given solutions or strategies used to obtain a solution to problems posed in class or on a common assessment instrument.

Strategy Three: Offer Regular Descriptive Feedback

Offer descriptive feedback instead of grades on work that is for practice during and after the unit. Descriptive feedback should reflect students' strengths and weaknesses with respect to the specific learning targets they are trying to achieve in a given assignment.

Figure 4.8: Formative assessment strategies for student action.   continued →

Feedback is most effective when it is timely and identifies what students are doing right as well as what they need to work on next and then requires students to act on that feedback.

Strategy Four: Teach Students to Self-Assess and Set Goals

Self-assessment is a necessary part of learning, not an add-on that we do if we have the time or the "right" type of students. Self-assessment includes asking students to do the following:

- Identify their strengths and areas for improvement for specific learning targets throughout the unit

- Offer descriptive feedback to classmates

- Use your feedback, feedback from other students, or their own self-assessment to identify what they need to work on and set goals for future learning and then take action on those goals.

Source: Adapted from Stiggins et al., 2006, pp. 42–46.

Visit **go.solution-tree.com/commoncore** for a reproducible version of this figure.

Steps two and three occur simultaneously during mathematics lessons. When implemented, these steps support you in informing students about their progress and designing activities that allow students to make their own learning adjustments, in addition to your own instructional adjustments in support of student learning. You and your students share responsibility for the effective implementation of formative assessment steps in the assessment cycle.

As your team plans the mathematics lessons for a unit of study, discuss the various formative assessment strategies that your team will use to ensure students know about their progress and act accordingly. You and your team must require student-led action steps for responding to the formative feedback students are receiving from you as well as *other students.*

Step Four: Students Take Action on In-Class Formative Assessment Feedback

As you read this chapter, it is possible the first three steps in the assessment cycle are already part of your current assessment paradigm. You and your team do write common formative assessment tasks and instruments together, you do design effective formative assessment classroom strategies, and you do ensure that students take action on the feedback you provide. However, it is very rare to find collaborative teams that use common assessment instruments such as chapter or unit tests as part of a formative process of learning. It is in this step that the old paradigm of testing for grading purposes (an end goal) and the new paradigm of assessment instruments and tools for formative assessment purposes (a means goal) emerges.

Wiliam (2007b) argues that summative assessment can take on three different purposes: (1) monitoring, (2) diagnosing, or (3) formatively assessing.

[Summative] assessment *monitors* learning to the extent it provides information about whether the student, class, school, or system is learning or not; it is *diagnostic* to the extent it provides information about what is going wrong, and it is *formative* to the extent it provides information about what to do about it. (p. 1062)

For example, the first-grade CCSS domain Operations and Algebraic Thinking includes the standard that students will, "Represent and solve problems involving addition and subtraction" (NGA & CCSSO, 2010, p. 15). Suppose the first-grade teacher team administers a summative assessment instrument at the end of instruction addressing this standard. If results of the summative assessment indicate 80 percent of the first graders meet or exceed the team's expectations according to a four-point grading rubric (4—exceeds the standard, 3—meets the standard, 2—approaches the standard, 1—does not meet the standard), then this represents the *monitoring* function of the assessment. Analysis of specific student performance is *diagnostic.* Suppose an individual first-grade student receives a 1 using the team's grading rubric. This is diagnostically indicating that he or she is not demonstrating success on that standard.

A *diagnostic* assessment, while necessary, is insufficient. *Diagnostic* assessment does not tell the student what he or she needs to do differently in order to make progress meeting the standard. The frequent admonition to "Try harder" or the tendency to assign more practice problems, is not likely to support the student in making progress. All too often, the solution when a student has not demonstrated mastery is to assign more practice. However, the primary function of practice is to solidify a student's current level of understanding. If the student does not understand the concept and continues to practice what he does not understand, then additional practice only results in the student solidifying his lack of understanding and increases his frustration. When you take the step to provide the student with additional instruction, such as by using concrete materials to support the student in visualizing addition and subtraction equations, then the summative assessment becomes *formative* for the student and has the potential to advance his learning. The important point is that any form of assessment becomes an opportunity to provide students with feedback, both with respect to their procedural fluency *and* conceptual understanding, to improve their learning.

It is the combination of formative assessment *with* feedback on the assessment instrument that has the largest impact on student achievement (Reeves, 2011). Reeves (2011) goes on to state that all forms of grading need to be viewed as formative feedback to students; and to be effective, feedback must have four characteristics.

1. **Accuracy:** Students and other teachers understand the evaluation criteria.

2. **Fairness:** Feedback is based solely on the student's work, not other student characteristics.

3. **Specificity:** Feedback occurs within agreed-on boundaries, and it is consistently applied to all students.

4. **Timeliness:** Students receive feedback in enough time to act on it and improve their performance.

As Wiliam (2011) describes it, effective feedback:

> should cause thinking. It should be focused; it should be related to the learning goals that have been shared with students; and it should be more work for the recipient than the donor. Indeed, the whole purpose of feedback should be to increase the extent to which students are owners of their own learning. (p. 132)

This will require that students are provided the time necessary to use the feedback they receive to improve their work (Wiliam, 2011).

When the collaborative team uses the summative assessment instrument (test or quiz) results for a first-grade class to modify instruction for the next instructional topic or modifies lessons within the assessed unit of instruction in advance of teaching the content the following year, then the summative assessment assumes a *formative* function for the collaborative team as well. Using assessment results to continuously improve instruction (lesson design) and student learning requires that each member of the collaborative team designs and uses common assessments.

Step Five: Collaborative Teams Use Ongoing Assessment Feedback to Improve Instruction

Step five is a critical component of the assessment cycle. It is during this step, at the end of a unit, that your collaborative team uses the results of assessment instruments and tools to analyze the effectiveness of the lessons you designed for the unit during step one. Assessment will continue to serve as an ends only and have limited impact, unless you and your collaborative team make necessary adjustments before teaching the same content. This investment in careful lesson planning and revision is strongly recommended as a lever to continually improve mathematics education and reduce inconsistencies in instructional quality (Morris & Hiebert, 2011; Morris et al., 2009).

A focus during collaborative lesson-planning sessions should be on the development of your pedagogical content knowledge—instructional strategies to help students learn specific mathematics content. Without strong pedagogical content-knowledge expertise, the ability of your collaborative team to affect increases in student achievement is lessened (Bausmith & Barry, 2011). Your collaborative team should use the critical lesson-planning and lesson-revision questions to support the inclusion of the high-leverage mathematics instructional practices (figure 1.2, page 15). Figure 4.9 highlights critical questions to guide your collaborative team during the lesson-planning and lesson-revision process.

Quality lesson planning that builds formative assessment *for* student learning into mathematics lessons is the first tier of an RTI approach to instruction (see chapter 5). Baroody (2011) writes, "The major source of most mathematical learning difficulties is how children are taught (psychologically inappropriate instruction), not their mental

1. How much of the lesson and material was approached through student investigation of cognitively demanding tasks or preplanned student questioning (instead of teacher-centered lecture and demonstration)?

   Is there evidence of a climate of mutual respect as students participate in mathematical discussions and provide meaningful feedback and critique the reasoning of other students?

   How will students make, test, and justify their mathematical conjectures and conclusions with the teacher and with one another?

2. What kinds of in-class formative assessments did the teacher use to reflect on the effectiveness of the lesson?

   Did the teacher provide descriptive feedback to students? Were students engaged in the lesson? Did the lesson design develop student interest and motivation to learn the content?

   Did the teacher seek evidence of student understanding?

   Did students have an opportunity to reflect on their learning as it relates to the learning target?

3. What CCSS Mathematical Practices did the teacher and students use to learn the mathematics content standards?

   Was there evidence that students were part of a learning community?

   Did students communicate their ideas to one another and the teacher?

   Did teacher questions elicit student thinking and other students' respectful critiquing of that reasoning?

4. What kinds of student-generated questions and conjectures were proposed in the lesson, and what type of student-led tasks were used to assess student understanding and learning?

Source: Adapted from Kanold et al., 2012.

Figure 4.9: Critical planning questions for formative assessment.

Visit **go.solution-tree.com/commoncore** for a reproducible version of this figure.

equipment (organic or cognitive dysfunction)" (p. 30). Therefore, in mathematics instruction, highly effective Tier 1 instruction—instruction that emphasizes the high-leverage instructional practices (figure 1.2) with planned formative assessment—is the most important tier and the tier that should receive the majority of your collaborative team's planning work. Research concerning the three-tier RTI model suggests that with effective Tier 1 instruction, approximately 80 percent of elementary students' mathematics learning needs can be met and learning difficulties are prevented (Gersten et al., 2009; Wixson, 2011).

Standards-Based Report Cards

The CCSS provide an excellent opportunity for you to implement standards-based report cards in the elementary grades. In kindergarten, for example, students could receive report card marks in each of the five mathematical content domains (NGA & CCSSO, 2010) and in Mathematical Practices for each marking period:

1. Counting and Cardinality

2. Operations and Algebraic Thinking

3. Number and Operations in Base Ten

4. Measurement and Data

5. Geometry

The marks students receive in each of these content domains (and Mathematical Practices) can be a direct result of their performance on summative assessments designed for each standard cluster under each domain. For example, under Counting and Cardinality, there are three content standard clusters (NGA & CCSSO, 2010):

1. Know number names and the count sequence.

2. Count to tell the number of objects.

3. Compare numbers. (p. 10)

A single summative assessment instrument would be designed to assess student mastery of each of these clusters and the connected Mathematical Practices. For example, a summative assessment instrument would be designed to measure student proficiency of the first standard cluster. This assessment instrument would have a number of tasks designed to measure proficiency in each of the three standards—count to 100 by ones and tens (K.CC.1), count forward beginning from a given number within the known sequence (K.CC.2), and write numbers from 0 to 20 and represent a number of objects with a written numeral 0–20 (K.CC3)—listed in this cluster. In addition, the tasks would be designed to assess student attainment of the Mathematical Practices addressed while teaching these content standards.

Suppose you grade student assessments and make report-card marks based on a 1–4 scale rubric:

1 = Does not meet the standard

2 = Approaches the standard

3 = Meets the standard

4 = Exceeds the standard

The mode of the marks students receive on the assessment tasks for each cluster would determine the overall cluster mark. The mode of the marks students receive on the three summative cluster assessment instruments for the domain Counting and Cardinality would be the grade they receive on their report card for this domain. Many teachers use the mean when determining students' grades. However, the mean is almost always an inaccurate reflection of what a student knows (Reeves, 2011). This is because the mean does not reflect student performance at the end of a grading period but rather the average performance over the length of the grading period, which may or may not reflect what the student knows at the end of instruction. The mode is also recommended over the mean because it functions better in a standards-based grading environment and avoids the creation of complicated rounding rules for determining grades.

Two formative assessment issues are important for you to keep in mind during summative assessment. First, within each lesson, ongoing formative assessment tasks must be embedded within instruction (as described in step two of the assessment cycle, figure 4.2, page 110) and used to continuously modify your instruction to prepare students for success on summative assessments. Second, the previously described summative assessment and grading process also serves a formative function. Results on summative assessment instruments serve a formative function because the results are used to identify students who may need additional and targeted instruction to reach proficiency.

Because the assessment cycle emphasizes the continuous modification of instruction and targeted reteaching with student re-engagement to meet individual student needs, it is important that students' grades also reflect this continued learning. For example, if a student's initial grade during a marking period for the domain Counting and Cardinality is a 2 (approaches the standard), but after six weeks of targeted additional instruction on the standard cluster within this domain, the student can then demonstrate proficiency, then the student's grade should be changed to reflect this new level of understanding and performance.

The CCSS Consortia Assessments

Preparing for and responding to large-scale mathematics assessments consume much of the focus and effort of grades K–2 teachers, elementary school principals, and school district administrators. Implementing the CCSS is unlikely to alter the scrutiny and pressure you face from large-scale assessments. Although accountability assessments are not planned to begin until grade 3, to maximize student performance in grade 3, the annual third-grade accountability assessment needs to be viewed as an assessment of cumulative learning across grades K–3. Therefore, K–2 teachers have a significant role to play in preparing students for success on accountability assessments.

In 2010, the U.S. Department of Education awarded $330 million in Race to the Top funds to two consortia, representing the majority of states, to develop assessments aligned with the CCSS. The SMARTER Balanced Assessment Consortium (SBAC), representing more than thirty states, received $160 million, and the Partnership for Assessment of Readiness for College and Careers (PARCC), representing more than twenty-five states, received $176 million. As of this publication, eleven states are members of both consortia (Porter et al., 2011). Both PARCC and SBAC intend to implement their new state-level common assessments for grades 3–8 and high school during the 2014–2015 school year.

Both assessment consortia aim to design *common* state assessments that are consistent with the vision of the CCSS to include items that assess higher-order thinking, reasoning and conceptual understanding, and problem-solving abilities. If the assessments take the form their designers intend, then these new common state assessments will go beyond assessment of low-level procedural skills that typify many current state adminis-tered assessments. Because "students' opportunities to learn mathematics are influenced by the assessment policies of the local district . . . [and influenced by] . . . the nature of pedagogy in the classroom" (Tate & Rousseau, 2007, p. 1222), these new common assessments can serve as a lever to promote desired instructional changes in favor of an emphasis on deep understanding and reasoning.

Both PARCC and SBAC intend to provide adaptive online tests that will include a mix of constructed-response items, performance-based tasks, and computer-enhanced items that require the application of knowledge and skills. Both assessment consortia are intending to provide a variety of assessment options within the assessment system. You should check your state website for the latest information about progress of the assessment consortia. You can also go to www.parcconline.org/about-parcc or www .smarterbalanced.org for information.

For the state assessments to function as a potential learning tool, you will need to ensure that they are used for formative purposes—that they are used to provide you and your students with accurate, timely, fair, and specific feedback that can move learning forward. This will require that you are provided time within your collaborative team to plan instructional adjustments and that students are supported in relearning content not yet mastered.

However, overreliance on the PARCC and SBAC interim assessments to provide a school district's formative assessment system is not recommended since the effectiveness of this structure to improve student learning is questionable (Popham, 2008). What will make the most difference in terms of student learning is the short-cycle classroom-based formative assessment described in this chapter. As Wiliam (2007a) writes, "If students have left the classroom before teachers have made adjustments to their teaching on the basis of what they have learned about students' achievement, then they are already play-ing catch-up" (p. 191).

It will be important for you to become engaged in your state and school's transition to the SMARTER or PARCC assessment initiative as you approach full implementation level for the Common Core. How and when will you use interim assessment? How will families and other members of the school community be informed? How will all chil-dren in your grade level or school be prepared? Such questions are appropriate as your district- and school-level PLC teams begin to link state-supported CCSS-related assess-ment to your implementation of the Common Core mathematics content and practices.

Assessment for Equity

When you work within your collaborative team to implement the assessment cycle, you and your team take significant steps toward reducing inequities in student learning generated when individual teachers make widely variable decisions. These decisions can be regarding instructional design issues, particularly the rigor of mathematical tasks and daily formative assessment and unit assessment task expectations (Kanold et al., 2012).

Ensuring all your collaborative team members implement the assessment cycle is a key strategy to promote the goal of equitable mathematics learning.

As research indicates, for assessment to be formative and lead to improvements in student learning, there needs to be an "explicit recipe for future action" (Wiliam, 2007b, p. 1062). Chapter 5 looks at the recipe your collaborative team can follow when assessment results indicate students have not met the learning targets during step two or step four in the assessment cycle.

Chapter 4 Extending My Understanding

1. Generate a list of common forms of assessment (such as teacher observations, teacher-made quizzes and tests, unit assessments, textbook chapter tests, district assessments, state-mandated assessments, and so on) that exist in mathematics at a particular grade level. Then classify these assessments as either formative or summative.

2. Examine all of the assessments your grade-level colleagues use, and determine which ones teacher teams collaboratively developed.

   ○ Which assessments incorporate the use of collaboratively developed scoring rubrics?

   ○ To what extent do the assessment items or tasks require students to demonstrate a balance of conceptual understanding and procedural fluency?

   ○ How are the results of each used to inform and improve teaching and learning (formative)? Measure proficiency (summative)?

   ○ Discuss your findings. How might you use this information to collaboratively develop common assessments in your grade-level collaborative team?

Online Resources

Visit **go.solution-tree.com/commoncore** for links to these resources.

- **Mathematics Common Core Coalition (www.nctm.org/standards /mathcommoncore):** This site includes materials and links to information and resources that the organizations of the coalition provide to the public and the education community about the CCSS for mathematics.

- **NCTM's Assessment Resources (www.nctm.org/resources/content .aspx?id=12650):** Resources such as a framework for evaluating large-scale assessments, NCTM's position statement on high stakes assessment, and various other publications are available through this web page.

- **Partnership for Assessment of Readiness for College and Careers (www .parcconline.org):** PARCC provides Common Core content frameworks, sample instructional units, sample assessment asks, professional development assessment modules, and more.

- **SMARTER Balanced Assessment Consortium (www.smarterbalanced .org):** This site provides grade-level content specifications for the summative assessment of the CCSS for mathematics, assessment development timelines and overviews, curriculum priorities and considerations, various assessment-related resources, computer adaptive testing fact sheets, sample grade-level tasks, and additional resources.

CHAPTER 5

Implementing Required Response to Intervention

All students are entitled to quality instruction within an equitable learning environment designed to meet their specific learning needs. You have a professional obligation to create and maintain an equitable learning environment and provide high-quality instruction. This chapter focuses on the final paradigm shift required to ensure successful CCSS implementation—the need to create directive response to intervention programs to support all students in meeting the expectations of the CCSS. When such programs are in place, then intervention serves the goal of equity.

The National Council of Teachers of Mathematics (2008) notes:

> Excellence in mathematics education rests on equity—high expectations, respect, understanding, and strong support for all students. Policies, practices, attitudes, and beliefs related to mathematics teaching and learning must be assessed continually to ensure that all students have equal access to the resources with the greatest potential to promote learning. A culture of equity maximizes the learning potential of all students. (p. 1)

A culture of equity that maximizes the learning of all students shifts the instructional focus from teaching to student learning and implements a system in which student learning is continuously monitored and instructional adjustments and targeted supports are put in place based on student need. Effective collaborative teams emphasize and foster this cultural shift from teaching to student learning.

Promoting and supporting equitable practices for students is a complex process and is best supported when your collaborative team examines several factors. The National Council of Supervisors of Mathematics' (2008) position statement on equity recommends that mathematics educators:

- Respond to equity as a meaningful process to address social justice issues of race, language, gender, and class bias

- Embrace a mindset shift from a student deficit perspective of equity to a focus on creating opportunities for equal access to meaningful mathematics

- Recognize underachievement not as a result of group membership but more likely a symptom of varying beliefs, opportunities, and experiences to learn mathematics

Recognizing and responding to these important facets of equity will promote the rich conversations needed in your collaborative team to promote high-quality instruction and equitable classrooms. Use the following discussion questions in your collaborative team to facilitate the conversation:

1. Do all students have access to high-quality, rigorous instruction regardless of mathematics placement? What evidence does and does not support this?

2. Are mathematics lessons planned with student strengths in mind (as opposed to only deficits)? How is this demonstrated?

3. Are lower-achieving groups overrepresented by ethnicity, sex, socioeconomic status, and so on in comparison to the student representation in other mathematics classes? If not, how might the collaborative team address this concern?

By examining the equitable practices in your school, in your grade-level collaborative team, and in your own classroom, you can have the deep and honest conversations necessary to promote a culture of equity.

Variation in student achievement among U.S. schools serving demographically similar students indicates that achievement gaps can be narrowed and that demographic factors are less likely to influence low student achievement if students receive high-quality instruction and targeted instructional supports (McKinsey & Company, 2009; Reeves, 2003). Research indicates that all students can learn mathematics when they have access to high-quality mathematics instruction and sufficient time and support to learn the curriculum (Burris, Heubert, & Levin, 2006; Campbell, 1995; Education Trust, 2005; Griffin, Case, & Siegler, 1994; Knapp et al., 1995; Silver & Stein, 1996; Slavin & Lake, 2008; Usiskin, 2007).

Far too frequently in the United States, mathematics has been perceived as a subject only a select few could master or should study. However, high-quality mathematics education is no longer just for those who want to study mathematics or science in college—it is a requirement for most levels of postsecondary education and careers (Achieve, 2005; American College Testing Program, 2006). In addition, the Common Core State Standards expect all students to study and attain at minimum the same set of high-quality standards. For too long too many students—especially students who are economically disadvantaged, English learners, or racial minorities or who have special needs—have been victims of low expectations in mathematics. For example, *tracking* has consistently deprived groups of students by relegating them to low-status mathematics classes in which they repeat basic skills year after year, fall further and further behind their peers, and do not experience significant mathematical substance (Boaler, Wiliam, & Brown, 2000; Stiff, Johnson, & Akos, 2011; Tate & Rousseau, 2002). To help close the achievement gap, students who have traditionally been identified as underperformers in mathematics must be exposed to more rigorous standards-based instruction and conceptually rich mathematical tasks. The CCSS require all students be held to and supported in meeting the same rigorous standards.

Equity does not mean that all students will receive identical instruction or the same amount and intensity of instruction. The National Council of Teachers of Mathematics (2000) propose, "Equity does not mean that every student should receive identical instruction; instead, it demands that reasonable and appropriate accommodations be made as needed to promote access and attainment for all students" (p. 12). These accommodations, or targeted supports, must be designed so that all students have the opportunity to experience success in the challenging grade-level mathematics content and practices outlined in the Common Core State Standards.

You can use the equity questions in figure 5.1 in your collaborative team to reflect on the degree to which all students are provided access to a rigorous mathematics curriculum based on grade-level CCSS. When using these questions, you should think about the evidence you use to support your responses. For example, if the least-experienced teachers on your team are teaching the most-challenged students, is it reasonable to argue that all students are receiving equitable instruction? Some of these team or school decisions are often made in an effort to reward teacher seniority but may inadvertently be contributing to inequitable learning opportunities and outcomes (Lubienski, 2007).

1. Do all students receive the same high-quality common instructional tasks by each teacher on our team?

2. Do all students receive equally rigorous instruction, balancing conceptual and procedural development and mathematical processes?

3. Do all students receive the same amount of teaching and learning time for mathematics each day?

4. Who teaches the most struggling students—the most experienced or least experienced teachers?

5. Do all students receive rich, compelling lessons with a focus on student understanding and learning?

6. Do all students receive grade-level (or above) mathematics instruction on the CCSS?

7. Are there any students identified as low achieving, and what is the team's intentional response for intervention and support?

Figure 5.1: Equity reflection questions.

Holding High Expectations for All Students

A component of promoting equity is holding and maintaining high expectations for all students: do all teachers on your team really believe all students can learn? Inherent in teaching are the beliefs teachers hold about the children they teach. While no teacher ever wants to admit that he or she has low expectations for any student, the reality is that many well-meaning, caring, and passionate teachers do in fact believe that some of their struggling students will not progress at the rate of other students and cannot meet grade-level standards. Do these low expectations derive from students' socioeconomic backgrounds, race, or ethnicity or the fact that students were placed in a low group? These are hard questions to ask but lie at the very heart of addressing equitable instruction.

Students inherently know the expectations their teachers hold for them, and research supports the powerful role self-efficacy plays in student achievement. As Bandura (1993) notes:

> People who have a low sense of self-efficacy in a given domain shy away from difficult tasks, which they perceive as personal threats. They have low aspirations and weak commitment to the goals they choose to pursue. They maintain a self-diagnostic focus rather than concentrate on how to perform successfully. When faced with difficult tasks, they dwell on their personal deficiencies, on the obstacles they will encounter, and on all kinds of adverse outcomes. They slacken their efforts and give up quickly in the face of difficulties. (p. 144)

In the following collaborative team activities, you can explore the influence of teacher and student self-efficacy on student achievement. Use the activities early in the school year to identify your beliefs about the students you teach, and then examine how those beliefs might influence your daily instructional decision making. You can use figure 5.2 to list the number of students you believe will easily make one year's academic progress in the Common Core State Standards, the number you believe will have to work hard to achieve one year's growth, and finally the number of students you believe will not make one year's progress. In the final row, provide a rationale for your predictions. After everyone in your collaborative team completes the table in figure 5.2 for their students, discuss the reflection questions.

Number of Students Who Will Easily Make One Year's Mathematics Growth	
Number of Students Who Will Need to Work Hard and Receive Additional Support to Achieve One Year's Mathematics Growth	
Number of Students Who Will Not Make One Year's Progress, Despite All Additional Support and Intervention	
Rationale for Predictions	

1. Think privately about your placement of the students. Does the placement of the students have any influence on your expectation for how they will achieve?

2. Does student placement change the delivery or content of your instruction in any way?

3. How might the expectations of the Common Core State Standards, both the content and the Mathematical Practices, influence the instructional decisions you will make regarding the students?

4. What teacher moves might you be making that demonstrate your beliefs about the mathematics progress your students are making?

Figure 5.2: Teacher expectations activity and reflection questions.

Visit **go.solution-tree.com/commoncore** for a reproducible version of this figure.

In discussing the reflection questions in figure 5.2, the focus should primarily be on developing a safe environment for you and your peers to think and reflect on your underlying expectations. It is critical for peers to develop a nonjudgmental atmosphere as you work together to reflect on the many classroom aspects that influence your beliefs about the students you teach.

In a follow-up activity, you can audio or video record yourself, or another team member, in short five- to ten-minute clips during key instructional times. As a collaborative team, you can then watch or listen to these audio or video artifacts and write down statements made and the levels of questions posed to students that may reveal the teacher's and students' learning expectations within the particular lessons. You can bring these statements to your collaborative team for discussion and reflection. These sessions will undoubtedly be revealing. In your practice are you promoting what's important? For example, are your questions during instruction focused on assessing depth of student understanding or only aimed at determining if students have correct answers? Are all the students engaged? These are just three examples of questions that may occur in such sessions. You may also opt to have another nonevaluative observer come in and record comments, statements, and questions. The purpose of this discussion is to create an awareness of teaching behaviors that signal to students the teacher's beliefs and expectations for them. Once again, a safe and encouraging environment is critical for this discussion to be productive.

The audio or videotaped vignettes will also provide indicators of teacher and student responses that can guide professional development relative to equity. For example, common statements teachers might make include, "You don't have to do that problem—it's pretty hard" or "You don't have to answer all the questions." Such comments may be intended to be nurturing and supportive but may also convey the message that the teacher does not believe the student can successfully complete the problems or assignment, and *that* may be the message the student hears. In an effort to nurture and support struggling students, teachers sometimes inadvertently lower their expectations for some students. A teacher who poses mostly recall versus analysis (inference) and synthesis questions might be doing this subconsciously but nevertheless demonstrates a sense of lowered expectations for her students. Often these students are relieved and do not aspire beyond the lower expectation. Additionally, teachers sometimes limit important student interaction and discussion in order to maintain a well-managed classroom. Together, the teacher and student have agreed that the material is too challenging, easier problems or tasks are more appropriate, and student learning is reduced. What a shame!

Using Required RTI in Mathematics

Intervention for students in mathematics has far too frequently been approached through a deficit model in which misconceptions and student shortcomings are identified and then addressed through targeted intervention groups, often in pullout programs that remove students from classroom instruction. Unfortunately, the net result is that students fall further behind their grade-level peers. Students receive this specialized or targeted instruction only after they have failed. The goal of these traditional intervention groups has been to improve achievement, but often the focus of this intervention has been on a narrow set of skills that is inconsistent with the broader set of instructional goals called for in the Common Core State Standards. The effect of this approach to intervention has been a superficial quick fix and a "hope for the best" attitude that in the long run does not serve students well, especially in the new, more rigorous environment of the Common Core State Standards. Clearly, students who have never been identified to receive intervention before may need additional support (NCTM, 2008) in content areas such as number and operations, with the increased expectation of conceptual understanding. The reality is that any student may require intervention; students who excel in some topics may need intervention support in others (NCTM, 2011).

In 2004, the reauthorization of the Individuals With Disabilities Education Act revised the law to align with the requirements of the No Child Left Behind Act. This change encouraged school systems to provide targeted interventions for all students in a delivery model commonly known as response to intervention. RTI is a framework to meet the needs of all learners and increase student achievement. At the elementary level, the purpose of RTI is to use screening to identify at-risk students, provide early intervention to all students, prevent misidentification, provide a system of early identification, prevent the need for special education identification, and use student interventions as part of disability determination (Johnson, Smith, & Harris, 2009). NCTM's (2011) position statement on intervention notes that "the long term goal of intervention should be to help students gain independent strategies and take responsibility for their own learning" (p. 1).

RTI is typically organized in a tiered intervention system that increases in intensity and is targeted to students' diagnosed needs to provide the support they need before they fall behind (Fennell, 2011). There are many forms of RTI, and all should be flexible in terms of implementation (NCTM, 2011). For the purpose of this book, the RTI model is a three-tiered system that includes the integration of research-based instructional practices, progress monitoring, and required support in a systematic approach to improve teaching and learning (Fuchs, Fuchs, & Vaughn, 2008; Fisher, Frey, & Rothenberg, 2011). The three tiers are summarized in figure 5.3.

Tier 1: Differentiated Instructional Response

Tier 1 comprises the instructional and curriculum program that all students receive. These classroom-based supports often include the following: high-quality, research-based instructional practices (figure 1.2, page 15); differentiated instruction; guided instruction with scaffolded support; additional time spent on developing concepts; use of specific or alternate models, materials, and tools; and more time to practice concepts. The mathematics instruction in Tier 1 is focused on differentiating grade-level instruction based on continuous formative assessment processes and supporting grade-level instruction. The classroom teacher typically provides Tier 1 support.

Tier 2: Targeted Response to Learning

Tier 2 encompasses targeted instructional time added to daily mathematics instruction for students whose needs are not met in Tier 1. This is typically not a pullout program. Instead, the classroom teacher or interventionist delivers it in small groups during additional mathematics instructional time. Tier 2 intervention still focuses on supporting grade-level instruction but with prioritized instructional focus on the grade-level CCSS critical areas for students whose Tier 1 differentiated instruction was insufficient. In addition, Tier 2 intervention typically provides instruction when a student is diagnosed with missing prerequisite grade-level skills and concepts.

Tier 3: Intensive Response to Learning

Tier 3 intervention is intensive instruction for students demonstrating greater need. This supplemental instruction is typically recommended for students with specific learning needs and might include small-group work or one-on-one tutoring with a supplemental program, in addition to remaining in Tier 1 classroom instruction to rebuild fundamental and missing foundational prerequisite grade-level skills and concepts. The classroom teacher, special educators, mathematics specialists, interventionists, or a combination of professionals may provide the concentrated mathematical conceptual work that provides the foundation for the more complex mathematical topics being covered in daily grade-level instruction.

Figure 5.3: Tiers of mathematics intervention.

Figure 5.4 illustrates the increasing intensity of the tiers of intervention.

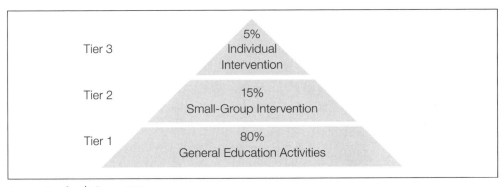

Source: Bender & Crane, 2011.

Figure 5.4: Pyramid of interventions.

Monitoring Grades K–2 Student Assessment Performance to Identify Student Needs

Most school districts first implemented RTI programs in reading. A key component of reading RTI programs is universal screening for students at risk in reading (Davis, Lindo, & Compton, 2007; Gersten et al., 2008; Jenkins, Hudson, & Johnson, 2007; Johnson, Mellard, Fuchs, & McKnight, 2006). As implementation of RTI programs was broadened beyond reading to mathematics, the universal screening component of reading programs was applied to mathematics. In some cases, this has resulted in school personnel utilizing assessments that are extraneous to the curriculum and used exclusively for the purpose of identifying students who require Tier 2 or 3 interventions. This creates yet another assessment system that consumes precious instructional time. The collaborative team approach we advocate for here, specifically with respect to the development and use of common formative assessments outlined in chapter 4, supersedes the need for the creation and implementation of a separate RTI screening and monitoring assessment.

The teaching-assessing-learning cycle in chapter 4 (figure 4.2, page 110) outlines a process in which you work within your collaborative team to develop common assessment instruments as well as formative assessment in-class strategies. These collaboratively developed assessments can and should also be seen and used as a universal system of screening and monitoring students for RTI services. This system of universal screening ensures all students an equal opportunity of having their learning needs identified. In addition, by using assessment instruments you collaboratively developed, the formative assessment in-class processes are more likely to be aligned with the CCSS content standards and Mathematical Practices. It is critical that test and quiz results not be seen as a way to place students into a low or slower-paced group for mathematics instruction but rather be used to design instructional interventions and supports *in addition to* grade-level instruction to meet the needs of individual students.

Diagnosing Needs for Targeted Intervention in Tier 2 and Tier 3

Your collaborative team will need to decide whether individual student needs can be met within the daily mathematics lesson (Tier 1) or whether supplemental interventions (Tier 2 or Tier 3) are required. In order to effectively implement Tier 2 or Tier 3 interventions, you need to use student performance on formative and summative assessments to identify *and then diagnose* the specific needs of students. Traditionally, teachers have not received preservice training or professional development in the area of diagnosing students' conceptual or procedural mathematical misconceptions and gaps in prerequisite knowledge. A thorough diagnosis of student learning needs to not only consist of the identification of the misconceptions and instructional needs involving both skills and concepts but also include an analysis of the underlying or prerequisite knowledge that may be causing the student's current level of difficulty. This must all be carefully considered in order for Tier 2 or Tier 3 interventions to be strategically implemented. Moderate prerequisite conceptual and procedural difficulties may signal that the student needs Tier 2 support in addition to whole-class instruction. More severe fundamental conceptual and procedural knowledge gaps may signal that students need supplemental Tier 3 services in order to rebuild critical foundational skills and address conceptual knowledge gaps.

As you work in your collaborative team to examine student performance on formative and summative assessments, you can begin to develop your own diagnostic skills.

As you examine student work to diagnose learning difficulties, you should consider the factors listed in figure 5.5.

1. **Student conceptual understanding:** Conceptual understanding is evidence of the student's knowledge of mathematical ideas and the ability to structure that knowledge in ways that facilitate making connections between ideas that are new to those that are known from prior experience.

2. **Student procedural fluency:** Procedural fluency refers to the development of procedures or algorithms for solving mathematical exercises. As an example, students learn to add by using terminology such as *carrying* and *borrowing* instead of using place-value manipulatives and vocabulary to develop rich understanding

3. **Student disposition:** This includes students' attitudes or beliefs about learning mathematics, including positive or negative behaviors and self-efficacy. Student perseverance is a critical component of disposition.

4. **Teacher-introduced ineffective strategies:** These are the specific strategies or practices that teachers use to teach topics to students that may not advance student understanding. An example of this is the *Pac-Man* or *alligator* technique to teach the symbols used (<, >) when comparing and ordering quantities.

5. **Student prerequisite misconceptions:** This includes student misunderstandings about necessary underlying concepts in mathematics. This may include difficulties with language, symbols, concepts, or procedures. A true misconception is when the student consistently makes the same error or types of errors and demonstrates a lack of prerequisite knowledge.

Figure 5.5: Student-work diagnoses and factors.

In order to more accurately diagnose a student's conceptual difficulties with grades K–2 mathematics, it may be necessary to conduct a *diagnostic interview*. A diagnostic interview consists of a series of prompts or questions that are asked to assess the considerations listed in figure 5.5. Table 5.1 (page 138) provides an example of a first-grade diagnostic interview. The power of the diagnostic interview lies in how you use the results. Every mathematics teacher also needs to be a diagnostician. An everyday need exists to quickly determine the challenges, misconceptions, lack of prerequisites, and other issues that influence student achievement and, sooner than one might think, interest in mathematics (Fennell, 2011). The diagnostic interview has the potential to influence long-term and short-term planning and certain considerations for instructional strategies for students receiving Tier 2 or Tier 3 intervention time in order to address the identified student needs. A productive activity for you to engage in while working in your collaborative team is the creation of other diagnostic interview protocols, using table 5.1 as an example. The interview is conducted when you ask a student to explain his or her thinking as you as a question or provide a prompt. You are able to ask clarifying questions as the student responds to determine the student's underlying conceptual understanding. When finished, you may want to make notes regarding the student's statements. Students should respond in writing so that you can analyze elements of each student's response.

Table 5.1: Sample First-Grade Diagnostic Interview

CCSS Domain and Standard (1.NBT)	Extend the counting sequence (NGA & CCSSO, 2010, p. 15).
Interview Prompt	"I am going to say a number and ask you to continue counting on from that number—97." Have the student continue counting until 120. "Write the numbers 97, 105, 115." Show the student a model using place-value materials (83), and ask the student to write a number to represent the value.
Conceptual Understanding	Have the student describe how he or she is solving the prompt. "How did you know what number comes next? How do you know what number to write? Which number matches the value in the model? What does that mean?" Ask students to think about the pattern in counting they know and to demonstrate place-value understanding. For example, "I know that this number is 105 because the digit 1 represents one hundred, and there are 0 tens and 5 ones." Does the student use correct language?
Procedural Fluency	Is the student fluent in the counting sequence? Is the student easily able to transition from values under 100 to over 100? Does the student have correct numeral placement? (A common misconception for 105 is often 1,005 as students attempt to account for the 100.)
Disposition	Does the student exhibit confidence and persist when solving the problem?
Ineffective Strategies	Does the student have to recount, start over, or write it down to count?
Student Prerequisites and Misconceptions	Does the student indicate misunderstandings in the counting sequence, place value, or understanding of place-value models?

Visit **go.solution-tree.com/commoncore** for a reproducible version of this table.

Planning Your RTI System of Support

Planning is integral to the actions of your collaborative team. The efforts you have put forth in examining Mathematical Practices, defining which content standards need particular attention, and determining student learning needs through formative assessment culminate in the decisions you make for your RTI system of support.

Tier 1 Instructional Strategies

Baroody (2011) proposes, "The major source of most mathematical learning difficulties is how children are taught (psychologically inappropriate instruction), not their mental equipment (organic or cognitive dysfunction)" (p. 30). The goal of Tier 1 instruction in the three-tier RTI model is to provide effective classroom instruction—instruction that emphasizes the high-leverage instructional practices from chapter 1, figure 1.2 (page 15).

Collaborative teams embedding assessment processes—emphasizing steps two and four from the assessment cycle—to develop alternative pedagogical strategies to support student learning of grade-level CCSS in the classroom characterize highly effective Tier 1 instruction. In fact, approximately 80 percent of elementary students' mathematics learning needs can be met and learning difficulties prevented with highly effective Tier 1 instruction (Gersten et al., 2009; Wixson, 2011).

As noted earlier, core instruction and related assistance has too often not focused on developing key mathematical practices or processes, like making sense of problems and critiquing the reasoning of others, but more on rote or procedural thinking limited to computational proficiency. Students who struggle in mathematics, however, deserve and should receive instruction that emphasizes all aspects of mathematical proficiency and should have the opportunity to experience the same high-leverage instructional practices that other students experience (Baroody, 2011). Both the National Mathematics Advisory Panel (2008) and the National Research Council (2001) argue that all students need to experience a balanced and comprehensive curriculum. The National Mathematics Advisory Panel (2008) recommends:

> To prepare students for Algebra, the curriculum must simultaneously develop conceptual understanding, computational fluency, and problem solving skills. Debates regarding the relative importance of these aspects of mathematical knowledge are misguided. These capabilities are mutually supportive, each facilitating learning of the others. Teachers should emphasize these interrelations; taken together, conceptual understanding of mathematical operations, fluent execution of procedures, and fast access to number combinations jointly support effective and efficient problem solving. (p. xix)

Therefore, it is critical that instructional efforts not only focus on the CCSS content standards but also address Mathematical Practices at all levels.

Tier 2 and Tier 3 Intervention Strategies

Intervention instructional strategies in mathematics cannot simply be more of the same. Specifically, more instruction that repeats exactly what was done in the classroom, only at a slower pace and with more practice, is doomed to fail. Students who have not been successful in Tier 1 instruction need alternate approaches in Tier 2 or Tier 3. *Assisting Students Struggling With Mathematics* (Gersten et al., 2009) makes several instructional recommendations to support intervention students. Figure 5.6 (page 140) lists these recommendations. Discussing and developing a shared meaning of each of

1. Instruction during the intervention should be explicit and systematic. This includes providing models of proficient problem solving, verbalization of thought processes, guided practice, corrective feedback, and frequent cumulative review.

2. Interventions should include instruction on solving word problems that is based on common underlying structures.

3. Intervention materials should include opportunities for students to work with visual representations of mathematical ideas, and interventionists should be proficient in the use of visual representations of mathematical ideas.

4. Interventions at all grade levels should devote about ten minutes in each session to building fluent retrieval of basic arithmetic facts.

5. Tier 2 and Tier 3 interventions should include motivational strategies.

Source: Adapted from Gersten et al., 2009.

Figure 5.6: RTI instructional strategies.

Visit **go.solution-tree.com/commoncore** for a reproducible version of this figure.

these strategies, and reflecting on their implementation and effectiveness during your collaborative meetings, are effective uses of your time.

Explicit Instruction

Research supports the use of explicit instruction for struggling or learning-impaired students (Clarke et al., 2011; Gersten et al., 2009; Gersten & Clarke, 2007; Jayanthi, Gersten, & Baker, 2008). Developing a shared understanding of explicit instruction is a particularly worthy topic of discussion in your collaborative team. Interpretations of *explicit instruction* can vary from teacher to teacher and often serve as a reason to begin *telling* students everything they need to know and encourage rote memorization and student mimicking of teacher-demonstrated methods. Explicit teaching is more accurately viewed as an approach that directs student attention toward specific learning in a highly structured environment, but that does not take away from students' opportunity to think meaningfully about the mathematics they are learning, make connections, and develop deep understanding—and this distinction is critically important.

The effective use of explicit instruction supports students in developing conceptual understanding. Instruction is purposeful and meaningful, and students understand why they are learning a particular technique or strategy. A key component in delivering explicit instruction is using corrective feedback for students as they learn the material. One example of an explicit instructional strategy includes using bar models as a representational tool to assist in the teaching of whole-number addition, subtraction, multiplication and division. (See figures 5.7 and 5.8.)

Figures 5.7 and 5.8 illustrate how students can be taught explicitly to recognize different types of problems and then use the bar diagrams to represent the problem's solution. Students are unlikely to generate this type of model or strategy on their own, so by explicitly modeling this technique with extensive guided practice and corrective feedback

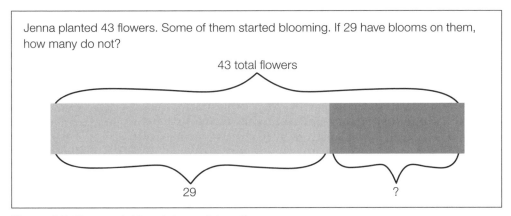

Jenna planted 43 flowers. Some of them started blooming. If 29 have blooms on them, how many do not?

Figure 5.7: Bar model involving subtraction.

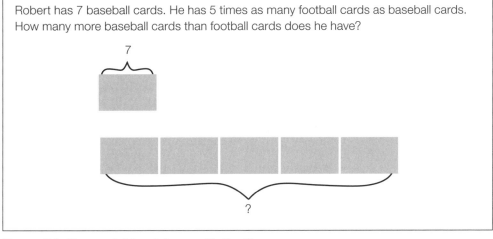

Robert has 7 baseball cards. He has 5 times as many football cards as baseball cards. How many more baseball cards than football cards does he have?

Figure 5.8: Bar model involving multiplication.

as students begin to use the representation, you empower students to recognize these problem structures and generalize solution strategies while building their understanding.

Word-Problem Structures

Word-problem structures are often confusing and difficult to interpret for students who need intervention. The language of word problems may appear to be misleading and confusing, especially if students have previously been taught keyword strategies (such as *how many in all, how many less*), which might actually inhibit understanding because students tend to focus on key words instead of the overall meaning of the problem. The Common Core State Standards (NGA & CCSSO, 2010) outline different types of word-problem situations students are likely to encounter. These common word-problem structures are found in table 5.2 (page 142) and table 5.3 (page 143). Explicit teaching of these word-problem structures during Tier 2 and Tier 3 intervention can enhance students' understanding and promote problem-solving success. These addition and sub-traction word-problem structures provide contexts for all decompositions of number.

Table 5.2: Common Core Addition and Subtraction Problem Situations

	Result Unknown	Change Unknown	Start Unknown
Add to	Two bunnies sat on the grass. Three more bunnies hopped there. How many bunnies are on the grass now? 2 + 3 = ?	Two bunnies were sitting on the grass. Some more bunnies hopped there. Then there were five bunnies. How many bunnies hopped over to the first two? 2 + ? = 5	Some bunnies were sitting on the grass. Three more bunnies hopped there. Then there were five bunnies. How many bunnies were on the grass before? ? + 3 = 5
Take From	Five apples were on the table. I ate two apples. How many apples are on the table now? 5 − 2 = ?	Five apples were on the table. I ate some apples. Then there were three apples. How many apples did I eat? 5 − ? = 3	Some apples were on the table. I ate two apples. Then there were three apples. How many apples were on the table before? ? − 2 = 3
	Total Unknown	**Addend Unknown**	**Both Addends Unknown**
Put Together or Take Apart	Three red apples and two green apples are on the table. How many apples are on the table? 3 + 2 = ?	Five apples are on the table. Three are red and the rest are green. How many apples are green? 3 + ? = 5, 5 − 3 = ?	Grandma has five flowers. How many can she put in her red vase and how many in her blue vase? 5 = 0 + 5, 5 = 5 + 0 5 = 1 + 4, 5 = 4 + 1 5 = 2 + 3, 5 = 3 + 2
	Difference Unknown	**Bigger Unknown**	**Smaller Unknown**
Compare	*How many more?* **version:** Lucy has two apples. Julie has five apples. How many more apples does Julie have than Lucy? *How many fewer?* **version:** Lucy has two apples. Julie has five apples. How many fewer apples does Lucy have than Julie? 2 + ? = 5, 5 − 2 = ?	**Version with *more*:** Julie has three more apples than Lucy. Lucy has two apples. How many apples does Julie have? **Version with *fewer*:** Lucy has three fewer apples than Julie. Lucy has two apples. How many apples does Julie have? 2 + 3 = ?, 3 + 2 = ?	**Version with *more*:** Julie has three more apples than Lucy. Julie has five apples. How many apples does Lucy have? **Version with *fewer*:** Lucy has three fewer apples than Julie. Julie has five apples. How many apples does Lucy have? 5 − 3 = ?, ? + 3 = 5

Source: Adapted from NGA & CCSSO, 2010, p. 88.

Table 5.3: Common Core Multiplication and Division Problem Situations

	Product Unknown	Group Size Unknown ("How Many in Each Group?" Division)	Number of Groups Unknown ("How Many Groups?" Division)
	$3 \times 6 = ?$	$3 \times ? = 18$ $18 \div 3 = ?$	$? \times 6 = 18$ $18 \div 6 = ?$
Equal Groups	There are 3 bags with 6 plums in each bag. How many plums are there in all? **Measurement example:** You need 3 lengths of string, each 6 inches long. How much string will you need altogether?	If 18 plums are shared equally into 3 bags, then how many plums will be in each bag? **Measurement example:** You have 18 inches of string, which you will cut into 3 equal pieces. How long will each piece of string be?	If 18 plums are to be packed 6 to a bag, then how many bags are needed? **Measurement example:** You have 18 inches of string, which you will cut into pieces that are 6 inches long. How many pieces of string will you have?
Arrays, Area	There are 3 rows of apples with 6 apples in each row. How many apples are there? **Area example:** What is the area of a 3 cm by 6 cm rectangle?	If 18 apples are arranged into 3 equal rows, how many apples will be in each row? **Area example:** A rectangle has an area of 18 square centimeters. If one side is 3 cm long, how long is a side next to it?	If 18 apples are arranged into equal rows of 6 apples, how many rows will there be? **Area example:** A rectangle has an area of 18 square centimeters. If one side is 6 cm long, how long is a side next to it?
Compare	A blue hat costs $6. A red hat costs 3 times as much as the blue hat. How much does the red hat cost? **Measurement example:** A rubber band is 6 cm long. How long will the rubber band be when it is stretched to be 3 times as long?	A red hat costs $18, and that is 3 times as much as a blue hat costs. How much does a blue hat cost? **Measurement example:** A rubber band is stretched to be 18 cm long, and that is 3 times as long as it was at first. How long was the rubber band at first?	A red hat costs $18, and a blue hat costs $6. How many times as much does the red hat cost as the blue hat? **Measurement example:** A rubber band was 6 cm long at first. Now it is stretched to be 18 cm long. How many times as long is the rubber band now as it was at first?
General	$a \times b = ?$	$a \times ? = p; p \div a = ?$	$? \times b = p; p \div b = ?$

Source: Adapted from NGA & CCSSO, 2010, p. 89.

Fact Fluency

The IES Practice Guide, *Assisting Students Struggling With Mathematics: Response to Intervention (RtI) for Elementary and Middle Schools* (Gersten et al., 2009), recommends that students spend approximately ten minutes a day building fluency in basic arithmetic facts, defined here as the addition and related subtraction facts and the multiplication and related division facts. This recommendation is based on research indicating that students who lack foundational skills are at a disadvantage in subsequent mathematics learning (Gersten et al., 2005; Wallace & Gurganus, 2005). This recommendation might be interpreted as an opportunity to administer basic fact tests in an effort to reach fluency in students, but that is not the intent. However, the implementation of this recommendation requires teachers to build basic fact strategy lessons for conceptual development, which build fluency. Fact fluency must be based on an understanding of operations and thinking strategies (Fuson, 2003; NRC, 2001). Students must be able to connect facts to those they know, use mathematics properties to make associations, and construct visual representations to develop conceptual understanding. Discussing appropriate strategies to develop fact fluency with understanding is a productive use of your time when you meet in your collaborative team. Use the questions in figure 5.9 during collaborative team discussions to reflect on the effectiveness of instructional strategies to develop fact fluency and to ensure that such fluency instruction does not devolve to mere rote memorization.

---

1. How might you use ten minutes a day to develop fact fluency?

2. How might you use fact strategies to develop conceptual understanding of facts so students can become fluent?

3. What fact fluency strategies might be best taught during this targeted instructional time?

4. What might be an effective method to screen for fact fluency?

5. How can fact fluency be monitored?

6. How might the use of the ten minutes be monitored?

Figure 5.9: Fact-fluency discussion questions.

Visit **go.solution-tree.com/commoncore** for a reproducible version of this figure.

Monitoring Interventions

The questions and monitoring chart in figure 5.10 can support you as you work in your collaborative team to monitor student progress in intervention. Your team should revisit these questions and the monitoring chart following every formative and summative assessment to ensure that all students who need intervention to learn grade-level standards are receiving the support they need to be successful.

1. When will Tier 2 and Tier 3 intervention support be provided? (Tier 1 support will typically occur in the regular classroom.) This should include amount of time spent, number of intervention sessions, and who will provide interventions. Who will provide Tier 1, 2, or 3 interventions to identified students?

2. Who will provide Tier 1, 2, or 3 supports to identified students?

3. What are the expected outcomes for students in Tier 1, 2, or 3?

4. What will be the focus (specific standards or prerequisite standards) of the intervention?

5. How are the content standards and the Mathematical Practices being addressed during intervention?

Student	Responsible Teacher	Time	CCSS Content and Mathematical Practices	Tier 1	Tier 2	Tier 3	Specific Instructional Strategies
Lauren	Mrs. K (Classroom teacher)	Twenty minutes—three times.	Grade 1 **Domain:** Operations and Algebraic Thinking Standard one	✓			Use small-group targeted instruction, using word-problem structures and manipulatives.
Jose	Mr. L (Interventionist)	2:00–2:30, Monday, Wednesday, and Friday	Grade 2 **Domain:** Number and Operations in Base Ten Standard five			✓	Use one-on-one instruction, using place-value cards and base-ten blocks to rebuild critical prerequisite place-value understanding before reteaching addition with regrouping.

Figure 5.10: Intervention assignment questions and monitoring chart.

Visit **go.solution-tree.com/commoncore** for a reproducible version of this figure.

Prioritizing Intervention Efforts

As the academic year continues, many students will seemingly need intervention support on many content standards. Intervention time is not infinite, and at some point it will become necessary to prioritize the content standards that will be the focus of intervention for some students. The standards and topics that fall under the Common Core State Standards' critical areas should be prioritized and emphasized during intervention. This will ensure a focus on the most important mathematics at each grade level. Table 5.4 lists kindergarten through grade 2 Common Core State Standards' critical areas.

Table 5.4: Common Core Critical Areas

Kindergarten Critical Areas	Grade 1 Critical Areas	Grade 2 Critical Areas
1. Representing, relating, and operating on whole numbers, initially with sets of objects 2. Describing shapes and space; more learning time in kindergarten should be devoted to number than to other topics.	1. Developing understanding of addition, subtraction, and strategies for addition and subtraction within 20 2. Developing understanding of whole-number relationships and place value, including grouping in tens and ones 3. Developing understanding of linear measurement and measuring lengths as iterating length units 4. Reasoning about attributes of and composing and decomposing geometric shapes	1. Extending understanding of base-ten notation 2. Building fluency with addition and subtraction 3. Using standard units of measure 4. Describing and analyzing shapes

Source: Adapted from NGA & CCSSO, 2010.

Developing Student Disposition and Motivation in Grades K–2 RTI

Developing productive student dispositions is central to the success of any mathematics program. The National Research Council (2001) defines *productive disposition* as "habitual inclinations to see mathematics as sensible, useful, and worthwhile, coupled with a belief in diligence and one's own efficacy" (p. 5). These beliefs are often developed as a result of the student's classroom experiences and greatly influenced by his or her daily interactions with the teacher and fellow students. The National Mathematics Advisory Panel's (2008) recommendation regarding student self-efficacy is clear:

> Children's goals and beliefs about learning are related to their mathematics performance. Experimental studies have demonstrated that changing children's beliefs from a focus on ability to a focus on effort increases their

engagement in mathematics learning, which in turn improves mathematics outcomes: When children believe that their efforts to learn make them "smarter," they show greater persistence in mathematics learning. (p. 20)

In a collaborative team activity focusing on student disposition, you may conduct interviews with students to assess student self-efficacy. For example, you could conduct three short interviews, using the sample interview questions in figure 5.11, with targeted students to determine their beliefs about their performance and progress. After interviewing the students, you could bring your notes from the interviews to a collaborative team meeting for discussion with your colleagues, using the reflection questions figure 5.11.

Student Interview

1. When you get frustrated in mathematics class, what do you think you could do to overcome that frustration? (diligence)

2. Does hard work make a difference in learning mathematics? (diligence)

3. Are you a good mathematics student? Why or why not? (self-efficacy)

4. Is it important to know mathematics? Why or why not? (worthwhileness)

5. Is there anything that gets in your way of being successful in mathematics? (self-formative assessment) What would help you be a better mathematics student?

6. What are your strengths in learning mathematics? (using formative assessment data)

7. What strategies work well for you? (using formative assessment data)

Teacher Reflection

1. Were you surprised by the student answers or comments? Why or why not?

2. Do you think the students' beliefs are tied to their performance? Why or why not?

3. Are there any teacher moves or practices that might be reinforcing negative beliefs or dispositions? What might they be?

4. Are there any teacher moves or practices that might be reinforcing positive beliefs or dispositions for students? What might they be?

5. What moves could teachers make in the classroom to support more positive or constructive beliefs?

6. What specific actions might you take as a teacher now that you are more aware of specific student beliefs?

Figure 5.11: Student disposition interview and reflection questions.

Visit **go.solution-tree.com/commoncore** for a reproducible version of this figure.

The interview and reflection questions can be quite revealing because they allow you to compare your own perceptions with your students' beliefs. This reflection can provide a rich opportunity for you to make important changes in your classroom environment. Ensuring that students have positive dispositions toward mathematics and that you and your colleagues believe your students are capable of learning challenging grade-level mathematics are crucial steps to positioning successful intervention programs.

Serving All Students Well

For too long, mathematics education has not served all students as well as it should have (NCTM, 2000). The expectations of the Common Core State Standards require that all students meet more rigorous grade-level standards in mathematics. Perhaps more importantly, equity concerns and economic demands make success in mathematics not only an immediate concern for all students but for society at large. The vast majority of students are capable of meeting these more rigorous expectations, but not necessarily within the same amount of instructional time or under the same instructional approach. An effective RTI program that systematically and continuously identifies student needs through a system of collaboratively developed assessments, and then provides students the appropriate targeted level of intervention support based on those assessment results, has the potential not only to ensure that all students have access to the conceptually rich mathematics outlined in the Common Core State Standards but also to close achievement gaps and promote equity in mathematics teaching and learning.

Chapter 5 Extending My Understanding

1. To what degree does your school provide RTI support as outlined in this chapter? Is there a systematic and timely structure that is a regular part of discussions in bimonthly grade-level or vertical collaborative team sessions?

2. Examine the descriptions of each tier of the RTI model (see pages 139–144). How might classroom teachers integrate this intervention model? How are students identified for targeted tier intervention? Do instructional approaches within the tiers supplement or replace whole-class instruction?

3. Considering your collaborative team's responses to questions one and two, how does the intervention reflect the CCSS for mathematics content standards and Mathematical Practices?

Online Resources

Visit **go.solution-tree.com/commoncore** for links to these resources.

-   **Assisting Students Struggling With Mathematics: Response to Intervention (RtI) for Elementary and Middle Schools (Gersten et al., 2099; http://ies .ed.gov/ncee/wwc/PracticeGuide.aspx?sid=2):** Developed by a panel of RTI experts, the eight recommendations in this guide are designed to help teachers, principals, and administrators use RTI for the early detection, prevention, and support of students struggling with mathematics. View the multimedia companion website Response to Intervention in Elementary-Middle Math (Doing What Works website—www.dww.ed.gov) to download state and district tools and resource materials.

- **Classroom-Focused Improvement Process (School Improvement in Maryland, 2010; http://mdk12.org/process/cfip):** The Classroom-Focused Improvement Process (CFIP) is a six-step process for increasing student achievement that grade-level or cross-level teacher teams plan and carry out as a part of their regular lesson-planning cycle.

- **National Center on Response to Intervention (www.rti4success.org):** This site provides a wealth of resources to plan, implement, and screen RTI, including professional development modules that teacher learning teams can use to initiate or improve an RTI program in schools, districts, or states.

- **NCTM's Intervention Resources (www.nctm.org/resources/content.aspx ?id=13198):** This site provides a collection of resources on creating or selecting intervention programs and identifying and addressing intervention issues as well as articles and research on intervention, Title 1 resources, and more.

EPILOGUE

Your Mathematics Professional Development Model

Implementing the Common Core State Standards for mathematics presents you with both new challenges and new opportunities. The unprecedented adoption of a common set of mathematics standards by nearly every state provides the opportunity for U.S. educators to press the reset button on mathematics education (Larson, 2011). Collectively, you and your colleagues have the opportunity to rededicate yourselves to ensuring that all students are provided with exemplary teaching and learning experiences, and you have access to the supports necessary to guarantee all students the opportunity to develop mathematical proficiency in the early grades that leads to successful student preparation for the CCSS K–12 college- and career-ready mathematics standards.

The CCSS college and career aspirations and vision for teaching, learning, and the assessment for student learning usher in an opportunity for unprecedented implementation of research-informed practices in your school or district's mathematics program. In order to meet the expectations of the five fundamental paradigm shifts described in this book, you will want to assess your current practice and clearly define your reality as a school against the roadmap to implementation described in figure E.1 (page 152).

Figure E.1 describes the essential paradigm shifts for your focus in the four critical areas of curriculum, instruction, assessment, and intervention for your teams and in your mathematics program. As you professionally develop one another through your interaction and work as members of a collaborative team, your students will not only be better prepared for the CCSS assessment expectations but also for the college and career readiness focus that is an expectation for all students K–12—whether your state is part of the CCSS or not. Each sector in figure E.1 describes three vital collaborative team behaviors for that area of change. If you hope to break through any current areas of stagnation in your mathematics programs and achieve greater student success than ever before, then it will require you to embrace these paradigms as part of a mindset for never-ending change, growth, and improvement within the reasoning and sense-making focus of the mathematics instruction your students receive in your school.

Working collaboratively in a grade-level team will make the CCSS obtainable not only for you but ultimately for your students. Working within a PLC culture is the best vehicle available to support you and your colleagues as you work together to interpret the Common Core State Standards, develop new pedagogical approaches through intensive collaborative planning, monitor student progress toward meeting the standards, and provide the targeted supports necessary to ensure that all students meet mathematical

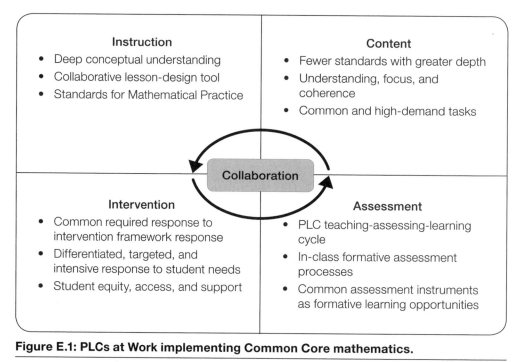

Figure E.1: PLCs at Work implementing Common Core mathematics.

Visit **go.solution-tree.com/commoncore** for a reproducible version of this figure.

opportunities of Common Core mathematics. But perhaps most significantly, your collaborative team and professional learning community culture will foster an environment in which you work to support one another as you focus on student learning and continuous instructional improvement in mathematics.

Sample Standards for Mathematical Content, PreKindergarten

The New York State Education Department and the Maryland State Department of Education have created their own set of preK content area standards in mathematics. Organized under "cognition and knowledge of the world," the New York standards present the following preK mathematics benchmarks:

- Children will demonstrate an understanding of numbers, ways to represent numbers, relationships among numbers, and the number system.
- Children will understand the beginning principles of addition and subtraction.
- Children will demonstrate understanding of geometric and spatial relations.
- Children will understand directionality, order, and position.
- Children will sort, classify, and organize objects by size, number, attributes, and other properties.
- Children will demonstrate knowledge of measurement.

New York's preK learning standards are available in the "New York State Pre-kindergarten Foundation for the Common Core" (New York State Education Department, n.d.; www.p12.nysed.gov/ciai/common_core_standards/pdfdocs/nyslsprek.pdf).

New York's preK mathematics benchmarks are very similar in language to the NCTM *Curriculum Focal Points* and *Connections to the Focal Points for the PreK Level* (NCTM, 2006).

The Maryland "look" for preK is essentially a backmapping of the kindergarten CCSS. Table A.1 presents the domains, clusters, and standards within the Maryland preK standards.

Table A.1: Maryland PreK Standards

Cluster	Standard
Domain: Counting and Cardinality	
Know number names and count sequence.	Count verbally to 10 by ones.
	Recognize the concept of just after or before a given number in the counting sequence up to 10.

continued →

Cluster	Standard
	Recognize written numerals 0–10.
Count to tell the number of objects.	Understand the relationship between numbers and quantities to 5, then to 10; connect counting to cardinality.
	When counting objects, say the number names in the standard order, pairing each object with one and only one number name.
	Recognize that the last number name said tells the number of objects counted.
	Recognize that each successive number name refers to a quantity that is one larger.
	Represent a number (0–5, then to 10) by producing a set of objects with concrete materials, pictures, and/or numerals (with 0 representing a count of no objects).
	Recognize the number of objects in a set without counting (subitizing). (Use 0–5 objects.)
Compare quantities.	Explore relationships by comparing groups of objects up to 10 to determine greater than/more or less than, and equal to/same.
	Identify whether the number of objects in one group is greater than, less than, or equal to the number of objects in another group (such as by using matching and counting strategies [including groups with up to 5 objects]).
Domain: Operations and Algebraic Thinking	
Understand addition as *putting together* and *adding to,* and understand subtraction as *taking apart* and *taking from.*	Explore addition and subtraction with objects, fingers, mental images, drawings, sounds (such as claps), acting out situations, and verbal explanations.
	Decompose quantity (less than or equal to 5, then to 10) into pairs in more than one way (such as by using objects or drawings).
	For any given quantity from (0 to 5, then to 10) find the quantity that must be added to make 5, then to 10, such as by using objects or drawings.
Domain: Number and Operations in Base Ten	
Work with numbers 0–10 to gain foundations for place value.	Investigate the relationship between ten ones and ten.

Cluster	Standard
Domain: Measurement and Data	
Describe and compare measureable attributes.	Describe measurable attributes of objects such as length and weight.
	Directly compare two objects with a measurable attribute in common, using words such as *longer/shorter*; *heavier/lighter*; or *taller/shorter*.
Sort objects into categories and compare categories.	Sort objects into given categories.
	Compare categories using words such as *greater than/more*, *less than*, and *equal to/same*.
Domain: Geometry	
Identify and describe two-dimensional shapes (circles, triangles, rectangles; including a square, which is a special rectangle).	Match like (congruent and similar) shapes.
	Group the shapes by attributes.
	Correctly name shapes (regardless of their orientations or overall size).
Work with three-dimensional shapes to gain foundation for geometric thinking.	Match and sort shapes.
	Describe three-dimensional objects using attributes.
	Compose and describe structures using three-dimensional shapes. Descriptions may include shape attributes, relative position, and so on.

Note: The Maryland State Department of Education website hosts the complete set of its preK mathematics standards (http://mdk12.org/instruction/commoncore/index.html).

APPENDIX B
Standards for Mathematical Practice

Source: NGA & CCSSO, 2010, pp. 6–8. © Copyright 2010. National Governors Association Center for Best Practices and Council of Chief State School Officers. All rights reserved. Used with permission.

The Standards for Mathematical Practice describe varieties of expertise that mathematics educators at all levels should seek to develop in their students. These practices rest on important "processes and proficiencies" with longstanding importance in mathematics education. The first of these are the NCTM process standards of problem solving, reasoning and proof, communication, representation, and connections. The second are the strands of mathematical proficiency specified in the National Research Council's report Adding It Up: adaptive reasoning, strategic competence, conceptual understanding (comprehension of mathematical concepts, operations and relations), procedural fluency (skill in carrying out procedures flexibly, accurately, efficiently and appropriately), and productive disposition (habitual inclination to see mathematics as sensible, useful, and worthwhile, coupled with a belief in diligence and one's own efficacy).

1. Make sense of problems and persevere in solving them. Mathematically proficient students start by explaining to themselves the meaning of a problem and looking for entry points to its solution. They analyze givens, constraints, relationships, and goals. They make conjectures about the form and meaning of the solution and plan a solution pathway rather than simply jumping into a solution attempt. They consider analogous problems, and try special cases and simpler forms of the original problem in order to gain insight into its solution. They monitor and evaluate their progress and change course if necessary. Older students might, depending on the context of the problem, transform algebraic expressions or change the viewing window on their graphing calculator to get the information they need. Mathematically proficient students can explain correspondences between equations, verbal descriptions, tables, and graphs or draw diagrams of important features and relationships, graph data, and search for regularity or trends. Younger students might rely on using concrete objects or pictures to help conceptualize and solve a problem. Mathematically proficient students check their answers to problems using a different method, and they continually ask themselves, "Does this make sense?" They can understand the approaches of others to solving complex problems and identify correspondences between different approaches.

2. Reason abstractly and quantitatively. Mathematically proficient students make sense of quantities and their relationships in problem situations. They bring two complementary abilities to bear on problems involving quantitative relationships: the ability to decontextualize—to abstract a given situation and represent it symbolically and manipulate the representing symbols as if they have a life of their own, without necessarily attending to their referents—and the ability to contextualize, to pause as needed during the manipulation process in order to probe into the referents for the symbols involved. Quantitative reasoning entails habits of creating a coherent representation of the problem at hand; considering the units involved; attending to the meaning of quantities, not just how to compute them; and knowing and flexibly using different properties of operations and objects.

3. Construct viable arguments and critique the reasoning of others. Mathematically proficient students understand and use stated assumptions, definitions, and previously established results in constructing arguments. They make conjectures and build a logical progression of statements to explore the truth of their conjectures. They are able to analyze situations by breaking them into cases, and can recognize and use counterexamples. They justify their conclusions, communicate them to others, and respond to the arguments of others. They reason inductively about data, making plausible arguments that take into account the context from which the data arose. Mathematically proficient students are also able to compare the effectiveness of two plausible arguments, distinguish correct logic or reasoning from that which is flawed, and—if there is a flaw in an argument—explain what it is. Elementary students can construct arguments using concrete referents such as objects, drawings, diagrams, and actions. Such arguments can make sense and be correct, even though they are not generalized or made formal until later grades. Later, students learn to determine domains to which an argument applies. Students at all grades can listen or read the arguments of others, decide whether they make sense, and ask useful questions to clarify or improve the arguments.

4. Model with mathematics. Mathematically proficient students can apply the mathematics they know to solve problems arising in everyday life, society, and the workplace. In early grades, this might be as simple as writing an addition equation to describe a situation. In middle grades, a student might apply proportional reasoning to plan a school event or analyze a problem in the community. By high school, a student might use geometry to solve a design problem or use a function to describe how one quantity of interest depends on another. Mathematically proficient students who can apply what they know are comfortable making assumptions and approximations to simplify a complicated situation, realizing that these may need revision later. They are able to identify important quantities in a practical situation and map their relationships using such tools as diagrams, two-way tables, graphs, flowcharts and formulas. They can analyze those relationships mathematically to draw conclusions. They routinely interpret their mathematical results in the context of the situation and reflect on whether the results make sense, possibly improving the model if it has not served its purpose.

5. Use appropriate tools strategically. Mathematically proficient students consider the available tools when solving a mathematical problem. These tools might include pencil and paper, concrete models, a ruler, a protractor, a calculator, a spreadsheet, a computer algebra system, a statistical package, or dynamic geometry software. Proficient students are sufficiently familiar with tools appropriate for their grade or course to make sound decisions about when each of these tools might be helpful, recognizing both the insight to be gained and their limitations. For example, mathematically proficient high school students analyze graphs of functions and solutions generated using a graphing calculator. They detect possible errors by strategically using estimation and other mathematical knowledge. When making mathematical models, they know that technology can enable them to visualize the results of varying assumptions, explore consequences, and compare predictions with data. Mathematically proficient students at various grade levels are able to identify relevant external mathematical resources, such as digital content located on a website, and use them to pose or solve problems. They are able to use technological tools to explore and deepen their understanding of concepts.

6. Attend to precision. Mathematically proficient students try to communicate precisely to others. They try to use clear definitions in discussion with others and in their own reasoning. They state the meaning of the symbols they choose, including using the equal sign consistently and appropriately. They are careful about specifying units of measure, and labeling axes to clarify the correspondence with quantities in a problem. They calculate accurately and efficiently, express numerical answers with a degree of precision appropriate for the problem context. In the elementary grades, students give carefully formulated explanations to each other. By the time they reach high school they have learned to examine claims and make explicit use of definitions.

7. Look for and make use of structure. Mathematically proficient students look closely to discern a pattern or structure. Young students, for example, might notice that three and seven more is the same amount as seven and three more, or they may sort a collection of shapes according to how many sides the shapes have. Later, students will see 7×8 equals the well remembered $7 \times 5 + 7 \times 3$, in preparation for learning about the distributive property. In the expression $x^2 + 9x + 14$, older students can see the 14 as 2×7 and the 9 as $2 + 7$. They recognize the significance of an existing line in a geometric figure and can use the strategy of drawing an auxiliary line for solving problems. They also can step back for an overview and shift perspective. They can see complicated things, such as some algebraic expressions, as single objects or as being composed of several objects. For example, they can see $5 - 3(x - y)^2$ as 5 minus a positive number times a square and use that to realize that its value cannot be more than 5 for any real numbers x and y.

8. Look for and express regularity in repeated reasoning. Mathematically proficient students notice if calculations are repeated, and look both for general methods and for shortcuts. Upper elementary students might notice when dividing 25 by 11 that they are repeating the same calculations over and over again, and conclude they have a repeating decimal. By paying attention to the calculation of slope as they repeatedly check whether points are on the line through (1, 2) with slope 3, middle school students might abstract the equation $(y - 2)/(x - 1) = 3$. Noticing the regularity in the way terms cancel when expanding $(x - 1)(x + 1)$, $(x - 1)(x^2 + x + 1)$, and $(x - 1)(x^3 + x^2 + x + 1)$ might lead them to the general formula for the sum of a geometric series. As they work to solve a problem, mathematically proficient students maintain oversight of the process, while attending to the details. They continually evaluate the reasonableness of their intermediate results.

Connecting the Standards for Mathematical Practice to the Standards for Mathematical Content

The Standards for Mathematical Practice describe ways in which developing student practitioners of the discipline of mathematics increasingly ought to engage with the subject matter as they grow in mathematical maturity and expertise throughout the elementary, middle and high school years. Designers of curricula, assessments, and professional development should all attend to the need to connect the mathematical practices to mathematical content in mathematics instruction.

The Standards for Mathematical Content are a balanced combination of procedure and understanding. Expectations that begin with the word "understand" are often especially good opportunities to connect the practices to the content. Students who lack understanding of a topic may rely on procedures too heavily. Without a flexible base from which to work, they may be less likely to consider analogous problems, represent problems coherently, justify conclusions, apply the mathematics to practical situations, use technology mindfully to work with the mathematics, explain the mathematics accurately to other students, step back for an overview, or deviate from a known procedure to find a shortcut. In short, a lack of understanding effectively prevents a student from engaging in the mathematical practices.

In this respect, those content standards which set an expectation of understanding are potential "points of intersection" between the Standards for Mathematical Content and the Standards for Mathematical Practice. These points of intersection are intended to be weighted toward central and generative concepts in the school mathematics curriculum that most merit the time, resources, innovative energies, and focus necessary to qualitatively improve the curriculum, instruction, assessment, professional development, and student achievement in mathematics.

Standards for Mathematical Content, Kindergarten

In Kindergarten, instructional time should focus on two critical areas: (1) representing, relating, and operating on whole numbers, initially with sets of objects; (2) describing shapes and space. More learning time in Kindergarten should be devoted to number than to other topics. (1) Students use numbers, including written numerals, to represent quantities and to solve quantitative problems, such as counting objects in a set; counting out a given number of objects; comparing sets or numerals; and modeling simple joining and separating situations with sets of objects, or eventually with equations such as $5 + 2 = 7$ and $7 - 2 = 5$. (Kindergarten students should see addition and subtraction equations, and student writing of equations in kindergarten is encouraged, but it is not required.) Students choose, combine, and apply effective strategies for answering quantitative questions, including quickly recognizing the cardinalities of small sets of objects, counting and producing sets of given sizes, counting the number of objects in combined sets, or counting the number of objects that remain in a set after some are taken away. (2) Students describe their physical world using geometric ideas (e.g., shape, orientation, spatial relations) and vocabulary. They identify, name, and describe basic two-dimensional shapes, such as squares, triangles, circles, rectangles, and hexagons, presented in a variety of ways (e.g., with different sizes and orientations), as well as three-dimensional shapes such as cubes, cones, cylinders, and spheres. They use basic shapes and spatial reasoning to model objects in their environment and to construct more complex shapes.

Grade K Overview

Counting and Cardinality

- Know number names and the count sequence.
- Count to tell the number of objects.
- Compare numbers.

Operations and Algebraic Thinking

- Understand addition as putting together and adding to, and understand subtraction as taking apart and taking from.

Number and Operations in Base Ten

- Work with numbers 11–19 to gain foundations for place value.

Measurement and Data

- Describe and compare measurable attributes.

- Classify objects and count the number of objects in categories.

Geometry

- Identify and describe shapes.

- Analyze, compare, create, and compose shapes.

Counting and Cardinality K.CC

Know number names and the count sequence.

1. Count to 100 by ones and by tens.

2. Count forward beginning from a given number within the known sequence (instead of having to begin at 1).

3. Write numbers from 0 to 20. Represent a number of objects with a written numeral 0–20 (with 0 representing a count of no objects).

Count to tell the number of objects.

4. Understand the relationship between numbers and quantities; connect counting to cardinality.

   a. When counting objects, say the number names in the standard order, pairing each object with one and only one number name and each number name with one and only one object.

   b. Understand that the last number name said tells the number of objects counted. The number of objects is the same regardless of their arrangement or the order in which they were counted.

   c. Understand that each successive number name refers to a quantity that is one larger.

5. Count to answer "how many?" questions about as many as 20 things arranged in a line, a rectangular array, or a circle, or as many as 10 things in a scattered configuration; given a number from 1–20, count out that many objects.

Compare numbers.

6. Identify whether the number of objects in one group is greater than, less than, or equal to the number of objects in another group, e.g., by using matching and counting strategies.

7. Compare two numbers between 1 and 10 presented as written numerals.

Operations and Algebraic Thinking K.OA

Understand addition as putting together and adding to, and understand subtraction as taking apart and taking from.

1. Represent addition and subtraction with objects, fingers, mental images, drawings, sounds (e.g., claps), acting out situations, verbal explanations, expressions, or equations.

2. Solve addition and subtraction word problems, and add and subtract within 10, e.g., by using objects or drawings to represent the problem.

3. Decompose numbers less than or equal to 10 into pairs in more than one way, e.g., by using objects or drawings, and record each decomposition by a drawing or equation (e.g., 5 = 2 + 3 and 5 = 4 + 1).

4. For any number from 1 to 9, find the number that makes 10 when added to the given number, e.g., by using objects or drawings, and record the answer with a drawing or equation.

5. Fluently add and subtract within 5.

Number and Operations in Base Ten K.NBT

Work with numbers 11–19 to gain foundations for place value.

1. Compose and decompose numbers from 11 to 19 into ten ones and some further ones, e.g., by using objects or drawings, and record each composition or decomposition by a drawing or equation (e.g., 18 = 10 + 8); understand that these numbers are composed of ten ones and one, two, three, four, five, six, seven, eight, or nine ones.

Measurement and Data K.MD

Describe and compare measurable attributes.

1. Describe measurable attributes of objects, such as length or weight. Describe several measurable attributes of a single object.

2. Directly compare two objects with a measurable attribute in common, to see which object has "more of"/"less of" the attribute, and describe the difference. For example, directly compare the heights of two children and describe one child as taller/shorter.

Classify objects and count the number of objects in each category.

3. Classify objects into given categories; count the numbers of objects in each category and sort the categories by count.

Geometry K.G

Identify and describe shapes (squares, circles, triangles, rectangles, hexagons, cubes, cones, cylinders, and spheres).

1. Describe objects in the environment using names of shapes, and describe the relative positions of these objects using terms such as above, below, beside, in front of, behind, and next to.

2. Correctly name shapes regardless of their orientations or overall size.

3. Identify shapes as two-dimensional (lying in a plane, "flat") or three-dimensional ("solid").

Analyze, compare, create, and compose shapes.

4. Analyze and compare two- and three-dimensional shapes, in different sizes and orientations, using informal language to describe their similarities, differences, parts (e.g., number of sides and vertices/"corners") and other attributes (e.g., having sides of equal length).

5. Model shapes in the world by building shapes from components (e.g., sticks and clay balls) and drawing shapes.

6. Compose simple shapes to form larger shapes. For example, "Can you join these two triangles with full sides touching to make a rectangle?"

APPENDIX D

Standards for Mathematical Content, Grade 1

In Grade 1, instructional time should focus on four critical areas: (1) developing understanding of addition, subtraction, and strategies for addition and subtraction within 20; (2) developing understanding of whole number relationships and place value, including grouping in tens and ones; (3) developing understanding of linear measurement and measuring lengths as iterating length units; and (4) reasoning about attributes of, and composing and decomposing geometric shapes.

(1) Students develop strategies for adding and subtracting whole numbers based on their prior work with small numbers. They use a variety of models, including discrete objects and length-based models (e.g., cubes connected to form lengths), to model add-to, take-from, put-together, take-apart, and compare situations to develop meaning for the operations of addition and subtraction, and to develop strategies to solve arithmetic problems with these operations. Students understand connections between counting and addition and subtraction (e.g., adding two is the same as counting on two). They use properties of addition to add whole numbers and to create and use increasingly sophisticated strategies based on these properties (e.g., "making tens") to solve addition and subtraction problems within 20. By comparing a variety of solution strategies, children build their understanding of the relationship between addition and subtraction.

(2) Students develop, discuss, and use efficient, accurate, and generalizable methods to add within 100 and subtract multiples of 10. They compare whole numbers (at least to 100) to develop understanding of and solve problems involving their relative sizes. They think of whole numbers between 10 and 100 in terms of tens and ones (especially recognizing the numbers 11 to 19 as composed of a ten and some ones). Through activities that build number sense, they understand the order of the counting numbers and their relative magnitudes.

(3) Students develop an understanding of the meaning and processes of measurement, including underlying concepts such as iterating (the mental activity of building up the length of an object with equal-sized units) and the transitivity principle for indirect measurement.

(4) Students compose and decompose plane or solid figures (e.g., put two triangles together to make a quadrilateral) and build understanding of part-whole relationships as well as the properties of the original and composite shapes. As they combine shapes, they recognize them from different perspectives and orientations, describe their geometric attributes, and determine how they are alike and different, to develop the background for measurement and for initial understandings of properties such as congruence and symmetry.

Grade 1 Overview

Operations and Algebraic Thinking

- Represent and solve problems involving addition and subtraction.
- Understand and apply properties of operations and the relationship between addition and subtraction.
- Add and subtract within 20.
- Work with addition and subtraction equations.

Number and Operations in Base Ten

- Extend the counting sequence.
- Understand place value.
- Use place value understanding and properties of operations to add and subtract.

Measurement and Data

- Measure lengths indirectly and by iterating length units.
- Tell and write time.
- Represent and interpret data.

Geometry

- Reason with shapes and their attributes.

Operations and Algebraic Thinking 1.OA

Represent and solve problems involving addition and subtraction.

1. Use addition and subtraction within 20 to solve word problems involving situations of adding to, taking from, putting together, taking apart, and comparing, with unknowns in all positions, e.g., by using objects, drawings, and equations with a symbol for the unknown number to represent the problem.

2. Solve word problems that call for addition of three whole numbers whose sum is less than or equal to 20, e.g., by using objects, drawings, and equations with a symbol for the unknown number to represent the problem.

Understand and apply properties of operations and the relationship between addition and subtraction.

3. Apply properties of operations as strategies to add and subtract. Examples: If 8 + 3 = 11 is known, then 3 + 8 = 11 is also known. (Commutative property of addition.) To add 2 + 6 + 4, the second two numbers can be added to make a ten, so 2 + 6 + 4 = 2 + 10 = 12. (Associative property of addition.)

4. Understand subtraction as an unknown-addend problem. For example, subtract 10 – 8 by finding the number that makes 10 when added to 8.

Add and subtract within 20.

5. Relate counting to addition and subtraction (e.g., by counting on 2 to add 2).

6. Add and subtract within 20, demonstrating fluency for addition and subtraction within 10. Use strategies such as counting on; making ten (e.g., 8 + 6 = 8 + 2 + 4 = 10 + 4 = 14); decomposing a number leading to a ten (e.g., 13 – 4 = 13 – 3 – 1 = 10 – 1 = 9); using the relationship between addition and subtraction (e.g., knowing that 8 + 4 = 12, one knows 12 – 8= 4); and creating equivalent but easier or known sums (e.g., adding 6 + 7 by creating the known equivalent 6 + 6 + 1 = 12 + 1 = 13).

Work with addition and subtraction equations.

7. Understand the meaning of the equal sign, and determine if equations involving addition and subtraction are true or false. For example, which of the following equations are true and which are false? 6 = 6, 7 = 8 – 1, 5 + 2 = 2 + 5, 4 + 1 = 5 + 2.

8. Determine the unknown whole number in an addition or subtraction equation relating three whole numbers. For example, determine the unknown number that makes the equation true in each of the equations 8 + ? = 11, 5 = □ – 3, 6 + 6 = □.

Number and Operations in Base Ten 1.NBT

Extend the counting sequence.

1. Count to 120, starting at any number less than 120. In this range, read and write numerals and represent a number of objects with a written numeral.

Understand place value.

2. Understand that the two digits of a two-digit number represent amounts of tens and ones. Understand the following as special cases:

    a. 10 can be thought of as a bundle of ten ones—called a "ten."

    b. The numbers from 11 to 19 are composed of a ten and one, two, three, four, five, six, seven, eight, or nine ones.

    c. The numbers 10, 20, 30, 40, 50, 60, 70, 80, 90 refer to one, two, three, four, five, six, seven, eight, or nine tens (and 0 ones).

3. Compare two two-digit numbers based on meanings of the tens and ones digits, recording the results of comparisons with the symbols >, =, and <.

Use place value understanding and properties of operations to add and subtract.

4. Add within 100, including adding a two-digit number and a one-digit number, and adding a two-digit number and a multiple of 10, using concrete models or drawings and strategies based on place value, properties of operations, and/or the relationship between addition and subtraction; relate the strategy to a written method and explain the reasoning used. Understand that in adding two-digit numbers, one adds tens and tens, ones and ones; and sometimes it is necessary to compose a ten.

5. Given a two-digit number, mentally find 10 more or 10 less than the number, without having to count; explain the reasoning used.

6. Subtract multiples of 10 in the range 10–90 from multiples of 10 in the range 10–90 (positive or zero differences), using concrete models or drawings and strategies based on place value, properties of operations, and/or the relationship between addition and subtraction; relate the strategy to a written method and explain the reasoning used.

Measurement and Data 1.MD

Measure lengths indirectly and by iterating length units.

1. Order three objects by length; compare the lengths of two objects indirectly by using a third object.

2. Express the length of an object as a whole number of length units, by laying multiple copies of a shorter object (the length unit) end to end; understand that the length measurement of an object is the number of same-size length units that span it with no gaps or overlaps. Limit to contexts where the object being measured is spanned by a whole number of length units with no gaps or overlaps.

Tell and write time.

3. Tell and write time in hours and half-hours using analog and digital clocks.

Represent and interpret data.

4. Organize, represent, and interpret data with up to three categories; ask and answer questions about the total number of data points, how many in each category, and how many more or less are in one category than in another.

Geometry 1.G

Reason with shapes and their attributes.

1. Distinguish between defining attributes (e.g., triangles are closed and three-sided) versus non-defining attributes (e.g., color, orientation, overall size); build and draw shapes to possess defining attributes.

2. Compose two-dimensional shapes (rectangles, squares, trapezoids, triangles, half-circles, and quarter-circles) or three-dimensional shapes (cubes, right rectangular prisms, right circular cones, and right circular cylinders) to create a composite shape, and compose new shapes from the composite shape.

3. Partition circles and rectangles into two and four equal shares, describe the shares using the words halves, fourths, and quarters, and use the phrases half of, fourth of, and quarter of. Describe the whole as two of, or four of the shares. Understand for these examples that decomposing into more equal shares creates smaller shares.

APPENDIX E

Standards for Mathematical Content, Grade 2

Source: NGA & CCSSO, 2010, pp. 13–16. © Copyright 2010. National Governors Association Center for Best Practices and Council of Chief State School Officers. All rights reserved. Used with permission.

In Grade 2, instructional time should focus on four critical areas: (1) extending understanding of base-ten notation; (2) building fluency with addition and subtraction; (3) using standard units of measure; and (4) describing and analyzing shapes.

(1) Students extend their understanding of the base-ten system. This includes ideas of counting in fives, tens, and multiples of hundreds, tens, and ones, as well as number relationships involving these units, including comparing. Students understand multi-digit numbers (up to 1000) written in base-ten notation, recognizing that the digits in each place represent amounts of thousands, hundreds, tens, or ones (e.g., 853 is 8 hundreds + 5 tens + 3 ones).

(2) Students use their understanding of addition to develop fluency with addition and subtraction within 100. They solve problems within 1000 by applying their understanding of models for addition and subtraction, and they develop, discuss, and use efficient, accurate, and generalizable methods to compute sums and differences of whole numbers in base-ten notation, using their understanding of place value and the properties of operations. They select and accurately apply methods that are appropriate for the context and the numbers involved to mentally calculate sums and differences for numbers with only tens or only hundreds.

(3) Students recognize the need for standard units of measure (centimeter and inch) and they use rulers and other measurement tools with the understanding that linear measure involves an iteration of units. They recognize that the smaller the unit, the more iterations they need to cover a given length.

(4) Students describe and analyze shapes by examining their sides and angles. Students investigate, describe, and reason about decomposing and combining shapes to make other shapes. Through building, drawing, and analyzing two- and three-dimensional shapes, students develop a foundation for understanding area, volume, congruence, similarity, and symmetry in later grades.

Grade 2 Overview

Operations and Algebraic Thinking

- Represent and solve problems involving addition and subtraction.

- Add and subtract within 20.

- Work with equal groups of objects to gain foundations for multiplication.

Number and Operations in Base Ten

- Understand place value.

- Use place value understanding and properties of operations to add and subtract.

Measurement and Data

- Measure and estimate lengths in standard units.

- Relate addition and subtraction to length.

- Work with time and money.

- Represent and interpret data.

Geometry

- Reason with shapes and their attributes.

Operations and Algebraic Thinking 2.OA

Represent and solve problems involving addition and subtraction.

1. Use addition and subtraction within 100 to solve one- and two-step word problems involving situations of adding to, taking from, putting together, taking apart, and comparing, with unknowns in all positions, e.g., by using drawings and equations with a symbol for the unknown number to represent the problem.

Add and subtract within 20.

2. Fluently add and subtract within 20 using mental strategies. By end of Grade 2, know from memory all sums of two one-digit numbers.

Work with equal groups of objects to gain foundations for multiplication.

3. Determine whether a group of objects (up to 20) has an odd or even number of members, e.g., by pairing objects or counting them by 2s; write an equation to express an even number as a sum of two equal addends.

4. Use addition to find the total number of objects arranged in rectangular arrays with up to 5 rows and up to 5 columns; write an equation to express the total as a sum of equal addends.

Number and Operations in Base Ten 2.NBT

Understand place value.

1. Understand that the three digits of a three-digit number represent amounts of hundreds, tens, and ones; e.g., 706 equals 7 hundreds, 0 tens, and 6 ones. Understand the following as special cases:

   a. 100 can be thought of as a bundle of ten tens—called a "hundred."

   b. The numbers 100, 200, 300, 400, 500, 600, 700, 800, 900 refer to one, two, three, four, five, six, seven, eight, or nine hundreds (and 0 tens and 0 ones).

2. Count within 1000; skip-count by 5s, 10s, and 100s.

3. Read and write numbers to 1000 using base-ten numerals, number names, and expanded form.

4. Compare two three-digit numbers based on meanings of the hundreds, tens, and ones digits, using >, =, and < symbols to record the results of comparisons.

Use place value understanding and properties of operations to add and subtract.

5. Fluently add and subtract within 100 using strategies based on place value, properties of operations, and/or the relationship between addition and subtraction.

6. Add up to four two-digit numbers using strategies based on place value and properties of operations.

7. Add and subtract within 1000, using concrete models or drawings and strategies based on place value, properties of operations, and/or the relationship between addition and subtraction; relate the strategy to a written method. Understand that in adding or subtracting three-digit numbers, one adds or subtracts hundreds and hundreds, tens and tens, ones and ones; and sometimes it is necessary to compose or decompose tens or hundreds.

8. Mentally add 10 or 100 to a given number 100–900, and mentally subtract 10 or 100 from a given number 100–900.

9. Explain why addition and subtraction strategies work, using place value and the properties of operations.

Measurement and Data 2.MD

Measure and estimate lengths in standard units.

1. Measure the length of an object by selecting and using appropriate tools such as rulers, yardsticks, meter sticks, and measuring tapes.

2. Measure the length of an object twice, using length units of different lengths for the two measurements; describe how the two measurements relate to the size of the unit chosen.

3. Estimate lengths using units of inches, feet, centimeters, and meters.

4. Measure to determine how much longer one object is than another, expressing the length difference in terms of a standard length unit.

Relate addition and subtraction to length.

5. Use addition and subtraction within 100 to solve word problems involving lengths that are given in the same units, e.g., by using drawings (such as drawings of rulers) and equations with a symbol for the unknown number to represent the problem.

6. Represent whole numbers as lengths from 0 on a number line diagram with equally spaced points corresponding to the numbers 0, 1, 2, . . . , and represent whole-number sums and differences within 100 on a number line diagram.

Work with time and money.

7. Tell and write time from analog and digital clocks to the nearest five minutes, using a.m. and p.m.

8. Solve word problems involving dollar bills, quarters, dimes, nickels, and pennies, using $ and ¢ symbols appropriately. Example: If you have 2 dimes and 3 pennies, how many cents do you have?

Represent and interpret data.

9. Generate measurement data by measuring lengths of several objects to the nearest whole unit, or by making repeated measurements of the same object. Show the measurements by making a line plot, where the horizontal scale is marked off in whole-number units.

10. Draw a picture graph and a bar graph (with single-unit scale) to represent a data set with up to four categories. Solve simple put-together, take-apart, and compare problems using information presented in a bar graph.

Geometry 2.G

Reason with shapes and their attributes.

1. Recognize and draw shapes having specified attributes, such as a given number of angles or a given number of equal faces. Identify triangles, quadrilaterals, pentagons, hexagons, and cubes.

2. Partition a rectangle into rows and columns of same-size squares and count to find the total number of them.

3. Partition circles and rectangles into two, three, or four equal shares, describe the shares using the words halves, thirds, half of, a third of, etc., and describe the whole as two halves, three thirds, four fourths. Recognize that equal shares of identical wholes need not have the same shape.

APPENDIX F

Changes in Mathematics Standards, 1989–2010

Helping students use their prior knowledge to enable them to recognize what is new and different in their learning is a key element of scaffolded instruction. Similarly, as you explore the CCSS for mathematics, it will be helpful to compare aspects of mathematics standards that have framed your previous instruction so that you can identify what is familiar, what is new and challenging, and what changes are required in the content delivered to your students. As you examine the CCSS mathematics standards for your grade level, you may find it helpful to refer to the standards that have formed the basis of your instruction recently. In all likelihood these standards are based on the landmark documents that have influenced mathematics instruction since 1989, when the National Council of Teachers of Mathematics published *Curriculum and Evaluation Standards for School Mathematics* (NCTM, 1989). In 2000, NCTM updated these curriculum standards in their *Principles and Standards for School Mathematics* (PSSM), which has served as the blueprint for revised state standards throughout 2000–2010.

The placement of content standards and mathematical processes is an important consideration in any set of standards. The content and process standards within the *Principles and Standards for School Mathematics* were the same across all the grade-level bands (preK–2, 3–5, 6–8, and 9–12).

The Common Core State Standards (NGA & CCSSO, 2010) differ significantly from the *Principles and Standards for School Mathematics* (NCTM, 2000) in the descriptive language used to define the content standards. The CCSS reference their content areas as *domains* rather than *content topics* or *strands*. Similarly, the content domains within the CCSS differ according to level rather than being the same from preK–12. These differences are illustrated in table F.1 (page 176) which shows content topics defined in the *Principles and Standards for School Mathematics* and the content domains defined in the Common Core State Standards. You can use this table with your collaborative learning team to focus discussion on these questions:

1. How familiar are the terms describing content topics and content domains?

2. How does the sequence of content compare to the sequence you have followed in the past?

3. What are your teacher professional development needs and differences between the *Principles and Standards for School Mathematics* and the Common Core State Standards content?

Table F.1: Mathematics Content—*Principles and Standards for School Mathematics* and the Common Core State Standards

PSSM—Content Topics Grades PreK–12	CCSS—Content Domains Grades K–5	CCSS—Content Domains Grades 6–8
Number and Operations	Counting and Cardinality (K only)	Ratios and Proportional Relationships (grades 6–7 only)
Algebra	Operations and Algebraic Thinking	The Number System
Geometry	Number and Operations in Base Ten	Expressions and Equations
Measurement	Number and Operations—Fractions (grades 3–5 only)	Functions (grade 8 only)
Data Analysis and Probability	Measurement and Data	Geometry
	Geometry	Statistics and Probability

Visit **go.solution-tree.com/commoncore** for a reproducible version of this table.

In 2006, NCTM released the *Curriculum Focal Points*. The *Curriculum Focal Points* were intended to serve as a discussion document for states, school districts, and local schools as they began a conversation around the more important or *focus* topics at particular grades for levels K–8. Many states saw the Focal Points as an opportunity for their schools or school districts to identify areas of curricular focus within particular grades and also to provide the grade-by-grade essentials for all students. The Focal Points became one of the foundational guides to the Common Core State Standards. One aspect of the CCSS is the *critical areas* presented at the beginning of each grade level's discussion (see appendix C, page 161, for example). The critical areas are grade-level emphasis points and are, in essence, the *Curriculum Focal Points,* with some revision. The critical areas for grades K–2 are shown in table F.2, which provides a second look at the important content across these grades. You can use this table to extend the discussion started with a review of table F.1 with your collaborative learning team. As your collaborative team begins work analyzing the content focus across the grades, you can draw on these questions to frame the discussion.

1. How much time do you think should be allotted for each critical area? How will these changes in time allocation be accommodated in schedule?

2. How are the critical areas similar to or different from topics you have emphasized in your teaching now or in the past?

3. What impact will work from the prior year have on the topics specified in the critical areas?

Table F.2: CCSS Critical Areas and NCTM Focal Points Grades PreK–2

Grade Level	CCSS Critical Areas	NCTM Focal Points
PreKindergarten	None	1. Develop an understanding of whole numbers, including concepts of correspondence, counting, cardinality, and comparison. 2. Identify shapes, and describe spatial relationships. 3. Identify measureable attributes, and compare objects by using these attributes.
Kindergarten	1. Represent and compare whole numbers, initially with sets of objects. 2. Describe shapes and space.	1. Represent, compare, and order whole numbers, and join and separate sets. 2. Describe shapes and space. 3. Order objects by measurable attributes.
Grade 1	1. Develop understanding of addition, subtraction, and strategies for addition and subtraction within 20. 2. Develop understanding of whole-number relationships and place value, including grouping in tens and ones. 3. Develop understanding of linear measurement and measuring lengths as iterating length units. 4. Reason about attributes of, and compose and decompose, geometric shapes.	1. Develop understandings of addition and subtraction and strategies for basic addition facts and related subtraction facts. 2. Develop an understanding of whole-number relationships, including grouping in tens and ones. 3. Compose and decompose geometric shapes. **Related Connection to the Focal Points*** 4. Measure by laying multiple copies of a unit end to end and then count the units by using groups of tens and ones.

continued →

Grade Level	CCSS Critical Areas	NCTM Focal Points
Grade 2	1. Extend understanding of base-ten notation. 2. Build fluency with addition and subtraction. 3. Use standard units of measure. 4. *Describe and analyze shapes.*	1. Develop an understanding of the base-ten numeration system and place-value concepts. 2. Develop quick recall of addition facts and related subtraction facts and fluency with multidigit addition and subtraction. 3. Develop an understanding of linear measurement and facility in measuring lengths.

Note: Italicized text indicates critical areas or elements of critical areas from the CCSS that were not considered Curriculum Focal Points *(NCTM, 2006).*

*The Curriculum Focal Points *(NCTM, 2006) present the most important mathematical topics and connections to the other content areas for each grade level. The listing of related connections to the Focal Points at grade 1 indicates that a connection to measurement was used to provide four critical areas for this grade.*

Visit **go.solution-tree.com/commoncore** for a reproducible version of this table.

The National Mathematics Advisory Panel (2008) identified the Critical Foundations of Algebra. These concepts and skills are essentials for all students prior to formal coursework in algebra and include the following major content topics, with suggested grade-level benchmarks. Clearly the benchmark regarding proficiency with addition and subtraction of whole numbers is grounded in experiences at the K–2 levels.

1. **Fluency with whole numbers:**

   a. By the end of grade 3, students should be proficient with addition and subtraction of whole numbers.

   b. By the end of grade 5, students should be proficient with multiplication and division of whole numbers.

2. **Fluency with fractions:**

   a. By the end of grade 4, students should be able to identify and represent fractions and decimals and compare them on a number line or with other common representations of fractions and decimals.

   b. By the end of grade 5, students should be proficient with comparing fractions and decimals and common percentages and with the addition and subtraction of fractions and decimals.

3. **Particular aspects of geometry and measurement:**

a. By the end of grade 5, students should be able to solve problems involving perimeter and area of triangles and all quadrilaterals having at least one pair of parallel sides (such as trapezoids).

Discussing the critical areas of the CCSS and the NCTM's Focal Points (see table F.2), as well as the NMAP's Critical Foundations will build on your team's initial examination of the general mathematics content (see table F.1, page 176) of the CCSS. This subsequent discussion of their similarities and how they outline points and emphasize topics within the CCSS provides a second-level professional development opportunity for collaborative teams on the important mathematics for grades K–2 This should prepare your collaborative teams to engage in meaningful discussions about what's important, mathematically, across these three grade levels. Additionally, these historical documents provide a precedent and eliminate any major surprises regarding actual content topics when experienced teachers review the CCSS domains, standards, and clusters for grades K–2.

References and Resources

Achieve. (2005). *Rising to the challenge: Are high school graduates prepared for college and work?* Washington, DC: Author.

American College Testing Program. (2006). *Ready for college and ready for work: Same or different?* Iowa City, IA: Author.

Baker, S., Gersten, R., & Lee, D. (2002). A synthesis of empirical research on teaching mathematics to low-achieving students. *The Elementary School Journal, 103*(1), 51–73.

Ball, D. L., & Bass, H. (2003). Making mathematics reasonable in school. In J. Kilpatrick, W. G. Martin, & D. Schifter (Eds.), *A research companion to principles and standards for school mathematics* (pp. 27–44). Reston, VA: National Council of Teachers of Mathematics.

Bandura, A. (1993). Perceived self-efficacy in cognitive development and functioning. *Educational Psychologist, 28*(2), 117–148.

Baroody, A. J. (1992). The development of kindergartener's mental-addition strategies. *Learning and Individual Differences, 4*(3), 215–235.

Baroody, A. J. (2011). Learning: A framework. In F. Fennell (Ed.), *Achieving fluency: Special education and mathematics* (pp. 15–53). Reston, VA: National Council of Teachers of Mathematics.

Bausmith, J. M., & Barry, C. (2011). Revisiting professional learning communities to increase college readiness: The importance of pedagogical content knowledge. *Educational Researcher, 40*(4), 175–178.

Bender, W. N., & Crane, D. (2011). *RTI in math: Practical guidelines for elementary teachers.* Bloomington, IN: Solution Tree Press.

Black, P., & Wiliam, D. (1998). Assessment and classroom learning. *Assessment in Education, 5*, 7–74.

Boaler, J., & Staples, M. (2008). Creating mathematical futures through an equitable teaching approach: The case of Railsdale School. *Teachers College Record, 110*, 608–645.

Boaler, J., Wiliam, D., & Brown, M. (2000). Students' experiences of ability grouping—disaffection, polarisation, and the construction of failure. *British Educational Research Journal, 26*, 631–648.

Bowman, B. T., Donovan, M. S., & Burns, M. S. (Eds.). (2001). *Eager to learn: Educating our preschoolers.* Washington, DC: National Academy Press.

Buffum, A., Mattos, M., & Weber, C. (2009). *Pyramid response to intervention: RTI, professional learning communities, and how to respond when kids don't learn.* Bloomington, IN: Solution Tree Press.

Burris, C. C., Heubert, J. P., & Levin, H. M. (2006). Accelerating mathematics achievement using heterogeneous grouping. *American Educational Research Journal, 43*(1), 105–136.

Bush, W. S., Briars, D. J., Confrey, J., Cramer, K., Lee, C., Martin, W. G., et al. (2011). *Common core state standards (CCSS) mathematics curriculum materials analysis project.* Accessed at www.mathedleadership.org/docs/ccss/CCSSO%20Mathematics%20Curriculum%20 Analysis%20Project.Whole%20Document.6.1.11.Final.docx on November 15, 2011.

Caldwell, J. H., Karp, K., & Bay-Williams, J. M. (2011). *Developing essential understanding of addition and subtraction for teaching mathematics in prekindergarten-grade 2.* Reston, VA: National Council of Teachers of Mathematics.

Campbell, P. F. (1995). *Project IMPACT: Increasing mathematics power for all children and teachers. Phase 1, final report.* College Park: Center for Mathematics Education, University of Maryland.

Campbell, P. F. (2011). Elementary mathematics specialists: A merger of policy, practice, and research. In W. F. Tate, K. D. King, & C. R. Anderson (Eds.), *Disrupting tradition: Research and practice pathways in mathematics education* (pp. 93–103). Reston, VA: National Council of Teachers of Mathematics.

Carpenter, T. P., Franke, M., & Levi, L. (2003). *Thinking mathematically: Integrating arithmetic and algebra in elementary school.* Portsmouth, NH: Heinemann.

Chetty, R., Friedman, J. N., Hilger, N., Saez, E., Schanzenbach, D., & Yagan, D. (2010). *How does your kindergarten classroom affect your earnings? Evidence from project STAR.* Cambridge, MA: Harvard Graduate School of Education.

Clarke, B., Smolkowski, K., Baker, S. K., Fien, H., Doabler, C. T., & Chard, D. J. (2011). The impact of a comprehensive Tier 1 core kindergarten program on the achievement of students at risk in mathematics. *The Elementary School Journal, 111,* 561–584.

Clements, D. H., & Sarama, J. (2009). *Learning and teaching early math: The learning trajectories approach.* New York: Routledge.

Clements, T. B. (2011). *The role of cognitive and metacognitive reading comprehension strategies in the reading and interpretation of mathematical word problem texts: Reading clinicians' perceptions of domain relevance and elementary students' cognitive strategy use.* Unpublished doctoral dissertation, University of Central Florida.

Cobb, P. (2000). Conducting teaching experiments in collaboration with teachers. In A. E. Kelly & R. A. Lesh (Eds.), *Handbook of research design in mathematics and science education* (pp. 307–333). Mahwah, NJ: Erlbaum.

Cohen, D. K., & Ball, D. (2001). Making change: Instruction and its improvement. *Phi Delta Kappan, 83*(1), 73–77.

Common Core State Standards Initiative. (2011). *Mathematics: Introduction: Standards for mathematical practice.* Accessed at www.corestandards.org/the-standards/mathematics/introduction/standards-for-mathematical-practice on November 15, 2011.

Darling-Hammond, L. (2010). *The flat world and education: How America's commitment to equity will determine our future.* New York: Teachers College Press.

Darling-Hammond, L., Wei, R. C., Andree, A., Richardson, N., & Orphanos, S. (2009). *Professional learning in the learning profession: A status report on teacher development in the United States and abroad.* Dallas, TX: National Staff Development Council.

Davies, A. (2007). Involving students in the classroom assessment process. In D. Reeves (Ed.), *Ahead of the curve: The power of assessment to transform teaching and learning* (pp. 31–57). Bloomington, IN: Solution Tree Press.

Davis, G. N., Lindo, E. J., & Compton, D. L. (2007). Childen at risk for reading failure: Constructing an early screening measure. *Teaching Exceptional Children, 39*(5), 32–37.

Dixon, J. K., Egendoerfer, L. A., & Clements, T. (2009). Do they really need to raise their hands? Challenging a traditional social norm in a second grade mathematics classroom. *Teaching and Teacher Education, 25,* 1067–1076.

DuFour, R., DuFour, R., & Eaker, R. (2008). *Revisiting professional learning communities at work: New insights for improving schools.* Bloomington, IN: Solution Tree Press.

DuFour, R., DuFour, R., Eaker, R., & Many, T. (2010). *Learning by doing: A handbook for professional learning communities at work* (2nd ed.). Bloomington, IN: Solution Tree Press.

Education Trust. (2005). *Gaining traction, gaining ground: How some high schools accelerate learning for struggling students.* Washington, DC: Education Trust.

Erwin, J. C. (2004). *The classroom of choice: Giving students what they need and getting what you want.* Alexandria, VA: Association for Supervision & Curriculum Development.

Fennell, F. (2011). *Achieving fluency: Special education and mathematics.* Reston, VA: National Council of Teachers of Mathematics.

Fernandez, C., & Yoshida, M. (2004). *Lesson study: A Japanese approach to improving mathematics teaching and learning.* Mahwah, NJ: Erlbaum.

Ferrini-Mundy, J., Gaham, K., Johnson, L., & Mills, G. (1998). *Making change in mathematics education: Learning from the field.* Reston, VA: National Council of Teachers of Mathematics.

Fisher, D., Frey, N, & Rothenberg, C. (2011). *Implementing RTI with English learners.* Bloomington, IN: Solution Tree Press.

Franke, M. L., Kazemi, E., & Battey, D. (2007). Mathematics teaching and classroom practice. In F. K. Lester (Ed.), *Second handbook of research on mathematics teaching and learning* (pp. 225–256). Charlotte, NC: Information Age.

Fuchs, D., Fuchs, L. S., & Vaughn, S. (2008). *Response to intervention: A framework for reading educators.* Newark, DE: International Reading Association.

Fuson, K. C. (1988). *Children's counting and concepts of number.* New York: Springer-Verlag.

Fuson, K. C. (2003). Toward computational fluency in multidigit multiplication and division. *Teaching Children Mathematics, 9,* 300–305.

Garet, M., Wayne, A., Stancavage, F., Taylor, J., Walters, K., Song, M., et al. (2010). *Middle school mathematics professional development impact study: Findings after the first year of implementation* (NCEE 2010–4009). Washington, DC: National Center for Education Evaluation and Regional Assistance.

Gersten, R., Beckmann, S., Clarke, B., Foegen, A., Marsh, L., Star, J. R., et al. (2009). *Assisting student struggling with mathematics: Response to intervention (RtI) for elementary and middle schools* (NCEE 2009–4060). Washington, DC: National Center for Education Evaluation and Regional Assistance.

Gersten, R., & Clarke, B. S. (2007). *Effective strategies for teaching students with difficulties in mathematics* (Research Brief). Reston, VA: National Council of Teachers of Mathematics.

Gersten, R., Jordan, N. C., & Flojo, J. R. (2005). Early identification and intervention for students with mathematics difficulties. *Journal of Learning Disabilities, 38*(4), 293–304.

Ginsburg, H. P., & Dolan, A. O. (2011). Assessment. In F. Fennell (Ed.), *Achieving fluency: Special education and mathematics* (pp. 85–103). Reston, VA: National Council of Teachers of Mathematics.

Gresalfi, M. S., & Cobb, P. (2011). Negotiating identities for mathematics teaching in the context of professional development. *Journal for Research in Mathematics Education, 42*(3), 270–304.

Griffin, S. A., Case, R., & Siegler, R. S. (1994). Rightstart: Providing the central conceptual prerequisites for first formal learning of arithmetic to students at risk for school failure. In K. McGilly (Ed.), *Classroom lessons: Integrating cognitive theory and classroom practice* (pp. 25–49). Cambridge, MA: MIT Press.

Hanley, T. V. (2005). Commentary on early identification and intervention for students with math difficulties: Make sense—do the math. *Journal for Learning Disabilities, 38*(4), 346–349.

Hiebert, J., & Grouws, D. A. (2007). The effects of classroom mathematics teaching on students' learning. In F. K. Lester (Ed.), *Second handbook of research on mathematics teaching and learning.* Charlotte, NC: Information Age.

Hiebert, J., & Stigler, J. W. (2004). A world of difference: Classrooms abroad provide lessons in teaching math and science. *Journal of the National Staff Development Council, 25*(4), 10–15.

Hill, H. C., Ball, D. L., & Schilling, S. G. (2008). Unpacking pedagogical content knowledge: Conceptualizing and measuring teachers' topic-specific knowledge of students. *Journal for Research in Mathematics Education, 39*(4), 372–400.

Individuals With Disabilities Education Improvement Act of 2004, Pub. L. No. 108–446, 118 Stat. 2647 (2004).

Inside Mathematics. (2010). *Common core standards for mathematical practice.* Accessed at http://insidemathematics.org/index.php/common-core-standards on November 15, 2011.

Jayanthi, M., Gersten, R., & Baker, S. (2008). *Mathematics instruction for students with learning disabilities or difficulty learning mathematics: A guide for teachers.* Portsmouth, NH: RMC Research Corporation.

Jenkins, J. R., Hudson, R. F., & Johnson, E. S. (2007). Screening for service delivery in an RTI framework: Candidate measures. *School Psychology Review, 36*, 560–582.

Jenkins, O. F. (2010). A professional collaboration model. *Mathematics Teaching in the Middle School, 16*(5), 288–294. Accessed at www.nctm.org/publications/article.aspx?id=27410 on November 15, 2011.

Johnson, E. S., Mellard, D. F., Fuchs, D., & McKnight, M. (2006). *Response to intervention: How to do it.* Lawrence, KS: National Research Center on Learning Disabilities.

Johnson, E., Smith, L., & Harris, M. (2009). *How RTI works in secondary schools.* Thousand Oaks, CA: Corwin Press.

Jordan, N., & Hanich, L. (2003). Characteristics of children with moderate mathematics deficiencies: A longitudinal perspective. *Learning Disabilities Research & Practice, 18,* 213–221.

Kanold, T. (2006). The flywheel effect. *Journal for Staff Development, 27*(2), 16–21.

Kanold, T., Briars, D., & Fennell, F. (2012). *What principals need to know about teaching and learning mathematics.* Bloomington, IN: Solution Tree Press.

Kantowski, M. G. (1980). Some thoughts on teaching for problem solving. In S. Krulik & R. Reys (Eds.), *Problem solving in school mathematics: 1980 yearbook* (pp. 195–203). Reston, VA: National Council of Teachers of Mathematics.

Kersaint, G. (2007). The learning environment: Its influence on what is learned. In W. G. Martin, M. E. Strutchens, & P. C. Elliott (Eds.), *The learning of mathematics: Sixty-ninth yearbook* (pp. 83–96). Reston, VA: National Council of Teachers of Mathematics.

Kinzer, C. J., Virag, L., & Morales, S. (2011). A reflective protocol for mathematics learning environments. *Teaching Children Mathematics, 17*(8), 480–484.

Knapp, M. S., Adelman, N. E., Marder, C., McCollum, H., Needels, M. C., Padilla, C., et al. (1995). *Teaching for meaning in high-poverty schools.* New York: Teachers College Press.

Larson, M. R. (2009). A curriculum decision-maker's perspective on conceptual and analytical frameworks for studying teachers' use of curriculum materials. In J. T. Remillard, B. A. Herbel-Eisenmann, & G. M. Lloyd (Eds.), *Mathematics teachers at work: Connecting curriculum materials and classroom instruction* (pp. 93–99). New York: Routledge.

Larson, M. R. (2011). *Administrator's guide: Interpreting the Common Core State Standards to improve mathematics education.* Reston, VA: National Council of Teachers of Mathematics.

Leinwand, S. (2009). *Accessible mathematics: 10 instructional shifts that raise student achievement.* Portsmouth, NH: Heinemann.

Leithwood, K., & Seashore Louis, K. (Eds.). (1998). *Organizational learning in schools.* Lisse, the Netherlands: Swets & Zeitlinger.

Lesh, R., & Zawojewski, J. (2007). Problem solving and modeling. In F. K. Lester Jr. (Ed.), *Second handbook of research on mathematics teaching and learning* (pp. 763–804). Reston, VA: National Council of Teachers of Mathematics.

Lester, F. K., Jr. (2010). Issues in teaching mathematical problem solving in the elementary grades. *School Science and Mathematics, 82*(2), 93–98.

Lezotte, L. W. (1991). *Correlates of effective schools: The first and second generation.* Okemos, MI: Effective Schools.

Little, J. W., & Horn, I. S. (2007). "Normalizing" problems of practice: Converting routine conversation into a resource for learning in professional communities. In L. Stroll & K. Seashore Louis (Eds.), *Professional learning communities: Divergence, depth, and dilemmas* (pp. 79–92). New York: McGraw-Hill.

Lubienski, S. T. (2007). What can we do about achievement disparities? *Educational Leadership, 65*(3), 54–59.

Marzano, R. J. (2006). *Classroom assessment and grading that work.* Alexandria, VA: Association for Supervision and Curriculum Development.

Marzano, R. J. (2007). Designing a comprehensive approach to classroom assessment. In D. Reeves (Ed.), *Ahead of the curve: The power of assessment to transform teaching and learning* (pp. 103–125). Bloomington, IN: Solution Tree Press.

McCall, M. S., Hauser, C., Cronin, J., Kingsbury, G. G., & Houser, R. (2006). *Achievement gaps: An examination of differences in student achievement and growth.* Lake Oswego, OR: Northwest Evaluation Association.

McKinsey & Company. (2009). *The economic impact of the achievement gap in America's schools.* Washington, DC: Author.

Morris, A. K., & Hiebert, J. (2011). Creating shared instructional products: An alternative approach to improving teaching. *Educational Researcher, 40*(1), 5–14.

Morris, A. K., Hiebert, J., & Spitzer, S. M. (2009). Mathematical knowledge for teaching in planning and evaluating instruction: What can preservice teachers learn? *Journal for Research in Mathematics Education, 40,* 491–529.

Mourshed, M., Chijioke, C., & Barber, M. (2010). *How the world's most improved school systems keep getting better.* Accessed at www.mckinsey.com/Client_Service/Social_Section /Latest-thinking/Worlds_most_improved_schools.aspx on January 10, 2012.

National Association for the Education of Young Children. (2010). *Early childhood mathematics: Promoting good beginnings.* Washington, DC: Author. Accessed at www.naeyc.org /files/naeyc/file/positions/psmath.pdf on January 11, 2012.

National Council of Supervisors of Mathematics. (2011). *Resources.* Accessed at www.mathed leadership.org/ccss/materials.html on November 15, 2011.

National Council of Supervisors of Mathematics. (2008). *Improving student achievement by leading the pursuit of a vision for equity.* Denver, CO: Author.

National Council of Teachers of Mathematics. (1980). *Agenda for action: Problem Solving.* Accessed at www.nctm.org/standards/content.aspx?id=17279 on June 25, 2011.

National Council of Teachers of Mathematics. (1989). *Curriculum and evaluation standards for school mathematics.* Reston, VA: Author.

National Council of Teachers of Mathematics. (2000). *Principles and standards for school mathematics.* Reston, VA: Author.

National Council of Teachers of Mathematics. (2006). *Curriculum focal points for prekindergarten through grade 8 mathematics: A quest for coherence.* Reston, VA: Author.

National Council of Teachers of Mathematics. (2007). *Mathematics teaching today: Improving practice, improving student learning.* Reston, VA: Author.

National Council of Teachers of Mathematics. (2008). *Equity in mathematics education: Position statement.* Reston, VA: Author.

National Council of Teachers of Mathematics. (2008–2011). *Teaching with curriculum focal points* (Vols. 1–13). Reston, VA: Author.

National Council of Teachers of Mathematics. (2010). *Making it happen: A guide to interpreting and implementing common core state standards for mathematics.* Reston, VA: Author.

National Council of Teachers of Mathematics. (2010–2012). *Developing essential understanding* (Vols. 1–10). Reston, VA: Author.

National Council of Teachers of Mathematics. (2011). *Intervention: Position statement.* Reston, VA: Author.

National Governors Association Center for Best Practices & Council of Chief State School Officers. (2010). *Common core state standards for mathematics.* Washington, DC: Authors. Accessed at www.corestandards.org/assets/CCSSI_Math%20Standards.pdf on November 22, 2010.

National Mathematics Advisory Panel. (2008). *Foundations for success: The final report of the National Mathematics Advisory Panel.* Washington, DC: U.S. Department of Education.

National Research Council. (2001). *Adding it up: Helping children learn mathematics.* Washington, DC: National Academies Press.

National Research Council. (2009). *Mathematics learning in early childhood: Paths toward excellence and equity.* Washington, DC: The National Academies Press.

New York State Education Department. (n.d.). N*ew York state prekindergarten foundation for the Common Core.* Albany, NY: Author. Accessed at www.p12.nysed.gov/ciai/common _core_standards/pdfdocs/nyslsprek.pdf on March 28, 2012.

No Child Left Behind Act of 2001, Pub. L. No. 107–110, 115 Stat. 1425 (2002).

Noguera, P. (2004). Transforming high schools. *Educational Leadership, 68*(8), 26–31.

Olson, J. (2007). Developing students' mathematical reasoning through games. *Teaching Children Mathematics, 13*(9), 464–471.

Partnership for Assessment of Readiness for College and Careers. (2011). *PARCC model content frameworks.* Accessed at www.parcconline.org/sites/parcc/files/PARCC-Overview _Dec2011.pdf on January 10, 2011.

Penuel, W. R., Fishman, B. J., Yamaguchi, R., & Gallagher, L. P. (2007). What makes professional development effective? Strategies that foster curriculum implementation. *American Educational Research Journal, 44*(4), 921–958.

Perry, B., & Dockett, S. (2002). Young children's access to powerful mathematical ideas. In L. D. English (Ed.), *Handbook of international research in mathematics education* (pp. 81–111). Mahwah, NJ: Erlbaum.

Perry, R., & Lewis, C. (2010). Building demand for research through lesson study. In C. E. Coburn & M. K. Stein (Eds.), *Research and practice in education: Building alliances, bridging the divide.* Lanham, MD: Rowman & Littlefield.

Pölya, G. (1957). *How to solve it.* Princeton, NJ: Princeton University Press.

Popham, W. J. (2008). *Transformative assessment.* Alexandria, VA: Association for Supervision and Curriculum Development.

Porter, A., McMaken, J., Hwang, J., & Yang, R. (2011). Common core standards: The new U.S. intended curriculum. *Educational Researcher, 40*(3), 103–116.

Rasmussen, C., Yackel, E., & King, K. (2003). Social and sociomathematical norms in mathematics classrooms. In H. L. Schoen & R. I. Charles (Eds.), *Teaching mathematics through problem solving: Grades 6–12* (pp. 143–154). Reston, VA: National Council of Teachers of Mathematics.

Rathouz, M. (2011). 3 ways that promote student reasoning. *Teaching Children Mathematics, 18*(3), 182–189.

Reeves, D. (2003). *High performance in high poverty schools: 90/90/90 and beyond.* Englewood, CO: Center for Performance Assessment.

Reeves, D. (2011). *Elements of grading: A guide to effective practices.* Bloomington, IN: Solution Tree Press.

Reys, B., & Fennell, F. (2003). Who should lead instruction at the elementary level. *Teaching Children Mathematics, 9,* 277–282.

Reys, R., & Reys, R. (2011). The high school mathematics curriculum—what can we learn from history? *Mathematics Teacher, 105*(1), 9–11.

Rivkin, S. G., Hanushek, E. A., & Kain, J. F. (2005). Teachers, schools, and academic achievement. *Econometrica, 73*(2), 417–458.

Saunders, W. M., Goldenberg, C. N., & Gallimore, R. (2009). Increasing achievement by focusing grade-level teams on improving classroom learning: A prospective, quasi-experimental study of Title I schools. *American Educational Research Journal, 46*(4), 1006–1033.

Schmidt, W. H., Cogan, L. S., Houang, R. T., & McKnight, C. C. (2011). Content coverage differences across districts/states: A persisting challenge for U.S. education policy. *American Journal of Education, 117*(3), 399–427.

Schmoker, M. (2006). *Results now: How we can achieve unprecedented improvement in teaching and learning.* Alexandria, VA: Association for Supervision and Curriculum Development.

Schmoker, M. (2011). *Focus: Elevating the essentials to radically improve student learning.* Alexandria, VA: Association for Supervision and Curriculum Development.

School Improvement in Maryland. (2010). *Introduction to the classroom-focused improvement process (CFIP).* Accessed at http://mdk12.org/process/cfip on November 15, 2011.

Seeley, C. L. (2009). *Faster isn't smarter: Messages about math, teaching, and learning in the 21st century.* Sausalito, CA: Math Solutions.

Shonkoff, J. P., & Phillips, D. A. (Eds.). (2000). *From neurons to neighborhoods: The science of early childhood development.* Washington, DC: National Academy Press.

Shuhua, A. (2004). *The middle path in math instruction: Solutions for improving math education.* Lanham, MD: Scarecrow Education.

Siegler, R., Carpenter, T., Fennell, F., Geary, D., Lewis, J., Okamato, Y., et al. (2010). *Developing effective fractions instruction for kindergarten through 8th grade: A practice guide* (NCEE

2010–4039). Washington, DC: National Center for Education Evaluation and Regional Assistance.

Silver, E. (2010). Examining what teachers do when they display their best practice: Teaching mathematics for understanding. *Journal of Mathematics Education at Teachers College, 1*(1), 1–6.

Silver, E. A., & Stein, M. K. (1996). The QUASAR project: The "revolution of the possible" in mathematics instructional reform in urban middle schools. *Urban Education, 30,* 476–521.

Slavin, R. E., & Lake, C. (2008). Effective programs in elementary mathematics: A best-evidence synthesis. *Review of Educational Research, 78*(3), 427–515.

SMARTER Balanced Assessment Consortium. (2010). Accessed at www.k12.wa.us/SMARTER/pubdoc/SBACSummary2010.pdf on January 10, 2012

Smith, M. S., & Stein, M. K. (2011). *5 practices for orchestrating productive mathematics discussions.* Reston, VA: National Council of Teachers of Mathematics.

Stein, M. K., & Kaufman, J. H. (2010). Selecting and supporting the use of mathematics curricula at scale. *American Educational Research Journal, 47,* 663–693.

Stein, M. K., Remillard, J., & Smith, M. S. (2007). How curriculum influences student learning. In F. K. Lester (Ed.), *Second handbook of research on mathematics teaching and learning* (pp. 319–370). Charlotte, NC: Information Age.

Stein, M. K., Russell, J., & Smith, M. S. (2011). The role of tools in bridging research and practice in an instructional improvement effort. In W. F. Tate, K. D. King, & C. R. Anderson (Eds.), *Disrupting tradition: Research and practice pathways in mathematics education* (pp. 33–44). Reston, VA: National Council of Teachers of Mathematics.

Stein, M. K., & Smith, M. S. (2010). The influence of curriculum on students' learning. In B. J. Reys, R. E. Reys, & R. Rubenstein (Eds.), *Mathematics curriculum: Issues, trends, and future directions, seventy-second yearbook* (pp. 351–362). Reston, VA: National Council of Teachers of Mathematics.

Stiff, L. V., Johnson, J. L., & Akos, P. (2011). Examining what we know for sure: Tracking in middle grades mathematics. In W. F. Tate, K. D. King, & C. R. Anderson (Eds.), *Disrupting tradition: Research and practice pathways in mathematics education* (pp. 63–75). Reston, VA: National Council of Teachers of Mathematics.

Stiggins, R. J., Arter, J. A., Chappuis, J., & Chappuis, S. (2006). *Classroom assessment for student learning: Doing it right—using it well.* Portland, OR: Educational Testing Service.

Stigler, J. W., Gonzales, P., Kawanaka, T., Knoll, S., & Serrano, A. (1999). *The TIMSS videotape classroom study: Methods and findings from an exploratory research project on eighth-grade mathematics instruction in Germany, Japan, and the United States.* Washington, DC: U.S. Department of Education, National Center for Education Statistics.

Stigler, J. W., & Hiebert, J. (1999). *The teaching gap: Best ideas from the world's teachers for improving education in the classroom.* New York: The Free Press.

Tate, W., & Rousseau, C. (2002). Access and opportunity: The political and social context of mathematics education. In L. D. English (Ed.), *Handbook of international research in mathematics education* (pp. 271–300). Mahwah, NJ: Erlbaum.

Tate, W. F., & Rousseau, C. (2007). Engineering change in mathematics education: Research, policy, and practice. In F. K. Lester (Ed.), *Second handbook of research on mathematics teaching and learning* (pp. 1209–1246). Charlotte, NC: Information Age.

Teacher Education Initiative Curriculum Group. (2008). *High-leverage teaching practices.* Unpublished manuscript, School of Education, University of Michigan, Ann Arbor.

Thompson, M., & Wiliam, D. (2007, April). *Tight but loose: A conceptual framework for scaling up school reforms.* Paper presented at the annual meeting of the American Educational Research Association, Chicago, IL.

Usiskin, Z. (2007). The case of the University of Chicago school mathematics project—Secondary component. In C. R. Hirsch (Ed.), *Perspectives on the design and development of school mathematics curricula* (pp. 173–182). Reston, VA: National Council of Teachers of Mathematics.

Walker, E. N. (2007). Why aren't more minorities taking advanced math? *Educational Leadership, 65*(3), 48–53.

Wallace, A. H., & Gurganus, S. P. (2005). Teaching for mastery of multiplication. *Teaching Children Mathematics, 12,* 26–33.

Waters, T., Marzano, R., & McNulty B. (2003). *Balanced leadership: What 30 years of research tells us about the effect of leadership on student achievement.* Denver, CO: McREL.

Wayne, A. J., Kwang, S. Y., Zhu, P., Cronen, S., & Garet, M. S. (2008). Experimenting with teacher professional development: Motives and methods. *Educational Researcher, 37*(8), 469–479.

Weiss, I. R., Heck, D. J., & Shimkus, E. S. (2004). Looking inside the classroom: Mathematics teaching in the United States. *NCSM Journal of Mathematics Education Leadership, 7*(1), 23–32.

Wiggins, G., & McTighe, J. (2000). *Understanding by design.* New York: Prentice Hall.

Wiliam, D. (2007a). Content then process: Teacher learning communities in the service of formative assessment. In D. Reeves (Ed.), *Ahead of the curve: The power of assessment to transform teaching and learning* (pp. 183–204). Bloomington, IN: Solution Tree Press.

Wiliam, D. (2007b). Keeping learning on track: Classroom assessment and the regulation of learning. In F. K. Lester (Ed.), *Second handbook of research on mathematics teaching and learning* (pp. 1053–1098). Charlotte, NC: Information Age.

Wiliam, D. (2011). *Embedded formative assessment.* Bloomington, IN: Solution Tree Press.

Wiliam, D., & Thompson, M. (2007). Integrating assessment with instruction: What will it take to make it work? In C. A. Dwyer (Ed.), *The future of assessment: Shaping teaching and learning* (pp. 53–82). Mahwah, NJ: Erlbaum.

Williams, B. (2003). Reframing the reform agenda. In B. Williams (Ed.), *Closing the achievement gap: A vision for changing beliefs and practices* (pp. 178–196). Alexandria, VA: Association for Supervision and Curriculum Development.

Wixson, K. (2011). A systemic view of RTI research. *The Elementary School Journal, 111*(4), 503–510.

Index

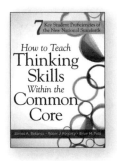

How to Teach Thinking Skills Within the Common Core
7 Key Student Proficiencies of the New National Standards
James A. Bellanca, Robin J. Fogarty, and Brian M. Pete
Empower your students to thrive across the curriculum. Packed with examples and tools, this practical guide prepares teachers across all grade levels and content areas to teach the most critical cognitive skills from the Common Core State Standards.
BKF576

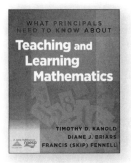

What Principals Need to Know About Teaching and Learning Mathematics
Timothy D. Kanold, Diane J. Briars, and Francis (Skip) Fennell
This must-have resource offers support and encouragement for improved mathematics achievement across every grade level. With an emphasis on Principles and Standards for School Mathematics and Common Core State Standards, this book covers the importance of mathematics content, learning and instruction, and mathematics assessment.
BKF501

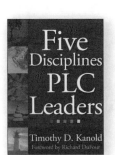

The Five Disciplines of PLC Leaders
Timothy D. Kanold
Foreword by Richard DuFour
Effective leadership in a professional learning community requires practice, patience, and skill. Through engaging examples and accessible language, this book offers a focused framework that will help educators maintain balance and consistent vision as they strengthen the skills of PLC leadership.
BKF495

Learning by Doing
A Handbook for Professional Learning Communities at Work™
Richard DuFour, Rebecca DuFour, Robert Eaker, and Thomas Many
Learning by Doing is an action guide for closing the knowing-doing gap and transforming schools into PLCs. It also includes seven major additions that equip educators with essential tools for confronting challenges.
BKF416

Solution Tree

Solution Tree's mission is to advance the work of our authors. By working with the best researchers and educators worldwide, we strive to be the premier provider of innovative publishing, in-demand events, and inspired professional development designed to transform education to ensure that all students learn.

NATIONAL COUNCIL OF
TEACHERS OF MATHEMATICS

The National Council of Teachers of Mathematics is a public voice of mathematics education, supporting teachers to ensure equitable mathematics learning of the highest quality for all students through vision, leadership, professional development, and research.